CULTURAL DIVERSITY IN TRADE UNIONS

Cultural Diversity in Trade Unions
A challenge to class identity?

Edited by
JOHAN WETS

Routledge
Taylor & Francis Group
LONDON AND NEW YORK

First published 2000 by Ashgate Publishing

Reissued 2018 by Routledge
2 Park Square, Milton Park, Abingdon, Oxon OX14 4RN
711 Third Avenue, New York, NY 10017, USA

Routledge is an imprint of the Taylor & Francis Group, an informa business

Copyright © Johan Wets 2000

All rights reserved. No part of this book may be reprinted or reproduced or utilised in any form or by any electronic, mechanical, or other means, now known or hereafter invented, including photocopying and recording, or in any information storage or retrieval system, without permission in writing from the publishers.

Notice:
Product or corporate names may be trademarks or registered trademarks, and are used only for identification and explanation without intent to infringe.

Publisher's Note
The publisher has gone to great lengths to ensure the quality of this reprint but points out that some imperfections in the original copies may be apparent.

Disclaimer
The publisher has made every effort to trace copyright holders and welcomes correspondence from those they have been unable to contact.

Typeset by
Sandra Volders
Hoger Instituut voor de Arbeid
E. Van Evenstraat 2e
B-3000 Leuven

A Library of Congress record exists under LC control number: 00131671

ISBN 13: 978-1-138-71567-7 (hbk)
ISBN 13: 978-1-138-71566-0 (pbk)
ISBN 13: 978-1-315-19742-5 (ebk)

Contents

List of Figures *vii*
List of Tables *viii*
List of Appendices *ix*
List of Contributors *x*
Acknowledgements *xii*

Introduction: Squaring the Circle? Trade Unions Torn between Class Solidarity and Regional and Cultural Identities in Western Europe
Patrick Pasture 1

1 Cultural Diversity and Politics: An Introduction
 Staffan Zetterholm 19

PART I: REGIONAL AND LOCAL CULTURAL DIVERSITIES

2 Divergent Developments, Regional Alliances and National Solidarity in Belgium
 Patrick Pasture 35

3 The Italian Trade Unions and the Local Challenge
 Giampiero Bianchi 71

4   Industrial Relations in Spain: Does Regional Diversity Awaken
    Union Tendencies to Divergence?
    Jacint Jordana   91

5   Industrial Relations and Trade Unions in Economic and Social
    Transformation in East Germany
    Volkmar Kreißig   119

PART II: TRADE UNIONS AND THE CHALLENGE OF IMMIGRANT WORKER CULTURES

6   Trade Union Policies towards Immigrants: The Case of Belgium
    (1944-97)
    Albert Martens   151

7   Trade Union Policies Regarding Immigration and Immigrant
    Workers in the Netherlands (1960-95)
    Judith Roosblad   169

8   Immigrants as a Special Target: Ambiguity of Solidaristic Action
    Maurizio Ambrosini   191

9   Organised Labour and the Black Worker in England: A Critical
    Analysis of Postwar Trends
    Satnam Virdee   207

10 The French Trade Union Movement and the Struggle Against
    Racism in the Workplace
    Philippe Bataille   227

List of Figures

Figure 5.1	The German system of industrial relations	120
Figure 5.2	Interaction of industrial relations, the welfare system and the labour market	122
Graph 6.1	Number of work permits issued annually to foreigners in Belgium, 1945-97	153
Figure 8.1	Labour supply and demand, and the role of the supporting institutions	195

List of Tables

Table 2.1	Unemployment rates and gross national product, 1995	56
Table 3.1	Priorities of trade union action in the north and in the south of Italy	79
Table 4.1	Structure and levels of collective bargaining in Spain, 1988-94	97
Table 4.2	Percentage of wage earners with temporary contracts and unemployed workers in relation to the active population, 1995	102
Table 4.3	Coverage of collective bargaining at the regional or infra-regional level, 1988-94	108
Table 8.1	Extra EEC dependent workers in firms, sectors and regional distribution, 1994	193
Table 8.2	Differences between the 'protective' and the 'bargaining' model	204
Table 9.1	Stewards' priorities ranking in top three	219

List of Appendices

Appendix 2.1	Trade Union Membership per **Region, 1910-95**	69
Appendix 2.2	Regional Distribution of Votes for the Workplace Health and Safety Committees, 1995	70
Appendix 4.1	Wage Earners: Regions, Sectors and Company Size, 1995	114
Appendix 4.2	Metal and Public Services Membership in the UGT by Regions, 1995	115
Appendix 4.3	Estimated Total Membership and Union Density by Regions, 1985-90-95	116
Appendix 6.1	Schematic Representation of Trade Union Logos, Praxis and Organisation Regarding Immigrants	163
Appendix 6.2	Summary of Trade Union Policy towards Immigration and Immigrants, 1945-97	166

List of Contributors

Maurizio Ambrosini is Professor of Sociology of Organisation at the Università Cattolica del Sacro Cuore, Mayland

Philippe Bataille is Maître de conférences at the University of Lille III and member of the Centre d'Analyse et d'Intervention Sociologiques (CADIS, EHESS/CNRS) in Paris

Giampiero Bianchi is historian, Head of the Study and Formation Department of the FISBA (CISL)

Jacint Jordana is Associate Professor at the Department of Political and Social Sciences of the Universitat Pompeu Fabra in Barcelona

Volkmar Kreißig is affiliated to WIESO-Europa in Chemnitz and currently Visiting Professor of Industrial Relations at the State University of St. Petersburg

Albert Martens is Professor of Urban Sociology and Sociology of Industrial Relations at the University of Leuven

Patrick Pasture, Ph D in History, is Research Associate of the Fund for Scientific Research - Flanders (Belgium), affiliated to the Faculty of Arts, and Project Manager at HIVA, University of Leuven

Judith Roosblad is researcher/Ph D student at the Institute for Migration and Ethnic Studies (IMES) at the University of Amsterdam

Satnam Virdee is Lecturer at the Sociology division of the Department of Government, University of Strathclyde, Glasgow

Johan Wets, Ph D in Political Science (1999), is Scientific Collaborator of HIVA, University of Leuven

Staffan Zetterholm is Associate Professor in European Studies, Department of Development and Planning, Aalborg University (Denmark)

Acknowledgements

This publication is based upon a seminar held in Leuven (Belgium) in February 1997, organised by the Higher Institute of Labour Studies (HIVA) of the University of Leuven in collaboration with the European Centre for Workers' Questions (EZA, Europäisches Zentrum für Arbeitnehmerfragen) and with the financial support of the European Community.

Johan Wets was responsible for the practical organisation of the seminar and the editing of the texts.[1] The administrative assistants of the HIVA, especially Evy Van Dael, Hilde Van Wijck, Liesbeth Villa, and Sandra Volders gave practical support at various times.

I would like to offer my sincere thanks to all those who made the seminar and this publication possible.

Patrick Pasture
Project Co-ordinator

---

[1] Unfortunately, my colleague Wets was unavailable for the introduction.

Introduction: Squaring the Circle? Trade Unions Torn between Class Solidarity and Regional and Cultural Identities in Western Europe

PATRICK PASTURE

This book is the second publication of the international research program 'The Culture Shock. Labour and the Integration of Europe', investigating how trade unions in Europe respond to challenges relating to the European integration. For once, the focus is not on economic and political problems arising from European integration. In this research program, the spotlight is directed towards cultural aspects of the action and organisation of trade unions. Our starting point is that trade unions are not only socio-economic and - not least - political pressure groups, but also communities with a collective identity, with distinctive shared values and patterns of behaviour; in the broad definition of 'culture' also used by Staffan Zetterholm (chapter 1). Our underlying assumption is that, only partially as a result of European integration, the unity of this collective identity has come under pressure towards the end of the twentieth century. The concept of Europe as used in this publication only serves to mark out the geographical area, and as a synonym for Western Europe. In this sense, the institutional infrastructure of the European community is not relevant, and does not actually feature at all in this publication.

Traditionally, the collective identity of the labour movement is, in the first place, shaped by class - a loaded concept, undoubtedly to some extent a product of its time, as it is defined or imagined by the labour movement itself. The concept of class nevertheless remains relevant, even if only because the trade union movement somehow remains an important factor in European society, and because it continues to define itself as working class, despite studies carried out by some social scientists into the disappearance or disintegration of the working class (e.g. Paluski and Waters, 1996). An in-depth analysis of this aspect is scheduled for a future edition in the present series (Van Gyes et al, 2000).

The identity of the labour movement is also defined by other factors, such as their political and ideological alignment. On the continent, the trade union movement has always contained different political and ideological tendencies, despite the never realised propensity towards unity (see Pasture et al, 1996; Ebbinghaus, 1993). Historic research has clearly demonstrated that the trade union movement adopted a national identity, even before World War I. The latter is naturally most significant in the context of the present research program: it can be safely assumed that a strong national identity constitutes a sizeable obstacle to international co-operation. The movement's national identity was not so much abstract as a very practical involvement in the setting-up of the national welfare state, and in the twentieth century the labour and trade union movement became an integral part of the fabric of the nation state (Van der Linden, 1988; Berger, 1995; Katznelson, 1986). Furthermore, the significance of national identity is particularly obvious in the context of immigration. If a conclusion can be drawn from the comparative study by Rinus Penninx and Judith Roosblad concerning the attitudes and actions of the trade unions towards immigrants and immigration in Europe between 1960 and 1993, it is that 'although the unions may commit themselves verbally in varying degrees to internationalist solidarity of all workers, the dominant frame of reference is that of the national state and the national arena' (Penninx and Roosblad, forthcoming).[1] Some labour and trade union movements have even linked up with nationalist and regionalist movements - the distinction between both is not always equally relevant: this issue was investigated in 1995 in the first seminar (Pasture and Verberckmoes, 1998).

In this book, the angle is reversed, as it were. Its starting point is the social and cultural divisions within the labour population and the trade union movement. Two themes are elaborated further in this book: regional divisions reinforced by increasing regionalism within Europe, and the challenge facing the trade unions when dealing with immigrants. On both issues, the ethnic component comes into play, although that particular aspect is not emphasised by the authors in the first part relating to regional diversity. The immigrants issue is inextricably linked with the upward surge in racism and right-wing extremism in large parts of Europe in the 1980s and 1990s; the latter became the main subject for some of the authors.

In a contribution mainly intended as background for the debate on cultural and regional diversity, Staffan Zetterholm wonders whether cultural homogeneity is a pre-condition for the legitimacy of a political system (chapter 1). His subject relates mainly to nation states, but his findings are

---

[1] See note 2.

of a more fundamental nature and are consequently relevant to both organisations and political systems, including trade unions. It is easy to acknowledge, as does Zetterholm, that cultural homogeneity is a myth. Culturally homogenous states are as few and far between as culturally homogeneous organisations. But this actual diversity based on 'private' culture (probably more distinguishable for social movements than for nation states), does not affect the scope for a common public culture consisting of shared myths and heroes. The labour movement has consistently helped to shape this common public culture, and it has always been mainly based on the class principle, to the extent that it has in fact managed to make the transition from '*Klasse-für-sich*' to '*Klasse-an-sich*'. Translated to the trade union movement, the common culture consists of trade union structures and practices or preferences for certain forms of organisation and action, such as recruitment levels or strike patterns.

Trade Union Movement and Regional Diversity

Europe has always been characterised by great regional ethnic diversity. The states were partially formed on that basis, although few states coincide with ethnic regional borders - however they may be defined - and most states by far contain several regions, languages and peoples. The same applies to the countries dealt with here: Italy, Spain, Germany, and Belgium are nation states with a long history of national diversity, and they all have gone through a laborious process of formation. However, this historical continuity is deceptive. Again, as will become apparent from the following contributions, the present regional and ethnic identities are not mere extensions of historic forerunners: they are re-defined every day, and the present-day product may only slightly resemble the so-called historical antecedents - which were, of course, equally indefinable and fluid.

Furthermore, the (re-)discovery of regions in Europe is entirely in keeping with an upsurge of regionalism or even nationalism. However, this regionalism is not happening everywhere, and the division of Europe into a large number of 'regions' (which do not always coincide with the regions envisaged by the regionalists) is largely an administrative exercise, although it usually corresponds to existing sub-national divisions (Keating, 1998) (for example, the departments in France and the Länder in Germany). Sometimes, however, the new divisions do not coincide with existing structures. Jacint Jordana deals with this issue in his contribution on Spain, where the provincial (subregional) level is very important for industrial relations (chapter 4). Most noticeable is the ongoing process of regional 'awakening' or imagination in Italy, which was only united in

1861 after existing as a colourful collection of small states dating back to town-states in the Middle ages.

Those local entities still characterise Italy today, but the great economic and industrial differences between the north and the south have caused the country to split into two or three, which left its mark not only in terms of statistics, but also on political practice and people's minds. The way in which the Lega Nord is cobbling together a new regional identity with elements of both, namely Padania, is intriguing, and it forms an almost perfect illustration of what historical anthropologists like Benedict Anderson (1991) have written regarding the process of nation-building. The question is whether such an almost conscious and forced application of theories aimed at explaining long-term developments can lead to a practical political result.

The admittedly relative success of the Lega suggests this may be the case indeed. Giampiero Bianchi (chapter 3) goes on to say that the upsurge of regional identities, also in trade union matters, does not stop with the more renowned 'Padania': regional trade union challenges also exist in Alto Adige, Val d'Aosta and Sardinia. He also demonstrates that older local identities in the Po Valley claim their own stake.

The much debated German example is obviously entirely different, although even Germany has known a complex and slow state formation, and the 'Länder' are very autonomous indeed. The former GDR, that was unified wit the FRG in 1989, has developed a different culture by undergoing an entirely different political system for forty years, which pervaded every aspect of communal life. Furthermore, of vital importance to the trade union movement, the economic conditions of the three 'ex-GDR' Länder and the former West Germany are separated by many miles.

Great economic divergence somehow seems to remain a constant factor. Without lapsing into primitive Marxian determinism, it is remarkable that the emergence of a strong regional identity seems to coincide, as if fortuitously, with large economic shifts. It would not be true to imply that the region emphasising its independence and renouncing another one, invariably has the most deprived economy, or, contrariwise, the best economic position, although the latter seems to ring true nowadays for Italy (Padania), Spain (Basque country) and Belgium (Flanders). The latter example demonstrates that, in the long term, the reverse may occur: until the 1950s, a still largely agrarian and parochial Flanders economically and culturally lagged far behind the more industrial areas in the South and the 'Frenchising' capital Brussels. However, it is obvious that awareness of a national or regional and ethnic identity often goes together with economic development, or, maybe more accurately, that it is aligned with it (which should illustrate the construed character of those relationships). On the other hand, not all remarkable economic differences lead to regional and ethnic diversification, at least not in the short to midterm. It remains unclear whether regional economic diversity in Europe is actually increasing, and whether that would explain the increasing regional tensions. A recent economic analysis of regional unemployment in Europe, carried out on behalf of the European Commission (DG II), indicates that centralised labour market policies increase the regional tensions in the labour market rather than reduce it. The authors of the study consequently conclude in favour of more regional 'subsidiarity' as far as labour market policies are concerned (Pench et al, 1999).

Although less than some authors expected, this last remark reminds that a general process of decentralisation definitely has taken place which focused not so much on the regional level as on the company level itself (see Ferner and Hyman (1998) for a short but lucid discussion of the subject). There are regional implications, nevertheless, not least because one of the strategies used by trade unions to cope with the downward pressure on industrial relations was the development of local and regional services and infrastructures, potentially resulting in regional collective bargaining. Meanwhile, there has been a noticeable revival of regionalism or nationalism - the distinction between them strikes us as simply a matter of degree, with regionalism aiming for greater autonomy for the region concerned within existing (federal) state borders, and nationalism striving for actual independence. According to Jacint Jordana (chapter 4), the above revival has produced regional forms of collective bargaining and social policy in Spain, while pressure from nationalists in the Basque country (particularly, in the 1990s, from the very successful nationalist trade unions) has resulted in their own strongly developed system of labour relations and regional labour policies.

Naturally, the various political, economic and social conditions of the regions will also have an effect on trade union organisation, even when structured at a national level, discounting for the moment the regional labour organisations - whether they are regionalist or nationalist. Wide variation exists in, for instance, recruitment levels, trade union praxis and, in countries with trade union pluralism (which applies to all European countries) the power distribution between different trade unions. Only Jacint Jordana for Spain (chapter 4), and, to a lesser extent, Patrick Pasture for Belgium (chapter 2), offer reliable figures for the distribution of power in trade unionism, highlighting huge differences. Jordana identifies at least three different types of trade union establishment: the little syndicated Mediterranean regions in the East; Madrid and the Southern regions, where syndicalism in the services and the public sector grew quite swiftly; and lastly the more syndicated regions in the North, still with significant diversities between the Basque country on the one hand and Asturias and Cantabria on the other hand. Trade union culture differs between the North and South of Belgium, too, with regard to recruitment levels, the distribution of power between the three confederations, and the strike patterns. Undoubtedly, considerable differences can also be found in Italian trade union culture between the North and Mezzogiorno. With the German reunification, two totally different worlds have actually been joined together; the former East-German trade unions were abolished as such, but there is no question of equal treatment at the moment. Judging from what Volkmar Kreißig writes (chapter 5), it will be a long time before both are fully integrated.

The way the trade union movement reacts to regional variations highlights some common developments, despite a number of differences. In all countries, the trade unions initially became organised at a national level and, historically speaking, they have favoured handling industrial relations at a national level. As stated by Jean Bunel, following on from Pierre Birnbaum, 'except for the Austro-marxists, socialists and communists have always searched to let the largest solidarities prevail theoretically within the nation states that were constituted and even beyond their borders' (Bunel, 1999, 20; Birnbaum, 1997) (transl. P.P.) - although we are inclined to underline the theoretical aspect of this affirmation, certainly regarding the last part of the quotation. This solidarity was naturally grafted onto the working class, demanding that regional conflicts should be overcome. In practice, it meant that regional differences were ignored. This is again most poignant in Italy, as is apparent from Bianchi's analysis (chapter 3), no matter how diversified that country in fact is. Although the combination of different language communities within the trade union movement in Belgium led to tensions from as early as the 19th century, the trade unions were structured nationally without discussion, and the industrial relations and social policies were shaped at a national level. The christian trade union movement sailed on a broadly nationalist course, i.e. it had a pronounced 'Flamingant' character in Flanders, calling for Flemish autonomy in a country where the culture, politics and economy were dominated by francophones, but it never questioned its loyalty to the Belgian state - quite the contrary (chapter 2; see also Pasture, 1998). Even after Spain, too, became a democracy, the trade unions CGT (socialist) and CC.OO. (communist) tried to establish a national system of labour relations.

The reunification of Germany did not bring an exception to the rule: the social structures existing in the Federal State of Germany where simply extended to cover the former GDR.

This does not detract from the pressure felt by trade unions from regionalisation. How they respond depends not only on their specific national context, but also on their own ideological and political traditions, and the response is not always evident. In Belgium, the christian labour movement has traditionally been one of the driving forces behind the regionalisation both of the political system and of economic policies (chapter 2). However, as the regionalisation unfolded, the movement lost its enthusiasm for moving further down the road; and in the fields of industrial relations and social security, it suddenly applied the brakes. The socialist trade union movement has only engaged itself in regional thinking after 1958, inspired by Wallonia's faltering economy, but it still gave priority to interregional solidarity. The diverging economies in the late 1990s provided a new impetus for the call for more regional economic management, threatening the traditional division in Belgium between economic and social policies.

In Italy, the discussion concerning recognition of the local and regional dimension in industrial relations reached a historic turning point in July 1993, according to Bianchi (chapter 3). The CISL in particular seemed to be playing the regional card, or at any rate to a higher extent than the CGIL - the parallel with the Belgian situation between the ACV and the ABVV (admittedly a social-democratic and not a communist organisation) is remarkable. The CISL seemed to feel most pressure to reform its internal organisation. In Jacint Jordana's view (chapter 3), the national confederations in Spain (the UGT and the CC.OO.), are leaving room for the regional dimension. Another factor in the equation is the very uneven distribution of regional sectors and hence also of sectorial unions. In a previous study (with Klaus-Jürgen Nagel) Jordana saw this as a partial explanation as to why no nationalist trade union could break through (Jordana and Nagel, 1998).

In an extension to Miroslav Hroch's theory regarding the development of nationalism (1985), it can indeed be argued that the existence of an organised labour movement may not prohibit the formation of a nationalist broad political movement (in Hroch's theory, the transfer to phase C in the development of nationalism), but it can stop the nationalist trade unions from breaking through. Both in Italy and in Spain, nationalist political parties seemed to become popular with the masses in the 1990s, inclusively and even particularly with the workers in industrial centres. The Basque country is an exception, and Ludger Mees has provided a strong analysis, in an adaptation of Hroch's theory, to explain that situation based on the differences in economic development and the specific political context (Mees, 1998). This does not prevent regional or nationalist trade unions existing in various regions, although they are not as successful as the Basque-nationalist trade organisations. In Italy, on the other hand, the regional nationalist trade unions do not seem to find favour at all. However, in this context, Giampiero Bianchi (chapter 3) does not contradict the conclusions of Michael Braun who pointed quite forcefully to the underlying regionalist thinking which is also penetrating the established national trade union federations, undermining the 'national' class solidarity (Braun, 1998). Bianchi seems to be of the opinion that the historically grown centralisation of the Italian trade unions is no longer adapted to the current situation, and that a certain internal regionalisation is necessary, certainly with relation to the development of and participation in a local or regional training and labour market management. Regional trade union services would reach the increasingly diversified working class, and they would benefit trade union activities in small and medium-sized companies. The same conclusion, though less explicitly, features in the contribution of Pasture from Belgium (chapter 2).

The Challenge of the Immigrants

More so than does regional diversity, immigrants confront European trade unions with the issue of identity, and they do it in two ways. Firstly, because, by definition, they bring their own values, norms and lifestyle to the host country. The question is how the local working class and its organisations will handle it. Secondly, the immigrants make the trade unions face up to the movement's own ideals and ideologies, namely the fundamental values of equality and internationalism. Hence, Albert Martens starts his contribution with a reference to the Communist Manifesto of 1848, in which Marx called all workers to unite (chapter 6). From that perspective, the contributions below are quite sobering.

In an important comparative study (still unpublished at the time of writing) of the attitudes and policies of trade unions in seven West European countries (Switzerland, the FRG, Austria, the Netherlands, France, the UK and Sweden) based on much the same premises as our program, Rinus Penninx and Judith Roosblad identified three basic dilemmas the unions faced regarding immigration and immigrants (Penninx and Roosblad, forthcoming; chapter 7).[2] (1) How should the trade unions react to immigration: should they resist immigration, or co-operate with governments and employers, and if so, under what conditions? (2) Should immigrants, once they are in a country, be considered as part of the normal workforce and citizenship, part of the same *working class*, and therefore actively recruited by the unions and receive the same rights as all other

---

[2] Rinus Penninx presented the conclusions of this study at the aforementioned conference of which this book contains the papers. Unfortunately, he could not deliver his text in the form of a chapter to this book, but he kindly allowed us to make use of the introduction and the conclusion of his edited volume, which we did, with some reluctance. We wish to express our thanks to Professor Penninx for his generous offer.

workers, or should they, as foreigners or temporary employees, be totally or partially excluded from these rights, in particular of trade union membership? (3) If the unions consider the immigrants as potential members, should they simply defend their general interests as workers, emphasising the collective stake in working class interests, while disregarding differences in 'material' and cultural positions, or should they develop specific policies and structures for them and give them preferential treatment at the risk of upsetting the indigenous workers? Incidentally, these three dilemmas do not exist totally independent of each other: answers to the first dilemma determine potential answers to the following one. For example, if the unions radically and successfully oppose immigration, the second and third dilemma become to some extent irrelevant, as is more or less the case in Austria (not dealt with in this volume). However, usually the unions oppose immigration to start with, with the intention of protecting the national labour market and the position of the indigenous workers, but they still have to face the second dilemma of how to respond to immigrants once the latter succeed in entering the labour market. As Castles and Kosack observed, it even becomes essential to organise these workers to avoid alienating them and, by dividing the workforce, to further weaken the union's strength culminating with 'the worst of both worlds' (Castles and Kosack, 1973, 128).

However, within the framework of this volume, we mainly concentrate on the second and third dilemma. Some contributions, especially by Roosblad (chapter 7), Martens (chapter 6) and Ambrosini (chapter 8), however, contain interesting facts and observations on the process of immigration and the introduction of immigrants into the labour market.

From the study by Penninx and Roosblad, it appears that trade unions have developed a wide range of changeable strategies which could not possibly be compiled into a realistic typology; in the end they found more or less as many types as there were cases. A few constant factors emerged, however. Trade unions tend to change tack as they are faced with the double dilemma described by Castles and Kosack. In the first phase, they oppose immigration, but in the second phase - involving a troublesome process occurring very unevenly in different countries and in different unions within the same country - when unions acknowledge that the immigrants are permanently settled, they actually take up their case. Albert Martens (chapter 6; see also Martens, 1996) illustrates this beautifully. Trade unions do not automatically adapt their own organisations to follow suit, but in time - again with great variations between countries and different trade unions - they eventually set up specific internal structures for the immigrants, some immediately, others after a delay spanning decades. The hardest adjustments involve specific cultural problems.

Penninx and Roosblad have tried to explain the great variation in trade union attitudes to immigration and immigrants. A crucial observation, relevant to our research theme, is that the culture and tradition of the immigrant workers does not particularly determine their attitude to the trade union, except in a few specific cases. For instance, the recruitment rate among Turkish workers in Sweden and Belgium is fairly high, but it is very low in France, the Netherlands and Switzerland (Penninx and Roosblad, forthcoming). It is not their own distinctive trade union traditions they grew up with that seem relevant to their attitude towards unionism, but the trade union culture of the country they work in, and how the policies of the local trade unions affect them. This applies both to recruitment levels, and to participation in collective actions, insofar it is possible to draw reliable conclusions based on the little factual data at our disposal.

The social and economic structures investigated by Penninx and Roosblad could only partly explain the variation in trade union positions and policies, although it turned out that the extent to which trade unions have pervaded the social, economic and political decision making process seemed to be significant for their attitude towards immigration and the time it took them to consider immigrants - particularly illegal immigrants - as fully-fledged citizens. Shifts in the trade union position (for instance, the great loss of political power in the UK and France) had consequences for their handling of the immigration issue. However, their relative power did not determine the *content* of trade union policies. As far as the content was concerned, the explanation had to be found in the specific national historical context of the different countries.

We have now returned to our first observations regarding the strong national identification of the labour movement with its nation state. Attempts have been made to detect systems in those national traditions. Emmanuel Todd (1994), for example, has reduced the widely varying policies on immigrants in Europe to a difference between the *jus sanguinis* and the *jus solis* - citizenship based on kinship, as in Germany, or founded on the principle of territorialism, which is much more inclusive, as in France. Although the variety of trade union attitudes towards immigrants clearly indicates that the issue is much more complex than Todd concludes - the case of France as discussed by Philippe Bataille (chapter 10) does not fit particularly well in Todd's somewhat 'idealistic' scheme either - the observation that unions largely adhere to national traditions and tendencies is valid, even if that may not be that surprising.

The contributions below complement those conclusions without refuting them. For example, they allow comparisons to be made between the Netherlands and Belgium, two countries with comparable industrial relations and trade union landscapes (although Belgium has a much higher trade union density rate than the Netherlands).[3] Belgium, however, experienced a massive number of immigrant workers much earlier, which was practically not questioned at the time (1st dilemma). The Belgian trade unions have from the start defended the foreign workers as 'class mates' (2nd dilemma) and adopted them to their ranks (3rd dilemma). The same happened, even to a greater extent, with the so-called second large wave of immigration from 1962 to 1965 (chapter 6). Even the Dutch trade unions took up a fairly positive position on this immigration, at least until a light economic depression in 1966/67 hardened their stance. Until the 'eighties, however, they harboured the illusion that the immigration - at least from the so-called 'guest workers' from the Mediterranean coast, as opposed to the colonial immigrants - was a temporary phenomenon, and that the immigrants would eventually return to their country of origin (chapter 7).

In Belgium, differences arose between how the immigrant workers were received by the socialist and the christian trade unions. The christian trade unions resolutely chose specific action and organisation, whereas the socialists advocated and practised a radical assimilation policy. In the Netherlands, too, protestant christian unions singled out the immigrants for specific attention and tailor-made provisions before the socialist and catholic unions started to act, but still extremely late compared with Belgium, even allowing for the different immigration pattern. The Confederation of Christian Trade Unions in the Netherlands CNV was motivated by religious considerations. Since the CNV had cancelled its federal debate with the other trade unions, it in fact emphasised its religious foundation (see also Pasture, 1996). The Dutch Confederation of Catholic Trade Unions NKV did not champion the same cause, probably not because its ideology had become watered down - as claimed by the CNV - but because it increasingly was influenced by social and democratic thinking, and the overriding importance of class solidarity; incidentally in 1973 the NKV federated with the socialist NVV. In Belgium, christian and socialist trade unions have come closer together with very similar immigration policies, under pressure from mutual rivalry.

---

[3] The volume by Penninx and Roosblad does not contain a contribution on Belgium. The explanation for the difference in recruitment levels between Belgium and the Netherlands is due mainly to two factors: firstly, the role played by Belgian unions in unemployment insurance, whereby they are in charge of paying out unemployment benefits, which is naturally an important factor for recruitment and retention of members. Secondly, the Belgian trade unions are present at all levels in the economy - at national, regional and industry level as well as at the workplace, right in the heart of companies through works councils and trade union delegations. Dutch trade unions are practically absent there.

This ideological component of postwar socialism is not easy to find in other countries. In this respect, Satnam Virdee (chapter 9) points out an entirely different view. In the 'sixties, the increasingly hard-line attitudes of the labour movement in Great Britain stimulated a more inclusive and international concept of social class, which also led to a shift in the British trade union movement. From an attitude towards black workers which was, at best, neutral and at worst, often sectionalist (if not even blatantly racist), towards a more inclusive approach, actively opposing racism at the workplace as well as in society in general. Growing class consciousness - the 'resurgence of the class struggle' in the terms of Crouch and Pizzorno (1978) - was more general in Europe in the late 1960s, but we could not find any evidence of such a large shift in attitude towards immigrant workers elsewhere, unless perhaps with the catholic union NKV in the Netherlands. However, nowhere else in Europe (except in Austria) had the unions adopted either such a sectionalist attitude towards immigrant workers, or had the immigrant issue been translated into terms of race.

The shift in policies of the British trade union movement occurred initially as a reaction against the extreme right, which stirred up xenophobic and even racist feelings in the 'seventies all over Europe - with varying results - against the immigrants (Betz, 1994; Hainsworth, 1992). As is apparent from the analysis by Philippe Bataille (chapter 10), racism also took hold in France, at times profoundly pervading French society and the workplace in particular. Bataille describes racism as a reaction to the crisis which continues to hit the underclass of the lowly skilled (despite more positive economic key figures in the mid-1990s), but also as an ideology construed by the extreme right, and as a cancer from outside the workplace which infiltrated both small and middle-sized companies, as well as the public services, and thus became part of a specific 'workers' culture' (defined as a total of values, discourses and practices). It has come to replace the value of class solidarity, traditionally held by the workers' movement, although this shocking observation does not feature as such in Bataille's text. This diffuse racism is difficult to identify with a particular 'party', and the trade union movement finds it hard to combat. Bataille's exposé further illustrates that if the trade union movement - which occupies the high moral ground with its ideals of equality - does not formulate an explicit reply to the first dilemma posed by immigration and the paradox of Castles and Kosack, it actually contrives to corrupt the situation. Virdee further demonstrates that the trade union movement in Great Britain can rectify the situation, and also in France, the confederations have now taken the fight against racism seriously. The top-down approach is necessary for this issue. Furthermore, a broad popular anti-racist movement has taken root in France, incorporating the trade unions. The French trade union movement has unfortunately become very weak, particularly within the companies themselves, where the struggle should be conducted in the first place. This makes it difficult to be optimistic.

In Flanders, too, where a strong extreme right movement advocates hatred for foreigners (targeting traditional, often impoverished workers' estates to that effect), the trade unions have picked up the gauntlet, albeit quite late and, in my opinion, at first with less conviction (see the contribution by Martens, chapter 6). Also in the Netherlands, the rise of the extreme right, which had remained on a much smaller scale there than in France and Flanders, generated a more positive attitude towards the immigrants within the unions, focusing on solidarity and equality. It is remarkable, however, that this solidarity, at first sight different from that in Great Britain, is expressed in humanistic terms rather than class terms. It undoubtedly points to a general trend in society, which became more widespread following the fall of the Berlin Wall and the bankruptcy of communism.

The extent to which their own national cultural experiences determine the relations between trade unions and immigrants is again obvious from the contribution by Maurizio Ambrosini regarding Italy (chapter 8). Even the 'first dilemma' mentioned above does not feature here: as a former place of emigration which is not short of labour and knows strong internal migration, the Italian trade unions did not view the newcomers on the labour market as a threat, nor, in the words of the author, as a 'remarkable phenomenon from an economic point of view'. In some respects, the Italian trade unions do not really seem to consider the immigrants as 'strangers'; they barely make the distinction between official and illegal immigrants - which is probably also related to the attitude of the Italians towards the State. Comparable tendencies, although less radical, can be found in Belgium, where the labour movement supported the legitimisation of illegal immigrants who had already spent a long time in the country, as well as the actions of refugee associations. The role of the trade union movement in the export of the welfare state undoubtedly influences its attitude towards immigrants. With its weak social structures, the trade unions in Italy largely retained control over the social provisions; the actions in support of the immigrants consequently somewhat remained in the charitable sector. It is remarkable how even this sort of attitude generates a response from the immigrants themselves. Parallels can be drawn with Belgium for that matter, too.

Ambrosini's text also demonstrates that the issue of the labour movement and the immigrants should not be narrowed to the trade unions. Trade unions only make up a part of the labour movement, and they further associate with other social movements that take the interests of the immigrants to heart and even grow to champion that cause when the unions fall short in their task of defending the immigrants. In France, the importance of the 'hand in hand' movement should be acknowledged. Paradoxically, but understandably so, the trade unions are weakest at defending the immigrants when it comes to the core issues of trade unionism, namely their position in the labour market and in the workplace. Various authors, particularly Roosblad, emphasise that tackling the issue through changes in legislation is often more effective than through the trade union movement - this also applies to other special groups, in the first place to female workers. In relation to their own organisation, trade unions seem most reticent to act, and also when strictly cultural issues are at stake (for example, the right to express religious beliefs - e.g. by wearing the *shador* - and to take holidays on particular religious feast days).

To conclude this introduction, we can ponder the question as to whether there are parallels in the way the trade union movement deals with regional cultural differences and with ethnic cultural differences as they emerge when dealing with immigrants. The answer is a resounding yes. After all, we notice that the trade unions - some more strongly than others, because the variation between trade unions of different ideological colours, but particularly of different countries, is very big - have not only identified themselves with the working class within the nation states, but also with the dominant ethnic group in that class, the 'native white worker'. The currently popular concept of *multiple identities* is, in fact, only of limited use in describing the problem highlighted: competing, or even rather contradictory identities, describes the reality in this case much better.

On a different note, it should be said that, because of its orientation to the nation state, the trade union movement finds it hard to differentiate internally. The class maxim - in practice restricted to the dominating ethnic working class - is opposed to a further division of the 'solidarity'; it is in that sense no coincidence that the christian trade unions in Belgium (and partly also in the Netherlands) are less susceptible to it, because they apply a slightly different, less adversary and exclusive class concept, while rejecting the class struggle. Probably due to the decline in class consciousness and also to the notion that the class concept tended to be interpreted in a rather exclusive way, we can see a clear trend in favour of clearing the way for increased diversity, for recognising regional entities on the one hand and ethnic and cultural identities and interests on the other.

A remarkable observation in this respect is that in both cases a link can be made with the rise of the extreme right, which manifests itself not only in increasing regionalism and nationalism but also in growing xenophobia, hatred for foreigners and racism. The recognition of distinctiveness, both of regions and of immigrants, is not, however, an expression of extreme right or neofascist infiltration, but rather a response to this threat. This is most obvious when the extreme right confronts the labour movement with the exclusive maxim that it has tolerated before, and probably even helped to uphold. The contributions by Satnam Virdee (chapter 9) and Philippe Bataille (chapter 10) are in this respect real eye openers. This observation reinforces our conclusions from the previous publication in this research program, which stated that the labour movement was actually able to carry a democratic, inclusive form of nationalism (Pasture and Verberckmoes, 1998), which has also been upheld by Stefan Berger and Angel Smith (1999).

This last observation returns us to our initial problem issue and the significance of cultural identity. I believe there can be little doubt that the cultural components as analysed in this publication and the previous one (or rather: contributed elements for such an analysis) are more than relevant for the trade union movement. However, a strong social and economic and political dimension remains, in the shape of the distribution of power.

References

Anderson, B. (1991), *Imagined Communities Reflections upon the Origin and Spread of Nationalism*, Verso, London/New York.
Berger, S. (1995), 'European Labour Movements and the European Working Class in Comparative Perspective', in S. Berger and D. Broughton (eds), *The Force of Labour. The Western European Labour Movement and the Working Class in the Twentieth Century*, Berg, Oxford/Washington, p. 245-61.
Berger, S. and Smith, A. (1999), 'Between Scylla and Charybdis: nationalism, Labour and ethnicity across five continents, 1870-1939', in S. Berger and A. Smith (eds), *Nationalism, Labour and Ethnicity 1870-1939*, Manchester UP, Manchester/New York, p. 1-30.
Betz, H.-G. (1994), *Radical Right-wing Populism in Western Europe*, Macmillan, Houndmills/London.
Birnbaum, P. (1997), *Sociologie des nationalismes*, PUF, Paris.
Braun, M. (1998), 'Regionalism Threatening Trade Unions in Northern Italy', in P. Pasture and J. Verberckmoes (eds), *Working Class Internationalism and the Appeal of National Identity. Historical Dilemmas and Current Debates on Western Europe*, Berg, Oxford/New York, p. 203-14.
Bunel, J. (1999), 'Espagne: syndicalisme et nationalisme au Pays Bas Espagnol', *Chronique internationale de l'IRES*, No. 56, p. 12-21.
Castles, S. and Kosack, G. (1973), *Immigrant workers and class structure in Europe*, Oxford UP, Oxford.
Crouch, C. and Pizzorno, A. (1979), *The resurgence of class conflict in western Europe since 1968*, Macmillan, London.
Ebbinghaus, B. (1993), 'Labour Unity in Union Diversity: Trade Unions and Social Cleavages in Western Europe, 1890-1989', Unpublished PhD thesis, European University Institute, Florence.

Ferner, A. and Hyman, R. (1998), 'Introduction: towards European Industrial Relations?', in A. Ferner and R. Hyman (eds), *Changing Industrial Relations in Europe*, Blackwell, Oxford, p. xi-xxvi.

Hainsworth, P. (ed) (1992), *The Extreme Right in Europe and the USA*, Themes in Right-Wing Ideology and Politics Series 13, Pinter, London.

Hroch, M. (1985), *Social Preconditions of National Revival in Europe. A Comparative Analysis of the Social Composition of Patriotic Groups among the Smaller European Nations*, Cambridge University Press, Cambridge.

Jordana, J. and Nagel, K.-J. (1998), 'Trade Unions in Catalonia: Have Unions Joined Nationalism?', in P. Pasture and J. Verberckmoes (eds), *Working Class Internationalism and the Appeal of National Identity. Historical Dilemmas and Current Debates on Western Europe*, Berg, Oxford/New York, p. 83-106.

Katznelson, I. (1986), 'Working-Class Formation: Constructing Cases and Comparisons', in I. Katznelson and A.R. Zolberg (eds), *Working-Class Formation. Nineteenth Century Patterns in Western Europe and the United States*, Princeton University Press, Princeton, p. 3-41.

Keating, M. (1998), *The new regionalism in Western Europe: territorial restructuring and political change*, Edward Elgar, Aldershot.

Martens, A. (1996), 'Trade Unions and Migrant Workers in Europe: A Changing Ideology as a Reflection of Variable Principles', in P. Pasture, J. Verberckmoes and H. De Witte (eds), *The Lost Perspective? Trade Unions between Ideology and Social Action in the New Europe*, Perspectives on Europe, Avebury, Aldershot, Volume 1, p. 200-17.

Mees, L. (1998), 'Social Solidarity and National Identity in the Basque Country: The Case of the Nationalist Trade Union ELA/STV', in P. Pasture and J. Verberckmoes (eds), *Working Class Internationalism and the Appeal of National Identity. Historical Dilemmas and Current Debates on Western Europe*, Berg, Oxford/New York, p. 43-82.

Paluski, J. and Waters, M. (1996), *The Death of Class*, Sage, London.

Pasture, P. (1993), 'The April 1944 "social pact" in Belgium and its significance for the postwar welfare state', *Journal of Contemporary History*, Vol. XXVIII, No. 3, p. 695-714.

Pasture, P. (1996), 'The Unattainable Unity in the Netherlands', in P. Pasture, J. Verberckmoes and H. De Witte (eds), *The Lost Perspective? Trade Unions between Ideology and Social Action in the New Europe*, Perspectives on Europe, Avebury, Aldershot, Volume 1, p. 136-79.

Pasture, P. (1998), 'The Temptations of Nationalism. Regionalist Orientations in the Christian Labour Movement in Belgium', in P. Pasture and J. Verberckmoes (eds), *Working Class Internationalism and the Appeal of National Identity. Historical Dilemmas and Current Debates on Western Europe*, Berg, Oxford/New York, p. 107-50.

Pasture, P. and Verberckmoes, J. (eds) (1998), *Working Class Internationalism and the Appeal of National Identity. Historical Dilemmas and Current Debates on Western Europe*, Berg, Oxford/New York.

Pasture, P., Verberckmoes, J. and De Witte, H. (eds) (1996), *The Lost Perspective? Trade Unions between Ideology and Social Action in the New Europe*, Perspectives on Europe, Avebury, Aldershot, 2 vols.

Pench, L.R., Sestino, P. and Frontini, E. (1999), *Some unpleasant arithmetics of regional unemployment in the EU. Are there any lessons for EMU?*, Economic Papers 134, European Commission, Brussels, April 1999 (http://europa.eu.int/comm/dg02/document/ecopap/ecp134en/htm; PDF file).

Penninx, R. and Roosblad, J. (eds) (forthcoming 2000), *Trade unions, immigration and immigrants in Europe 1960-93. A comparative study of attitudes and actions of trade*

unions in seven West European countries, Berghahn, Oxford (introduction and conclusion).
Todd, E. (1994), *Le destin des immigrés. Assimilation et ségrégation dans les démocraties occidentales*, Seuil, Paris.
Van der Linden, M. (1988), 'The National Integration of European Working Classes. Explaining the Causal Configuration', *International Review of Social History*, No. XXXIII, p. 285-311.
Van Gyes, G. c.s. (eds) (forthcoming 2000), *Can Class Still Unite? Trade Unions, Class Solidarity and the Differentiated Workforce in Late Modernity*, Ashgate, Aldershot.

1 Cultural Diversity and Politics: An Introduction

STAFFAN ZETTERHOLM

A 'natural' starting point for a discussion of cultural diversity and politics is the common sense notion that the 'natural' borders of a political system coincide with cultural borders, which is another way of saying that they ought to coincide.[1] This notion is expressed *inter alia* in the normative political principle of the *right to self-determination* of peoples, where the 'people' more often than not is defined in terms of ethnicity or culture. The principle of the popular right of self-determination has been very dominant in the last hundred years (or more) and is, of course, related to the establishment of a new fundamental basis for political legitimacy after the French revolution and the demise of other principles such as a religious base of political power. The people as sovereign, the base for all political power, also finds its expression in democratic forms of government. Thus, our starting point seems to imply a rather close link between democratic forms of governance and the requirement of cultural homogeneity. As John Stuart Mill said in the last century:

> Free institutions are next to impossible in a country made up of different nationalities. Among a people without fellow-feeling, especially if they read and speak different languages, the united public opinion, necessary to the working of representative government, cannot exist (Mill, 1958, 230).

---

[1] 'The idea of a culturally homogeneous political community consisting of autonomous, rational individuals has continued to dominate those forms of political thought in which the people are regarded as taking an active part in governing themselves' (Hindess, 1992, 160).

Thus, cultural diversity according to common conceptions of politics - as defined in terms of democratic nation-states - may seem detrimental to both the legitimacy and the efficiency of the democratic political system.

The cultural homogeneity of a political system as an ideal may be defended both by the need for cultural autonomy (in order to preserve the culture,[2] something which is seen as a value in itself) and by the need for effective political governance.

Cultural Autonomy

Cultural autonomy may be viewed as the right of societal groups to maintain and develop their own culture, and the only or the best way to secure the autonomy of the cultural group is to give it political autonomy - political independence. The level of political autonomy may differ: from total political self-determination, expressed in an independent state, to different forms of restricted autonomy, power sharing and constitutional guarantees within a broader political framework. But there are - it is argued - Rights of Minority Cultures, which should be secured by legal/constitutional means. Such rights of cultural groups are either founded in the liberal argument that every individual has a right to preserve and develop his or her own culture, or they are framed in collective terms, as group rights, which are not reducible to individual rights.

Stability and Efficiency of Government

But the argument for cultural homogeneity may also focus on the need for governmental efficiency in democratic political systems. According to this line of reasoning, a democracy needs higher levels of loyalty and solidarity between the members of the political system if it is to be legitimate even when the government makes decisions which are seen as costly - even sacrifices - to some groups. The basic logic is that a democracy does not have the possibility of using coercive means to secure effective implementation, but must rather rely on the acceptance by the citizens of the proposition that the decisions are for 'the common good'. Such an acceptance requires a strong identification with the political system as a collective unit. Sacri-

---

[2] The concept of culture used in this presentation is a broad anthropological concept: culture is seen as a 'way of life', a setup of beliefs, norms and ideas, which is common to a social group and which is expressed in the practices of the group. A more narrow concept of culture, defined in terms of the arts and literature and other symbolic expressions of the world-view of the group, will be included in our broad concept.

fices are not endured for 'them', for some strangers outside the social group, but for 'us', the political community. Only if such strong feelings of community - of loyalty and solidarity with the collective unit - prevail, can democratic government be stable and efficient. This strong identification with the political community might be labelled 'nationhood' (cf. Canovan, 1996), which is the base of the nation-state. To the extent - I underline to the *extent*, and this is really the crux of the matter - that cultural homogeneity is needed for such a strong identification with the political community to emerge, one can argue that cultural homogeneity is required for the stability and efficiency of democratic political systems. The argument reversed: cultural diversity within the political system will contribute to lower levels of loyalty and solidarity, and thus to a weaker and less legitimate government.

The Political Community

Central to the discussion is the concept of the political community, which denotes the political system as a membership organisation and thus stands for the individuals or groups which are members of the same political system. This is a multifaceted concept, from which at least three different aspects may be singled out in our context:

a) the political community as defined by citizenship, of rights and obligations;
b) the political community as defined by a feeling of identity;
c) the political community as defined by borders, i.e. the inclusion of some people and the exclusion of others.

Since the development of the modern idea of 'democracy' in political theory and in politics, conceptions of self-government and representative government have focused upon the people and the characteristics of the people in their double capacity as both rulers and ruled, or, in other words, as citizens and subjects. The contract theories of the 17th century focused primarily on the individual as a rational actor, able to organise the 'state of nature' into a suitable political structure through a reciprocal commitment to certain political principles. Locke speaks of 'any number of men' making a covenant, and Hobbes states that a 'commonwealth is said to be instituted when a multitude of men do agree' (quoted in Van Dyke, 1996, 34). In this case the political community seems to be given a rather minimal definition: the common aspect can be reduced to the acceptance of the political institutions - through the contract.

The concept of 'political community' in modern political theory also denotes the people who are members of the same political system, in their double capacities as subjects and citizens. It is differentiated from 'the government' or the 'authorities', on the one hand, and from the 'political regime', or the specific political institutional arrangements, on the other (cf. Easton, 1965, passim). The delimitation of the political community draws the boundaries around those who are citizens as well as subjects (and thus subject to the political decisions), and those who are not. This is the uncomplicated definition of the political community, which bypasses any differentiation between a community of subjects and a community of citizens, by means of which it is possible to avoid taking a position on the problem of non-citizens within the boundaries of the political system, i.e. those who are bound by the political decisions without having (full) rights as citizens to participate in the political system. Categories of such non-citizens have throughout the course of history included slaves, foreigners, women and children. In the political theory discourse of the 1990s, the groups that are being focused upon in particular are immigrant groups and minority ethnic/cultural groups.

The other aspect concerns the preconditions of the existence or development of cohesion and a fellow-feeling. According to Paul Howe, such preconditions of communal cohesion may 'change quite dramatically over time... At a different historical stage, people, by attaching importance to different shared elements, can come to have new notions of the boundaries of a community' (Howe, 1995, 30). At the same time, he argues, traditional theories of cohesion emphasise a 'significant degree of tangible homogeneity among community members' (Howe, 1995, 30), such as common ethnic origin (even if it is 'imagined' or fabricated by nationalist leaders), or the level of communication,[3] both quantitatively and qualitatively, between the members of a system, be it a social, a political, or an international political system. Thus, an assumption of (some sort of) cultural homogeneity seems to loom large in the idea of political community.

In summary, we can differentiate between two basic dimensions or ingredients in our presentation of common assumptions about the normative links between cultural homogeneity and the democratic political system: (1) a strong identification with the political community is needed for a stable and efficient democracy to maintain itself, and (2) cultural homogeneity is required for the maintenance of a strong identification with the political community, and, thus, cultural diversity weakens community feelings and the legitimacy of the system.

---

[3] The classic representative being Deutsch (1966).

Multicultural Political Systems

So far we have concentrated on the normative idea of cultural homogeneity as a necessary or at least fairly integrated aspect of the political community. At the same time, political realities seem to include cultural diversity in many cases. Thus, many, if not most, political units do not consist of only one, homogeneous people, but they contain different ethnic/cultural groupings. This is definitely true of big countries like Germany, Britain or France. The only really reliable example of nation-state homogeneity, which is often mentioned in the literature, seems to be Iceland (Hedetoft, 1995, Chapter 5; Canovan, 1996). This creates a problem of explanation if we accept that most political systems, including most democratic systems, have a certain amount of cultural heterogeneity. Heterogeneity can in this context mean (at least) two things. (1) The concept of common culture is a myth, as no country can be said to have a common culture. Modern life with a comprehensive division of labour and differences in education, social life, etc. means that the different social and professional and political groups have very different ideas and values. They do not share 'meaning' as implied by the concept of 'common culture'. (2) Many countries include different ethnic/cultural groups, both in their self-understanding and in the opinion of others. Quite apart from the fact that some well-functioning democracies consist of several cultural groups, as for example Switzerland, there are in many countries minority cultural/ethnic groups which do not opt for secession or cause serious disruptions in the political system.

Thus, political systems may be defined as 'multi-cultural' in two different ideal-typical ways.

a) Cultural complexity with a monocultural image:
   Every large-scale political system exhibits cultural complexity (in the sense defined by Hannerz (1992)) to the extent that it is impossible, or - in a more cautious formulation - very difficult, to talk about a common culture for a state. The distribution of existential and practical knowledge over the population in modern times - with the highly complex division of labour and with the different uses of different media and the different educational paths - makes the lack of a common world view or a common approach to life and societal affairs probable. Apart perhaps from some very small and isolated states, cultural homogeneity is nonexistent. This does not imply, however, that it does not exist as an 'imagined culture' in the self-understanding of the populations. Examples of this type may include the Nordic countries or Ireland.

b) Cultural diversity with a multicultural image:
Some political systems are openly recognized, also by their populations, as being multi-cultural, i.e. as including different ethnic/cultural groups, which are considered, both in their self-understanding and in the understanding of others, to be culturally diverse. Examples are not hard to find. Most countries recognize the existence of ethnic/cultural subcommunities. For example, the United Kingdom, Canada and the United States all belong to this category. This may be the result of earlier conquests and the forced inclusion of certain peoples into a new political structure, but it can also be the result of large-scale migration, which creates new ethnic/cultural communities within the borders of another country. The situation here can also be described with the term 'cultural complexity' - both within the cultural communities and between them. That is to say, one cannot presuppose cultural homogeneity within the cultural subcommunities. But the self-understanding of the population in such cases involves the parallel existence of several different and more or less homogeneous cultures.

In both of these types there seems to be a tension between the definition of the 'nation-state polity' and the existing political realities of cultural diversity which, according to the argument presented above, would lead to a weaker identification with the political community, less legitimacy accorded to the political decisions, and less loyalty and solidarity between different cultural groups. Is this in fact the case?
Different answers could be given to this question.

a) The strong identification with the political community is not dependent on cultural homogeneity. There might be other bases for political support. One very lively debate has been about the case of *Verfassungspatriotismus*, or consensus about the basic political rules and norms of the polity. The common acceptance of these basic rules is enough to rally the people behind the government, and to create solidarity and feelings of community.
Empirically there is some evidence that cultural homogeneity is not a precondition of the strong identification with the political community. It is possible to point to multi-cultural political systems which, all the same, can be characterized as being nation-states, i.e. where among the citizens there is a strong identification with the system and a high level of loyalty and solidarity. An example often given is Switzerland, which combines strong allegiance to the political system with different cultural identities, different languages, etc. Another example sometimes given is the USA, with the metaphor of the 'melting pot', which implies the emergence of a new identity, very much related to the political

community. Thus, the link between cultural homogeneity and the strong identification with the political community seems rather tenuous or contingent, as strong identification seems possible within a multi-cultural political population. There are many different views as to the conclusions that should be drawn by such (counter-) examples. The very specific position and history of Switzerland, and the very special constitutional arrangements, including a high degree of regional (and thus cultural group) autonomy and the extensive use of direct democracy in the form of referenda, are emphasized as making Switzerland an exceptional case, not transferable to other political systems. And the exceptional character of the USA is linked, on the one hand, to its being an immigrant country, where the immigrants have voluntarily left their own cultural group and in a sense have already accepted cultural change and, on the other, to the existence of a dominant white, Anglophone culture, which forms the basis for a cultural homogeneity, or rather cultural dominance. It is not possible within the present context to discuss further the reasonableness of these different interpretations.

In this context I want to draw attention to the existence of two concepts of culture which sometimes are mixed, or are not clearly separated, and which therefore may create some confusion when the argument is about multi-cultural political systems. It may be useful to differentiate between two parts of the overall culture of a society (the culture itself, being defined broadly in an anthropological fashion as a '"way of life", as a distinct set of beliefs and norms and the concurrent social practices of a societal group'): between what we can call the 'private' culture and what we can call the 'public' culture. Of course, the distinction is often blurred, as the private culture and the public culture overlap and interact within the societal group. Furthermore, language is both private and public and defies the distinction. The point I want to make is only that in some - and perhaps in many - political systems, which are thought of as being multi-cultural, there is a common public culture expressed through the acceptance of the political institutions, and a common 'national history' and a 'national heritage' of public myths and heroes, which form the basis for a strong identification with the political community. The more private aspects of the culture may still be different and distinct. Thus, a common history, interpreted in nation-building terms, may be a part of the explanation of the strong political community in Switzerland.

Such an argument does point to the importance of *time* in including different cultural/ethnic groups within one national community. Groups dominated by - and in opposition to - another political regime may over time come to feel integrated with and identify with the political community.

b) There is a false picture of harmony and tolerance between different cultural groups within a single political community. The absence of conflict does not exclude the existence of latent tensions between different cultural groups within one polity, but their relative size and the power distribution between them restricts the politicisation of the cultural dimension within the polity. For the minority groups, there may be insufficient political resources to better the political or cultural situation for themselves. Passivity, based on powerlessness, instead of open political opposition and mobilisation may contribute to a false impression of acceptance and strong identification with the political community.

c) One might also try to combine the two earlier answers, by saying that both harmony and conflict may emerge as a result of political conditions or the use of culture as a political mobilisation resource. The requirement of cultural homogeneity is a political ideology which may or may not be activated and accepted, and which, if activated, may create a political dynamic of its own, leading to a widening cleavage between the cultural groups, social and economic discrimination, and a growing alienation and hostility between the groups.

In order to analyse a bit further the character of the tension between cultural diversity and politics, it is necessary at this point to introduce the question as to what status this idea has. Or in other words: 'Is the idea given, is it changing, and is it changeable? Is it a part of politics as such, or is it a part of present-day conceptions of politics which may change (or which may be changed by conscious efforts)? Is the principle of national/cultural self-determination part and parcel of our understanding of democratic politics?'

Analytical Frameworks

There seem to be many different answers and different models as to the character of the idea of the desirability of cultural homogeneity within the political community. In order to facilitate the discussion, we can distinguish four different approaches concerning the 'cultural' idea of cultural homogeneity of the political community. (The nation-state idea is of course part of our culture!)

a) The (perceived) need for cultural homogeneity is based upon 'human nature' itself. Man is a social and collective animal, whose existence and well-being is dependent upon the individual being a member of a group, which establishes, develops and maintains a common system of ideas and norms, i.e. a common culture, which is a necessity for individual growth and for the social identity of the members of the group. Therefore the group can be regarded as being the natural environment of the individual. From this perspective it seems natural to view political self-determination of the societal group as only a continuation and an expansion of the identity and pride of the group and its culture - 'its way of life'.

b) The (perceived) need for cultural homogeneity is based on certain *functional requirements* in terms of economic and social developments within a given historical period. Many theories of nationalism see the establishment of the nation-state and its emphasis on national culture and national identity in terms of a 'necessary' adaptation to the requirements of new technologies, new production structures and the expansion of trade to larger areas (the Gellner thesis). New needs for political centralisation and more extensive political regulation of the economy (and other societal sectors) mean that there is also a functional imperative to create a strong feeling of community within the political system and a strong political identity in order to mobilise support for strong government intervention and control.

c) The (perceived) need for cultural homogeneity - and thus for the exclusion of other groups from political participation and influence - is based upon a certain definition of the ideal political community, which in turn is the result of processes of *social construction*, or, to use other terminology, is based upon the production and dissemination of a certain ideology. In this case, or rather group of cases, the idea of a culturally homogeneous political community is seen is being more or less produced and maintained by political or social forces, be they the aggregate outcome of many political discourses, or be they generated and upheld by specific political strata or groupings in an effort to preserve their political or societal power. In this perspective, power and the political control of 'the construction of collective meaning' become central analytical foci.

d) One might add a fourth paradigm, which sees the dominance of the idea of cultural homogeneity of the political system as being the result of experiences and *calculations of rational actors* who are the members of the political system. In terms of the narrow goal of 'maximisation of political influence and of the utility of the political decisions', resistance to a multicultural political system may seem to be a rational reaction on the part of the citizens. The existence - or the probability - of the introduction and legitimacy of ideas and norms which are viewed as being culturally distant from one's own will expand the uncertainty of political outcomes (i.e. it will expand the win-set in other directions than one's own) and reduce the future benefits from the political output.

Now, looking at the different reasons for the idea of cultural homogeneity, it is clear that the different paradigms lead to very different conclusions and to different recommendations as to how to handle a situation within the context of a multi-cultural political system.

The first paradigm, in which cultural homogeneity is seen to be a prerequisite for a 'good social and political life', views cultural diversity as a directly negative feature of political life which must in some way or another be corrected or at least neutralised. The political autonomy of the social group is to be strengthened, either by the establishment of a totally independent political unit, a state, or through a high level of political independence within a constitutional framework which is common for different cultural communities. Particularly areas defined as having a high cultural impact are singled out for autonomy, such as educational, linguistic and cultural policy areas. The discussion in political philosophy of legal rights for minority cultures, including collective rights as opposed to individual human rights, will enter into the picture here (Kymlicka, 1996).

The second analytical perspective, which views the functional requirements of cultural homogeneity (e.g. in terms of educational and linguistic qualifications) as being necessary for efficient communication, for mobility and flexibility of the labour force, and for the efficient mobilisation of political support and allegiance, will have to raise the question as to whether the same functional requirements still exist in the present period, or whether the processes of globalisation, internationalisation and regionalisation, where the borders of the nation-states seem to be restricting in a detrimental way the transnational economic and political interactions, will require a change in the definition of politics and a rethinking of the link between culture and politics. At the same time, international political co-operation, also in the form of political integration, raises the question as to whether the strong identification with the nation-state is compatible with the changes in the political landscape. Instead of one central government, politics has to be multi-centred, comprising many centres with overlapping competencies. Instead of the cultural definition of the political community, we need to develop a definition of politics in multi-cultural or a-cultural terms.

As a matter of fact, this question about the long-term changes of the political landscape as a result of economic globalisation is central to the ongoing discussions about future models of governance, particularly, though not exclusively, in relation to the future political structure of the European Union. The conflict between those who define politics in terms of the nation-state, with its implication of cultural homogeneity (as ideal type, if not in reality) as the basis of political identity and of state sovereignty, and those who define politics in terms of transnational governance structures, either in the form of federal structures or in the form of 'post-parliamentarian' policy networks consisting of experts, politicians and civil servants from the different member countries (cf. Andersen and Burns, 1995), has a bearing on how the link between culture and politics is going to be defined.

The third perspective - focusing upon the social construction and maintenance of our definitions, our understanding of politics - may lead to very different conclusions as to whether the idea of the desirability of cultural homogeneity of the political community will continue, or even be strengthened, or possibly be changed into an acceptance and support of a multicultural political community. The conclusions are dependent upon how one perceives the processes of social construction, and particularly how possible and effective it is to control and consciously change collective ideas and norms. There are two very divergent points of view. These can be described as the two end-points of a continuum. On the one hand, the social construction is controllable by political and media elites, which may change the concepts and norms of people by comprehensive efforts. This idea of politically directed cultural change has had many proponents throughout history. We could mention the concept of a 'totalitarian political system', in which a comprehensive effort is made to create 'a new man' with new ideas, norms and emotions. But such extremes are only one type of endeavour. Educational campaigns through mass-media and through the school system which are aimed at changing ideas are a common element in many political and social elites, both on the nation-state level and on the European level. We could mention the European Commission project to launch the rewriting of the History of Europe without adopting a national perspective. The other end-point is an understanding of the social construction processes in terms of extreme complexity, where institutions and habits, which are generated and supported by the interactions and expectations of millions of people, resist conscious change. According to this view, cultures do change, of course, but consciously manipulated change is very difficult or impossible, because people are not the passive recipients of messages from political or social elites but active generators of new ideas and expectations as a result of changes in their environment. Most analysts, I think, are situated somewhere on the continuum between these two extremes. The position one holds will influence one's policy proposals in relation to the question of multi-cultural politics, whether one favours a policy of interaction and integration between different cultural groups or whether one prefers a policy of relative cultural autonomy as a way of handling the risks of a multi-cultural political community (in terms of lower levels of social solidarity and the legitimacy of the political decisions).

The policy conclusions of the fourth analytical perspective - the rational choice perspective - are dependent upon the means and resources which the political or social elites have at their disposal for influencing the calculus of the rational citizens. Different policies can be implemented to reduce the costs of multicultural political systems, both in the form of constitutional guarantees and the granting of cultural autonomy to the cultural groups. But, of course, costs can also be reduced by excluding cultural groups from full citizenship or by denying them the political resources that would enable them to claim full equal rights. The rejection of political integration with other groups, especially with those that take the form of supranational institutions (which thus, by implication, are creating a new political community), or the expulsion of culturally different groups from the existing political community could be viewed as a 'rational' course of action for the purpose of 'solving' the problem of a multi-cultural policy through the preservation or reestablishment of a culturally homogenous political community.

Thus, the different explanatory models have different implications as to the 'problem of a multi-cultural political community', i.e. the latent or conscious tendency to exclude the culturally different from full and equal membership in the political system.

Conclusion

I have attempted to examine the link or tension between cultural diversity and politics as based in culture, i.e. as originating in our conceptions of how to define politics, and particularly the political community. Thus my focus has been on cultural change: 'What is the character of our beliefs about the most desirable political community and how stable are they?' Views of cultural change differ and the different models of cultural change imply different options and possibilities for conscious political change. Thus there are no easy answers, but there can be a value in making more explicit the assumptions lying behind the different arguments and recommendations.

References

Andersen, S.S. and Burns, T.R. (1995), 'The European Union and the Erosion of Parliamentary Democracy: a Study of Post-parliamentary Governance', in S.S. Andersen and K. Eliassen (eds), *The European Union: How Democratic is it?*, Sage, London, p. 227-53.
Canovan, M. (1996), *Nationhood and Political Theory*, Edward Elgar, Cheltenham.
Deutsch, K. (1966), *Nationalism and Social Communication*, MIT-Press, Cambridge, Mass. (second edition).
Easton, D. (1965), *A Systems Analysis of Political Life*, Wiley, New York.
Hannerz, U. (1992), *Cultural Complexity: a Study in the Social Organisation of Meaning*, Columbia University Press, New York.
Hedetoft, U. (1995), *The Signs of Nations*, Dartmouth, Aldershot.
Hindess, B. (1992), 'Power and Rationality: the Western Concept of the Political Community', *Alternatives*, Vol. 17, No. 2, p. 149-73.
Howe, P. (1995), 'A Community of Europeans: the Requisite Underpinnings', *Journal of Common Market Studies*, Vol. 33, No. 1, p. 27-46.
Kymlicka, W. (1996), *The Rights of Minority Cultures*, Oxford University Press, Oxford.
Mill, J.S. (1858), *Considerations on Representative Government*, Liberal Arts Press, New York.
Van Dyke, V. (1996), 'The Individual, the State and Ethnic Communities in Political Theory', in W. Kymlicka (ed), *The Rights of Minority Cultures*, Oxford University Press, Oxford, p. 31-56.

PART I
REGIONAL AND LOCAL CULTURAL DIVERSITIES

PART I
REGIONAL AND LOCAL CULTURAL DIVERSITIES

2 Divergent Developments, Regional Alliances and National Solidarity in Belgium

PATRICK PASTURE[1]

Small as it is, Belgium is infamous for its social and political schisms and in particular for the regional divide between Flemings and Walloons (Fitzmaurice, 1996; McRae, 1986; Lijphart, 1981). However, in most surveys of industrial relations these divisions are not taken into account.[2] In this article, we will redress the balance and assess, in particular, the impact of the regional divide on the labour movement. Therefore, we will first emphasise the historical and continuing - even increasing - relevance of the regional divisions for the Belgian economy and the social realities. Given the highly politicised nature of the Belgian labour movement, we have to deal with the political as well as the economic and social aspects of the regional question. Subsequently, we will analyse the implications the regional diversities have for the labour movement and the responses of the trade unions.

Political Schisms, Divergent Economies and Regional Movements

The Church-State schism is the oldest division line - its origins go back to the late eighteenth century, although it only materialised into a political division in the middle of the following century. Although its relevance may be declining, it gave rise to powerful political families of christian demo-

---

[1] I wish to thank Peter van der Hallen and Guy Van Gyes for their fruitful comments on an earlier version of this text as well as Sandra Volders for the technical assistance and Anne Lee for reviewing my English. However, only I remain responsible for errors that may remain.
[2] E.g. Luyten, 1995; Spineux, 1990. Vilrokx and Van Leemput (1992; 1998) constitute a notable exception.

crats and anticlericals (socialists and liberals); even today, notwithstanding secularisation, the christian democrats, at least in Flanders, remain the largest political movement. The industrial revolution led to the formation of an industrial working class; however, only in the industrial areas of Wallonia and the major industrial cities did a neat labour-capital class division develop - when the Flemish countryside became industrialised, the social stratification remained more complex. Nevertheless, a strong labour movement came into being, politically divided though between socialists, christian democrats and liberals, and the social struggle, including the fight for universal suffrage, had a major impact on the social and political history of the country. A high level of organisation is one of the features of this kind of 'pillarised' country, and this is particularly true for the workers: with 51.9 per cent of the employees affiliated to one of the three trade union confederations (1995), Belgium is one of the most unionised countries in the Western world (ILO, 1997).

The origins of the regional division are more complex than may appear at first sight (cf. Deprez and Vos, 1998). In 1830, the new state of Belgium was linguistically composed of a French- (and Walloon-dialect!) speaking part and the Flemish provinces, where the ordinary people used Dutch (Flemish) dialects but the elite communicated in French.[3] Only in 1898 was Dutch recognised alongside French as an official language. The bilingual perspective being unacceptable to the Walloons, the Flemish movement from that date onwards strove for the Dutchification of Flanders. This would gradually become realised with the language laws of the 1920s and 1930s and the fixation by law of the language borders in 1963. A series of constitutional reforms - in 1970, 1980, 1988 and 1993 - transformed Belgium into a federal state.

The federalisation of Belgium, however, certainly was not just the outcome of the action of the Flemish movement but of the Walloon movement as well. This Walloon movement originated mainly from Francophone reactions - in particular in Flanders and Brussels rather than Wallonia - against the Flemish movement, even if it gradually came to identify somehow with Wallonia as a separate region (leading to tensions with Francophones in Flanders and Brussels) (Wils, 1992). The demographic evolution of the regions is very divergent, particularly since the 1920s. While the Flemish population until the late 1960s had the advantage of a relatively high birth rate - a result of its more rural, economically and culturally underdeveloped and largely catholic character - Wallonia's population in

---

[3] Dutch was only used in primary education, lower courts of justice, some general educational books, etc., but not in the administration, the army, the courts, higher education, etc.

the industrialised and urbanised areas stagnated already around 1880-1910 and started to decline around 1930 (Saey et al, 1998; Quévit, 1978). Fear of being outnumbered stimulated in the 1960s a natalist immigration policy, but also greatly influenced the thinking of many Walloons about the idea of a federal organisation of the state. However, economic changes carried even more weight in this development (cf. Destatte, 1997; Kesteloot, 1988; 1993; 1997).

Economic evolutions had a considerable impact on the community divide with special repercussions on the labour movement. From the outset, the industrialisation of Belgium developed very unevenly geographically. Early industrialisation concentrated on the coal fields along the River Meuse, while the capital Brussels quickly 'Francosised' as the administrative, commercial and cultural centre of the country. Apart from Brussels, Ghent and Antwerp, the Northern Dutch-speaking part of Belgium remained economically underdeveloped. Until the early 1960s, in Flanders structural unemployment remained high, pushing many Flemish workers to search for work, temporarily or permanently, outside their region, in particular in the Walloon industries or in Northern France (Saey et al, 1998; Vandermotten, 1990; Veraghtert, 1981). The Flemish movement, supported by christian democracy, in the 1950s therefore not only strove to remove the social and cultural barriers for Flemish-speaking people in their professional lives, but also argued for a regional employment policy for Flanders (Pasture, 1992).

However, since the discovery of coal fields in the Flemish province of Limburg around 1900, things started to change - very slowly but fundamentally, resulting in a complete transformation of the Belgian economy and in particular of the economic conditions of the regions (De Brabander, 1988; Kumps and Witterwulghe, 1981; Vandermotten, 1990; Veraghtert, 1981). On the one hand, the Walloon economy stagnated and then declined rapidly from the mid-1950s onwards and especially in the 1970s and 1980s. Flanders, on the other hand, in the 1960s managed to attract new industries thanks to its strategic location near the North Sea, with easy access to the European hinterland, and its highly trained population; it developed a particularly dynamic economy which, after a serious setback during the worldwide recession of 1974-82, resumed again in the 1990s (Monfort et al, 1998; Bismans, 1998).

The Walloon economy indeed relied largely on its natural resources of coal and concentrated almost exclusively on the heavy industries of iron and steel around the coal-mines and the Rivers Sambre and Meuse, without much diversification. However, already in the 1920s and 1930s these industries showed certain structural rigidities (Hogg, 1986). Since the Belgian industrial apparatus survived the 1940-44 war mostly undamaged, industrial production after the war resumed almost immediately, leading to a quick recovery of the Belgian economy (the 'Belgian miracle'). However, this fortunate evolution masked a lack of investment in innovation and diversification, in particular in Wallonia (Cassiers et al, 1993; Mommen, 1994, 99-105). When in 1955/58 the demand for coal dropped, the economic backbone of Wallonia was severely hit. The closure of many coal-mines suddenly shocked the Walloon masses and caused social unrest, culminating in the winter 1960/61 uprising against the so-called Unity Law of Prime Minister Gaston Eyskens (Mommen, 1994, 99-111; 127-130; Neuville and Yerna, 1990; Quévit, 1978). Yet the fate of the Walloon industry opened the way to the gradual implementation of economic 'programming', allowing for regional investments, as was demanded by the Flemish movement as well.

Parallel to the decline of the Walloon economy, new (mostly foreign) investments were located in new industrial sites near Flanders' ports. They created new jobs that by 1962 eradicated the age-old Flemish unemployment. The favourable economic climate during the 'golden sixties' also profited Wallonia, although its structural problems remained unsolved, while no work came from new economic development (Mommen, 1994, 127-130; Bismans, 1998). The economic stagnation and gradual deterioration became quite clear in the second half of the 1960s, until the crisis of the 1970s and 1980s virtually ruined the remaining factories of iron and steel, turning the once blooming industrial heart of Wallonia into pure wasteland. From 1969 onwards unemployment remained much more important in Wallonia than in Flanders, even if the coal-mines of Limburg (Flanders) started to share the same fate as the Walloon mines a decade earlier.

Regional Differences and the Alliances of the Workers

Political Divisions

The political divisions of Belgian society have particularly affected the working class. The Belgian socialist labour movement has become one of the major political forces in Belgium and even a model for socialists in other countries, but it never managed to get a majority of Belgian workers behind it. Its major competitor was the christian labour movement, which came into being roughly between 1890 and 1906 as a result of the reaction against the mounting influence of socialism with its strong anticlericalism and internationalism. After World War II, the christian labour movement even exceeded the socialists in numbers as well as political influence

(Annex 1). Apart from socialist and christian labour movements, there also exists a small liberal trade union confederation, mainly confined to Brussels.

All of these workers' organisations are fully integrated with their respective political families and, in varying ways and often only implicitly, tied to their corresponding political parties in a system usually described as 'pillarisation'. This applies to the trade unions as well, although their importance in the socio-economic system has become such that in the post-World War II period they obtained a decisive influence upon socio-economic policy (Pasture, 1993).

From the outset, the social geography of the country has had a considerable impact on the unions (cf. Strikwerda, 1997). The socialist trade unions were the first to rise among the artisans and textile workers of Brussels and Ghent and among the industrial workers of the coal-mines and factories of Wallonia. They became part of the Belgian Workers' Party (BWP, 1885), which pursued a reformist political course fighting for universal suffrage, even if in some Walloon centres revolutionary-syndicalist factions survived. After World War I, the socialist unions made a breakthrough, although after a few years many of the new members were lost again. Belgian unions got their mass character mainly during the 1930s due to the unemployment insurance they organised (Vanthemsche, 1989); their membership figures continued to mount steadily after World War II, when their power extended in the new collective bargaining system which recognised their participation at all levels of the Belgian economy - including plant level - and the unions continued to pay out unemployment benefits. For a number of reasons, the christian trade unions benefited most from this growth (Spineux, 1981; Pasture, 1993; 1996).

At the time the catholic church started to recognise the importance of the social question and to open the door for genuine workers' organisations and unions (Rerum novarum, 1891), the immense majority of the working class in industrial Wallonia were definitively lost for the church. However, Flanders (except for Antwerp and especially Ghent), was still hardly touched by modernity and not (yet) de-christianised. With the ground prepared by the revival of nineteenth century catholicism and the activities of the many pious associations, when the Flemish provinces gradually lost their agrarian character, the christian unions found an environment where they could successfully compete with the socialist unions (Mampuys, 1994; Strikwerda, 1997). Political catholicism or christian democracy therefore turned out to prevail in Flanders, even in industrialised and urban centres. In Wallonia socialism has dominated the political landscape since World War I, although in the peripheral areas political catholicism or liberalism are stronger (Saey et al, 1998).

Apart from the position of catholicism, the socio-economic and socio-geographical structure of Flanders remained different from the industrial provinces of Wallonia. The industrialisation was accompanied by the development of infrastructure, as a deliberate policy to avoid massive migration to the cities. The distances between social classes, in particular between blue- and white-collar workers, lower middle-classes, small farmers and agricultural workers were smaller; they lived more together and often joined the same (catholic) associations. Apart from Ghent where the first anti-socialist unions arose and which has since remained one of its strongholds, the christian labour movement fitted particularly well in the many mid-size Flemish towns. To avoid the dominant position of the socialists in the big companies, the christian unions developed local activities and services attracting the workers in their home-towns alongside the workplace. So they became more centralised and apparently also more effective in offering services, such as unemployment insurance, which was the major factor for union growth in the interwar period, as well as legal advice and social assistance. After 1945, the christian unions especially directed their action towards new industries and activities, and set up specific bodies for minority groups and special categories of workers such as women (!) and migrants, something the socialists only did reluctantly (Pasture, 1996; Spineux, 1981; see also Chapter 7).

These economic and political divergences entailed some important consequences for the trade union movement (see Annex 1 and 2 for figures). Somewhat surprisingly, unionisation in Flanders even before World War I was higher than in Wallonia, although the latter was far more industrialised (Neuville, 1959; 1973). The main explanation for this remarkable phenomenon probably lays in the impact of pillarisation or, in other words, the different associational political culture in Flanders: more so than Wallonia, the region since the mid 19th century is covered with numerous associations and mass organisations, often closely interrelated and part of a politically integrated subculture (comp. Hellemans, 1990; Billiet, 1988). Around 1957 the membership of the christian unions exceeded the number of affiliates of the socialist unions.

The Flemish in every confederation constitute the majority, but within the socialist unions, Francophones and Flemish were more or less of equal strength and in some affiliated professional unions Walloons dominated. Within the christian labour movement Flemings hold an overwhelming majority in almost every single organisation, but the Francophones enjoy guaranteed representation in the highest governing bodies of the movement. This is particularly the case in the trade union confederation. So the president and the secretary general of the CSC always belong to a different language community; since 1947 the president has been Flemish (but bilingual) and the secretary general Francophone (Pasture, 1992). In the FGTB a similar arrangement exists between the secretary general and his deputy (Messiaen, 1997).

According to Lode Wils, the christian labour movement owed its success mainly to its association with the Flemish movement (Wils, 1986; Gerard, 1998). Although we believe other factors carry more weight in explaining the growth of the christian unions (see Pasture and Mampuys, 1990), its Flemish character certainly did favour the christian labour movement, while the perception of the socialist workers' organisations, with their anticlericalism, their rhetoric of the international class struggle and their many Francophone foremen, hampered their breakthrough in a still very parochial Flanders (see also Strikwerda, 1997).

Basic Regional Alliances

Wils, however, touches upon an important phenomenon that needs to be revealed in the context of this article, i.e. the regional alliances of the labour movement. From its origins the christian labour movement indeed supported the Flemish cause, although it also remained loyal to the Belgian state: it never engaged in the nationalist, exclusive anti-Belgian politics of the political nationalists, even if a certain compliance did exist, and it did not join the Flemish political collaboration with the German occupiers in 1914 and 1940 (!) (Pasture, 1998; Gerard, 1998). In the 1920s and 1930s, the Flemish cause formed the basis of a factual broad popular alliance of workers, farmers and lower middle-class within the Catholic Party striving for the so-called 'minimum programme' for the recognition of a unilingual Flanders; the christian labour political representatives (= christian democrats) were known for their Flemish militancy (Wils, 1992; Gerard, 1994b). Very likely this Flemish orientation prevented the breakthrough of a Flemish nationalist workers' movement in the 1930s, when such an attempt was undertaken by the Flemish-nationalist party (De Wever, 1995, 81-2 and 277-83; see also Pasture, 1995). How much this Flemish militancy directly involved the christian *trade unions*, however, is hard to tell; apart from general political support for the christian democratic Flamingants, the unions hardly ever engaged in collective action in support of specific Flemish demands (e.g., for the Dutchification of enterprises - although this in the 1950s and 1960s was part of their programme). However, the christian unions in the 1950s did advocate a regional economic policy, although not very successfully until 1959 (Pasture, 1992, Chapter 5; see also Gerard, 1998).

Apart from some isolated figures, one may observe that the organised socialist labour movement largely ignored the Flemish cause. This was not just the result of a presumed dominance of Francophone workers in the movement, who often tended to look down on their Flemish comrades (we shall return to this issue), but had particular strategic motivations and ideological roots as well. Indeed, this disregard of nationalist aspirations is common among social democrat movements throughout Europe. Reference to the internationalism of the class struggle gives only a partial answer. After all, socialists in 1914 - and of course in 1940 as well - fully and enthusiastically supported their governments in the war effort, putting all internationalist rhetoric aside. The Belgians did not constitute an exception to this phenomenon either. Indeed, the majority of Belgian socialists before 1914 already identified with the Belgian state (Vanschoenbeek, 1997).

One reason is undoubtedly the socialist's fixation on the state, which is considered to be a condition for capitalist development and consequently also an indispensable transitory phase for the socialist revolution (Schwarzmantel, 1991). Through the fight for and the achievement of universal suffrage, increasing social legislation, and the recognition of the workers by the state, the latter became, in the terms of René Galissot, 'la patrie des prolétaires' (the fatherland of the workers). Although the socialist unions especially remained often very suspicious towards too much authority in the state until the 1930s, the basic re-alliance of the socialist movement with the nation state was completed well before 1914 (Van der Linden, 1988; Galissot, 1989).

But the political context was equally important. Already before 1914, nationalist movements by socialists were considered to be reactionary by definition, precisely because they constituted a threat to the strong national states that the socialists advocated (cf. Forman, 1998). Moreover, after the militant separatist Flemish nationalists had collaborated in 1914 and again in 1940, favouring a fascist New Order, anything like an alliance with the Flemish movement was virtually impossible, including the democratic forms supported by their main competitors. For the christian labour movement, things were different because of the strong catholic outlook and the popular roots of Flemish political nationalism; the christian labour movement did distance itself from the collaboration, even if it maintained, however, some sympathy for presumed 'idealists' (see extensively Pasture, 1998).

However, already around the turn of the century, the first *'Wallingant'* and Francophile resentments found an echo within the socialist labour movement, especially in trade union circles. Jules Destrée, for example, expressed the anti-Flemish frustrations in his famous *Lettre ouverte au roi* (Open letter to the King, 1912) where he declared 'Sire, il n'y a pas de belges' (Sire, there are no Belgians) (see Kesteloot, 1998; Wils, 1992, 211 ff.; Schreiber, 1995). Anti-Flemish stereotypes referred sometimes to the Flemish 'immigrants' in Wallonia, but were fuelled foremost by the Flemish advance, for instance in the administration, as well as by the preferential treatment of Flemish by the Germans in 1914-18 and 1940-44 (the so-called *Flamenpolitik* to divide the Belgian resistance) and the Flemish-nationalist collaboration. But as Philippe Destatte recently underlined, the Walloon movement also had economic complaints; Walloon militants already in 1910 opposed a (presumingly) preferential treatment of Flanders by the federal government (Destatte, 1997).[4] Demographic considerations played their part as well, since Wallonia's population stagnated since 1910 and the Walloons therefore feared being outnumbered by the Flemings. The anti-Flemish and Francophile resentments were particularly strong and widespread in 1945, although the favourable economic development of Wallonia after the war and the political divisions surrounding the King's question and, more, the so-called 'school war' of the 1950s overshadowed the linguistic issues - even if the attitudes towards these questions were quite different in both regions and they therefore also contributed to deepening the community divide (Wils, 1992).

Things changed, however, after the end of the 'school war' when christian democrats and anticlericals reached an agreement on the role of the state and of free - mostly catholic - initiatives in education and social services (1958/63), and when the Walloon economy suffered a severe setback due to the European coal crisis (Pasture, 1992; Tyssens, 1997). The latter seemed to confirm the Wallingants' greatest fears.

Radicalisation in the 1960s

The new political and economic conditions, combined with a reinforcement of the neocorporatist basic compromise between employers and unions which was expressed in the productivity protocols of 1954 and 1957, favoured the first initiatives towards a regional and planned economic policy. The so-called 'Unity Law' introduced before Parliament in November 1960 by the christian democrat Prime Minister Gaston Eyskens was, in fact, one of these, but it also contained a package including important cuts and savings. It were these that provoked such an angry reaction in Wallonia, especially (but not only) among socialists. Incidentally, while the christian unions shared to a large extent the criticisms of the socialists, they continued to support the government and opposed the general strike called by the socialists, not only because of their relationship of trust with the

---

[4] However, at that time Flanders was largely underdeveloped and the government exclusively Francophone (see the particularly critical review of Destatte's essay by Kesteloot (1997)).

prime minister, but in particular because Eyskens had granted some Flemish demands (Joye and Lewin, 1967). Needless to say, that this attitude caused much dissent among the Francophone christian workers. However, in the socialist unions the Flemings also appeared to be considerably less eager to fight than the Walloons (Neuville and Yerna, 1990; Pasture, 1992).

The division of the Belgian working class pushed the radical Walloon socialist strike leader André Renard, secretary general of the powerful metalworkers union and vice-secretary general of the socialist trade union confederation FGTB, to advocate a federal solution to the social struggle. In his opinion, the structural reforms that the socialists demanded - in short, the socialisation and planning of production - never could be implemented within a Belgian framework because of the too compliant attitude of the Flemish. Hence, federalisation became a prerequisite for a socialist society. To promote his views, Renard launched a new political movement, the Mouvement Populaire Wallon (MPW), which grew fast among syndicalist circles. However, most Flemish socialists were weary of any federalisation, since in Flanders they constituted a minority and they would be overshadowed by the christians. The few Flemish-minded socialists grouped around the weekly review *Links* found little support; but they too advocated some form of federalism only from 1963 onwards. The leadership of the socialist labour movement, of the unions as well as of the party, wanted to save the unity of the movement and opposed Renard's radical and federalist discourse. They formally broke with the MPW, which lost much of its appeal after the sudden death of its charismatic leader in July 1962. Nevertheless, Renard's ideas continued to influence the Walloon socialist labour movement, that in the later 1960s increasingly identified with the fate of Wallonia (Messiaen, 1997; Destatte, 1995; 1997; Kesteloot, 1988; 1993; Moreau, 1984; Neuville and Yerna, 1990; Beaufays, 1985; Pletinckx, 1985; Wils, 1992; Francq, 1990).

In the 1960s, the linguistic dispute more and more came to the fore and divided the population regardless of class. In particular, the Dutchification of the University of Leuven, bilingual but situated in Flanders, worked as the catalyst for the Flemish-Francophone separation. In 1968, the French section of the university had to leave Leuven for a new campus in the Walloon countryside, *Louvain-la-Neuve*. In the aftermath, the Christian Democratic Party split into a Flemish- and a French-speaking party (CVP/PSC). The umbrella organisation of the christian labour movement, after years of internal divisions and disputes due to different political orientations of Dutch- and French-speaking militants, in 1964 stopped acting as a unitary organisation and no more common meetings of the statutory bodies with Francophones and Flemings were held (Pasture, 1992; Gerard, 1994c). Incidentally, it is remarkable that within the Francophone catholic community, the workers were the first to develop regional sympathies and were perhaps the most outspoken federalists (Pasture, 1992; 1998; Seiler, 1975). This was mainly due to the minority position they occupied in Wallonia, but especially in the catholic community and in the christian labour movement itself, which enticed them to escape from isolation and marginality, and to search for alliances.[5]

These developments did affect the Belgian trade unions considerably. During the uprising against the Unity Law in December 1960 within the FGTB, a non-statutory Walloon regional body was created under the leadership of André Renard, to co-ordinate the strike actions in Wallonia. It became Renards power base and the nucleus of the MPW. The defeat of the actions against the Unity Law and the tensions that had risen between Flemish and Walloon trade unionists led to some organisational and political adaptations within the unions. After difficult internal negotiations the FGTB in 1963 introduced parity between French- and Dutch-speaking in its secretariat and its governing bodies, and recognised the right of the regions to consult separately about certain regional issues and to express their own views (the 'tendency-right'); in this way the FGTB was the first to take steps towards regional decentralisation. Within the christian unions, the anger of the Francophones in 1960-61 was appeased once more with guaranteed representation - even if in practice this did not entail a larger representation (Pasture, 1992, 289). Although the CSC stood under heavy pressure from its Walloon militants, partly in reaction to the competing Walloon socialist labour movement, the CSC leadership pushed back any attempts to decentralise the trade union's structures along regional lines, fearing the unity of the movement would be at stake. Obviously it was the Francophones who strove for a regionalisation of the union, since the Flemish by their sheer size dominated its governing bodies.

The economic deterioration of Wallonia, however, modified the attitude of the socialist labour movement towards the question of regional autonomy. More and more, the ideas of the late André Renard found their way. Francophone socialist politicians focused on the Walloon and Francophone interests, often still imbedded in an anti-Flemish discourse, however, the fact that multinational firms preferred to invest in Flanders was even interpreted as a conspiracy of the Flemish politicians and Brussels capitalists against the Walloon working classes (Mommen, 1994, 128-9). Such perceptions were fuelled by the linguistic dispute and in particular by the *Walen buiten* slogan addressed to the Francophones by the Flemish stu-

---

[5] Compare the different attitude of the socialist Flemings, which is more comparable with catholic conservatives who also relied on the majority of their fellows in the other region, at least until the school pact of 1958.

dents in Leuven. By 1967, the MPW, who had somewhat moderated its demands, could manifest itself again as an internal pressure group within the socialist movement. Socialist and former trade unionists in 1968, together with other currents in the Walloon movement (in particular the progressive catholics of the movement *Rénovation wallonne*), created a new political party, the *Rassemblement Wallon* (RW), giving priority to their regional alliance (Destatte, 1995; 1997).

These developments also affected the FGTB. In February 1967 the Walloon trade unionists adopted a Manifesto on the economic reconversion of the Walloon industry and in November they subscribed to a radical regionalist economic programme. In 1968 a Walloon and a Flemish regional organisation - called *interrégionales* ('interregional' because it grouped together different territorial, 'regional', organisations) - were created and recognised by the national authorities of the FGTB. These regional organisations had a large degree of autonomy in establishing their own organisation, objectives and action (Messiaen, 1997; Beaufays, 1985; Pletinckx, 1985; Arcq, 1980; Moreau, 1984; Neuville and Yerna, 1990). Although the Walloon *interrégionale* remained remarkably moderate regarding institutional reforms, with Jacques Yerna and André Genot it strongly associated itself with the MPW (Destatte, 1995).

The regional question was perceived in a fairly similar way by the Walloon militants in the socialist and the christian trade unions. This in the late 1960s contributed to a real rapprochement between both movements, leading to the establishment of a relatively strong united trade union front and culminating in the 1969 appeals to working class unity by a new progressive movement *Objectif '72 Wallonie-Bruxelles*, which involved Jacques Yerna, and by the president of the Socialist Party Leo Collard. For reasons that go beyond the scope of this article, these initiatives did not find the necessary popular support and failed (see extensively Pasture, 1992).

The interest of the unions in a real federalisation of Belgium, however, remained limited. On the contrary, while the labour movement welcomed regional economic policy, it opposed any regionalisation of industrial relations and social security, considering them to be the cornerstones of the Belgian social model. In particular, the leadership of the christian trade unions believed that further federalisation would lead to a falling apart of their movement (Pasture, 1992, 390-2), while the Flemish socialists also feared being outnumbered in Flanders. Such developments could easily put the entire power base of the labour movement at risk and could alter the power balance with the employers at their expense. Incidentally, the latter were not inclined to modify the basic structures of the industrial relations scheme either, which had finally proved to be fairly beneficial for all partners involved. From their point of view, regionalisation of industrial relations would have disastrous effects in Wallonia. Since the social partners virtually monopolised collective bargaining and also played a predominant role in social security, they easily managed to keep these out of the federalisation process of 1970-93, although recently pressures also arose on these issues. From this perspective, it becomes obvious that the unions also tried to thwart internal decentralising tendencies.

Regionalisation Step by Step (1970-93)

Unfinished Business

With the revision of the constitution in 1970, the process of federalisation of Belgium was set in motion. The 1970 revision provided for the creation of four regional cultural councils (for Flanders, Wallonia, bilingual Brussels and for the German-speaking linguistic area) and the recognition of three regions: Flanders, Wallonia (including the German-speaking area) and Brussels - largely leaving it to the legislator to confine concretely the powers of these regions. The implementation of these provisions and, in particular, the question of Brussels as a separate region, lasted an entire decade. However, political regionalisation was not necessary to institutionalise some regional economic collaboration. The Terwagne Act of July 1970 created regional tripartite economic councils for Flanders, Wallonia and for the province of Brabant (which included Brussels together with the French-speaking and the Dutch-speaking part of the province), with advisory capacity regarding economic planning.

When in 1974 the first oil-shock immersed the Western economies in a long-lasting depression, Belgium was severely hit. For the obsolete Walloon enterprises, the repercussions were particularly disastrous (Mommen, 1994; De Grauwe, 1993). The linguistic problems contributed largely to paralyse political life - between January 1972 and December 1981 twelve different government coalitions were formed, most of them ending because of community disputes - which prevented an effective industrial policy from being implemented and hampered the recovery. Economic decentralisation had been introduced in 1970, but the regions lacked the political powers as well as the financial resources to develop an active industrial and labour market policy. Therefore, the most affected industrial sectors - steel, coal-mines, shipbuilding, textile and glass - were granted a 'national' status as 'national industries in difficulties', by which they escaped from the responsibility of the regional authorities. In practice, a financial scheme developed (called 'wafer iron') whereby subsidies and investments in one industry or region had to be compensated for by similar investments in the other region as well. These kind of financial compensations were nothing new: the technique had been used many times before to appease political conflicts. However, given the economic constraints, the price paid was particularly high and public expenditure, especially after the second oil crisis of 1978, expanded beyond control (see Mommen, 1994; Buyst, 1993; Cassiers et al, 1993; De Grauwe, 1993).

The trade unions, although united in a so-called 'trade union unity front' remained quite inoffensive in the 1970s. Union proposals to combat the crisis emphasised greater planning, state support for the declining industries to maintain employment and purchasing power, a reduction in working time and the creation of an alternative labour circuit by the state (Pasture, 1996; see also Heylen and Van Gompel, 1992). However, the renowned Belgian industrial relations scheme became stuck; between 1976 and 1981 central talks between business and unions failed to reach any intersectoral agreement. Collective bargaining decentralised and became tougher. In 1980, the leadership of the christian labour movement concluded that the recovery of the economy needed a complete change of tack and a reconstitution of state finances, which were deteriorating quickly, particularly since 1979. This opened up the way for a more orthodox economic and financial policy, but destroyed the trade union front (Mommen, 1994; Vilrokx and Van Leemput, 1992).

Federalism and the New Economic Politics

In 1980 a new constitutional revision settled some enduring community disputes, profoundly changing the institutional shape of Belgium and introducing a special kind of federalism (regionalism). The new constitution recognised the autonomy of three *communities* (the Dutch, the French and the German community - the Dutch and French community both being mandated for bilingual Brussels) along with three socio-economic *regions* (Flanders, Wallonia and Brussels). The *communities* are empowered for so-called 'person-related' matters: culture, education (including professional education and training), and welfare (excluding social security) such as social welfare, social integration, family care, health care, care for elderly, youth and disabled persons. The *regions* deal with employment policy (esp. employment-finding), regional economic and industrial policy, energy policy, public works, transport, research and technology, town and country planning, and environment. It should be noted that, even if important parts of social and economic policy were regionalised, some key aspects of it remained subject to the federal authority, such as social security (including unemployment benefits), financial policy, and income and price policy. In Flanders, the regional parliaments and governments (called respectively councils and executives until 1988) for the Flemish region and for the Flemish community (with authority also for the Dutch-speaking people in Brussels) fused, but this did not happen in the French community - mainly because of the strong opposition of the Francophones in Brussels. Incidentally, the organisation of Brussels as a separate region only materialised in 1988. The result of this gradual federalisation is, to say the least, extremely complex, and the delimitations of federal and regional competencies looks often most unclear and illogical.[6] Further constitutional revisions in 1988-89 and 1993-94 explicitly recognised and reinforced the federal character of Belgium, including the regions' right (albeit limited) to levy taxes and to conclude international agreements (for English introductions to the federalisation of Belgium see Falter (1998) and Fitzmaurice (1996)).

The 1980 revision of the constitution certainly contributed to the new economic and political course, which was implemented from 1981 onwards by the christian democrat/liberal coalition headed by Wilfried Martens. This coalition managed to set the communal *contentieux* aside, imposed a policy of restraints, and opted for an economic policy aimed at restoring the competitiveness of the enterprises. However, the Walloon enterprises were in a much worse shape than their counterparts in the North of the country and could hardly compete in the international markets. So the Flemish economy recovered relatively well, which resulted in an extraordinary economic boom in the mid-1990s, while Wallonia needed much more time to restructure. So, notwithstanding relatively favourable economic conditions, the economies of the North and the South (and Brussels) further drifted apart (Descamps, 1998).

In 1983, after the government had secured the future of the Cockerill-Sambre steel factories with one final big capital injection, the responsibility for the so-called 'national industries in difficulties' was handed over to the regions (Mommen, 1994, 206-8; Capron, 1987). It was only from that date onwards that they could really develop a regional economic and industrial policy. That year the Walloon Regional Economic Council (CERW) was transformed into an Economic and Social Council for the Walloon Region (CESRW), composed of representatives of the employers, middle-class, agriculture and workers. It became a crucial organisation in the development of the Walloon economic and social policy. In 1985 the Flemish government installed a tripartite Flemish Social and Economic Consultation Committee (VESOC) (which, in fact, already worked on an informal basis from 1980), and is entitled to advise the Flemish region on all aspects of

---

[6] E.g. regarding employment and health care, which are partly subject to the federal, partly to the regional authorities, or regarding unemployment (federal), work-finding (regional) and vocational training (community matter).

socio-economic policy which involve the government (executive) of the region. The bipartite Social and Economic Council for Flanders (SERV), also established in 1985 - replacing the Regional Economic Council for Flanders - has an important mandate for consulting the Flemish government as well, but can also take public stances and is the major place for consultation between the social partners in the Flemish region. The Brussels Economic and Social Council (replacing the Regional Economic Council for Brabant) and the Brussels Committee for Economic and Social Consultation only came about in 1997.

The Labour Movement in a Federal State in Construction

While political parties split along regional lines - after the christian democrats in 1968; also in the liberal and socialist parties in 1972 and 1978 respectively Flemings and Francophones decided to go separate ways - the trade unions, with the exception of the unions for white-collar workers (which in reality never united Flemings and Francophones), remained federal (national), although regional consultation existed in the FGTB. The *interrégionales* of the FGTB were charged with the FGTB representation in the regional economic councils that were created after the Terwagne Act of July 1970 (Messiaen, 1997). In 1978, after the government had reached an agreement on further federalisation (the 'Egmont-pact', which, incidentally, was broken afterwards and caused the fall of the cabinet), the FGTB actualised its statutes: it stressed its unitary and 'indivisible' character, but emphasised its will to develop a trade union 'countervailing power' in the new regional structures; it officially gave the *interrégionales* a place in its statutes and created a bilingual *interrégionale* for Brussels (Messiaen, 1997).

Also the CSC had to concede, in November 1970, the formation of a Walloon committee, followed one year later by a similar Flemish committee. These regional committees, however, only enjoyed an informal status. In 1974, the CSC formally accepted the possibility of regional advisory committees, although still subsumed and supervised by the national governing authorities. Four years later, in 1978, the confederation decided to establish regional committees for Brussels, Flanders and Wallonia with ruling authority regarding the regionalised social and economic matters (CSC-activity report 1977-79). Incidentally, the Brussels Regional Committee in practice only met for the first time in 1983. The CSC modified its regional structures again after the 1980 constitutional revision and its implementation, and created a Committee for the French Community separate from the Walloon Regional Committee and the Brussels Regional Committee; however, it took some years before they actually started (incidentally we did not find any trace of a CSC Committee for the German Community). Only in 1984 did the CSC adapt its statutes to the new situation; apart from the Regional and Community Committees it also created a co-ordinating National committee (ACV, 1994; www.acv-csc.be).

The FGTB did not make a distinction between regional and community responsibilities. The question of the distribution of the competences between the French community and the regions, was disputed between Francophones stressing the importance of the Francophone community and the so-called 'Renardistes' or Walloon regionalists. The latter came to the fore at the congress of the Walloon *interrégionale* of October 1990 *Réussir la Wallonnie* and the congress of the Walloon socialists of December 1990, where the then president of the *interrégionale wallonne FGTB*, Urbain Destrée, argued that education should be transferred from the communities to the regions (Destatte, 1995 76-7; 1997, 381-3).

The main remit of the regional trade union structures concerned co-operation with the new regional institutions and the development of regional policy, but they also played a role in the development of the trade union movement in their region. From the outset, the Walloon Regional Committee strove for the realisation of a trade union front with the FGTB. Parallel to the extension of social and economic regionalisation, the authority of these regional bodies, both in the FGTB and the CSC, also expanded. However, the French community appeared to be very reluctant to become involved with the unions. This did not prevent them, though, to advance specific demands, particularly regarding vocational training, permanent education, working conditions in schools and non-profit enterprises, and to organise training for militants on issues within the community's mandate, including the environment. It seems that the regional or communal structures play a key role in developing the broader interests that Belgian unions promote to present themselves as contemporary social movements in the 1990s (comp. Van Gyes and De Witte, forthcoming; Pasture, 1996). The Brussels regional organisations have, among other things, distinguished themselves in combating racism. In general, however, this larger political orientation seems more strongly implemented within the christian unions than within the socialist, at least for those issues that are most remote from the traditional workplace, such as environment; the christian trade unions also appear to be more inclined to favour outspoken local initiatives.

In the 1980s, the regional organisations of the unions developed successfully. This evolution is partly the result of the increasing importance of the regional authorities in general but, obviously, the regional union bodies also develop a dynamic or inner logic that increases their own power and importance. This should come as no surprise since the reinforcement of the regional institutions is part of their program. In the initial years, most attention was devoted to co-operation with the development of the regional institutions. Only recently has there been a clear increase in attention to the content of the regional trade union action.

Remarkably, while the FGTB was the first to create regional structures (although one should be aware that in the socialist trade union movement the centre of power remained with the affiliated national unions and these did not follow this partial regionalisation), it seems to us that since the late 1980s in the CSC the regional dimension has had a stronger impact than in the FGTB, in particular in Flanders.[7] The FGTB interregional organisations seem to be more integrated within the national structures of the confederation than the regional committees of the CSC. For example, the president of the Flemish interregional is also the FGTB national secretary general Mia De Vits. On the other hand, it has to be noted that the interregional organisations dispose of their own research department, while the regional committees CSC have to rely on the national research department (where there is some regional specialisation however). Although both unions stress the importance of national solidarity, in particular of social security, this seems to be more clearly the case for the FGTB than for the CSC; it also appears that the almost instinctive socialist abhorrence towards mounting 'nationalist' resentments - in particular of the Flemish - may help to explain this situation. In this context, it may be useful to note that in 1994 - indeed as late as that - all three trade union confederations adopted an internal code against militants of the Flemish-nationalist party Vlaams Blok (Van Gyes and De Witte, forthcoming). It should also be observed, however, that this step was motivated by this party's extreme right and anti-immigrant attitude and not so much by its political nationalism - even if, for many, rightly or wrongly, they are related. The stronger outlook of the christian unions' regional action may also be related to their somewhat broader view of trade unionism. They, indeed, appear more inclined to include non-workplace-related issues in their action, such as environment, education and training, and poverty. Nevertheless, his relatively 'moderate' image in 1999 allowed the president of the Flemish regional committee, Luc Cortebeeck, to succeed to Willy Peirens as president of the CSC.

---

[7] In any case the difference in internal representation - e.g. in the representation of the regional activities in the national activity reports - is particularly striking. It also appears to us that the regional trade union leaders in the CSC play a more prominent role than in the FGTB.

Regional Pressures on the Federal Welfare State in the 1990s

Some specific recent developments in industrial relations and socio-economic politics change the outlook of the community problem for the unions as well. As became apparent in the above, the federalisation of Belgium did not directly involve collective bargaining nor social security; the social partners, with the exception of the pressure group of the Flemish-minded employers VEV (which, however, is not directly involved in collective bargaining) never demanded this regionalisation either. However, since the 1970s, the Flemish movement has regularly denounced so-called 'unexplainable flows' of social security funds from Flanders to Wallonia, especially in health insurance and unemployment benefits. These flows are attributed to a presumed irresponsible spending culture of the Walloon (Francophone) socialists, even when the existence of structural differences between both regions, such as an older population and higher unemployment in Wallonia, are recognised. Therefore, the Flemish movement, backed up by some leading Flemish economists, does advocate a regionalisation of social security. However, the unions, supported in this by the mutualities,[8] always opposed any threat to the 'national solidarity', which in their view constitutes the essence of social security. For the Walloon socialist labour movement, maintaining the national social security scheme is an absolute condition for safeguarding Belgian unity. However, it appears to us that the argument for federalisation of social security is gaining ground among Flemish employees, especially among christian white-collar workers.

Some recent developments seem to increase the relevance of the regional dimension in labour relations. As in many other countries, industrial relations in Belgium came under pressure to decentralise (Van Gyes and De Witte, forthcoming; Vilrokx and Van Leemput, 1992; 1998). However, due to the very elaborate system of collective bargaining, involving all levels of industry, and especially including the enterprise itself, this never had a similarly destructive effect (Vilrokx and Van Leemput, 1992; 1998). Nevertheless, national intersectoral collective bargaining became increasingly difficult from the time of the oil crisis in 1974; no central collective agreements were concluded between 1975 and 1986. The agreements signed after that date were also very meagre, 'unable to support the objective of collective solidarity', as two observers of Belgian industrial relations commented (Vilrokx and Van Leemput, 1998, 335). In 1993, the social partners could not reach a 'Social Pact on employment competitiveness and employment' as suggested by the federal government. Finally the government

---

[8] Mutualities: (private) health insurance funds organised by the social organisations.

imposed its 'Global Plan' itself. Also in 1995 and 1997, negotiations between the social partners to reach a consensus on these matters failed, while in 1996 the tripartite 'Pact for the Future' was rejected by the FGTB, disavowing the central leadership which had subscribed to it (Dryon and Krzeslo, 1997; Vilrokx and Van Leemput, 1998). At the time of writing (December 1998), the social partners, however, have finally succeeded in signing a substantial intersectoral agreement.

It is undeniable that the inability of the social partners to conclude important intersectoral agreements on employment and wage policy has undermined their authority (especially of the union confederations). In particular, the militant socialist national unions, with their power base in Wallonia, are blamed for this failure. A major consequence of the inability to conclude intersectoral agreements was that it has given way to greater state intervention by imposing clear restraints on wage formation - what historically was the prerogative of bipartite collective bargaining - and determining working conditions and employment policy, which further threatens the authority of the unions. It also contributed to decentralisation of collective bargaining at company level (Vilrokx and Van Leemput, 1992; 1998).

For some, the regions could provide an opportunity for the unions to regain some authority, which they lost on a national level. The unions may indeed profit from the need of the new regional institutions for social recognition, and to become rooted in the social and political environment. Particularly in Flanders, voices are raised in demanding regional co-operation, particularly regarding employment - which, in turn, also increases pressure to regionalise the budget for unemployment insurance (Dryon and Krzeslo, 1997; Arcq, 1997). Incidentally, this is exactly the evolution that the Walloon unionists fear the most, and probably also explains to a considerable extent the more flexible attitude of the socialist unions, which facilitated the agreement of November 1998. Nevertheless, the position of the trade unions is also difficult at the regional level. In 1994, for example, the unions were excluded from the management boards of the Flemish investment committees; instead, the Flemish government decided to create a tripartite Consultation Committee on Public Initiative (OVO). Even now, this initiative has not yet materialised.

This issue is connected to another development that affects the nature and content of intersectoral collective bargaining. Intersectoral collective bargaining as it developed in the 'golden sixties' mainly concerned the distribution of wealth and income (Bundervoet, 1973). However, since the economic crises of the 1970s and 1980s, employment policy has become more important. Employment policy in the eyes of labour was seen mainly as a question of increasing the demand for labour by public works and incentives for employers to engage, and of limiting manpower, in particular by working time reductions (Heylen and Van Gompel, 1992; Pasture, 1992). However, in the 1980s, Belgium also seems to have discovered the importance of a more active labour market policy. So the unions developed initiatives in the fields of vocational training and continuous education (comp. Streeck, 1992), which since 1980 have become part of regional or community responsibilities. The unions were involved in the establishment of the regional placement and vocational training services (1985), of sub-regional employment committees and in the development of industrial reconversion. The problem of working time is still considered to be a federal matter, however, mainly because of its implications for social security; working time and flexibility are also part of the stalemate between unions and employers at federal level. However, in 1994, the Flemish government, in accordance with the regional organisations of the trade unions, introduced a system of incentives for career breaks and reducing working time provided it is made within a collective framework (Serroyen and Delcroix, 1997). This may constitute the start of a new phase in industrial relations.

However, some of the activities mentioned, in particular in the field of vocational training, are developed by the affiliated national unions, which have not yet (or hardly) developed regional structures. This situation inevitably creates tensions between the affiliated national unions and the intersectoral regional bodies, which therefore seem to adopt merely a political role. This is particularly true for the socialist unions, while in the christian trade union movement the intersectoral level is more developed and the confederation has greater authority over the affiliated national unions.

The present developments not only follow from the internal dynamics of the different regional and community structures, but are inevitably also the result of the continuing drifting apart of the regions. Compared with regional diversities in other (much larger) European countries (table 2.1), the differences in economic performance, employment and income (to mention just the most important parameters) between Flanders, Wallonia and Brussels remain relatively small - but they are increasing considerably. While Flanders has become one of the most prosperous and dynamic regions in Europe, signs of a recovery south of the linguistic border remain scarce; in particular, unemployment in Brussels and the Walloon provinces is higher than the European average and in the neighbouring countries. The difference in the standard of living between Flanders and Wallonia today amounts to 24 per cent. This divergence puts the existing solidarity input from Flanders to Wallonia (and Brussels) - which plays a huge part in explaining why the social situation in Wallonia is not even worse - under a lot of pressure (Descamps, 1998). Moreover, according to many in Flanders, these divergent economic prospects do not just come from different economic conditions, but are also the result of different policies; in any case, the reasoning goes, divergent economic situations demand divergent policies - hence the belief that Flanders needs the necessary instruments to follow its own socio-economic policy even more, which implies more regulatory powers, in particular regarding wage and price policy, and more means, thus more control over its own resources. In particular, in the Social and Economic Council of Flanders (SERV) voices are raised to increase the powers of the regions, including unemployment and health insurance. Informally, many trade unionists subscribe to greater regionalisation, also of union structures, both in the CSC and in the FGTB.

Table 2.1   Unemployment rates and gross national product, 1995

	(a)		(b)	
	1983	1995	1980	1995
Belgium	11.9	9.4	93.3	104.5
Flanders	11.3	6.9	92.4	107.6
Brussels	13.1	13.3	150.2	158.0
Wallonia	12.5	12.9	77.0	83.4
The Netherlands	11.7	7.0	93.1	98.8
Germany*	6.8	8.2	102.5	101.5
France	7.6	11.5	98.9	98.1

Legend: (a) Unemployment rate, Eurostat definition.
(b) Gross National Product per capita (real value parity, indexed Eur3 = 100).

* Germany before 1983: FRG.

Source: Descamps, 1998, 17, 23, 29.

The Flemish government in particular would like to see regional collective agreements come about, especially on regional or communal issues such as professional training, technological innovation, and employment-finding - among other things to avoid the regional government having to pay the bills arising from tripartite bargaining. This may explain why the Flemish government has committed itself to expedite all unanimous decisions of the VESOC. Already in 1993, such an attempt was undertaken by Leona Detiège, the Flemish Minister of Employment, but it failed. In 1996 and 1997 her successor Theo Kelchtermans and Luc Van den Brande, the Flemish Minister-President, in a more favourable political context, reiterated the idea. The reactions of the social partners are ambiguous: the FGTB seems to be the most fervent opponent of it, but Robert Voorhamme, the former secretary general of the Flemish interregional organisation, today a socialist representative in the Flemish parliament, has recognised that a differentiation of collective bargaining becomes unavoidable. In particular, the pressure group of the Flemish-minded employers VEV, criticising especially the national Federation of Belgian Enterprises (FEB) because of its unwillingness to reach an agreement (although the FEB, contrary to the VEV, is recognised as a representative organisation for the employers and thus competent for concluding collective agreements), seems to favour regional collective bargaining. The trade unions fear possible competition between both employers' federations, leading to a further deterioration in working conditions. However, it seems that the Flemish ACV is also welcoming the VEVs present willingness to compromise. Incidentally, in some industrial sectors, in particular textiles and transport, bipartite regional bargaining is already taking place indirectly via local negotiations (Muelenaer, 1997).

In July 1997, an important step in this process was taken when in Leuven sixteen prominent Flemish unionists, employers, social scientists and politicians signed a charter - in their own names, however, not binding their organisations - containing proposals to halve unemployment in Flanders by 2003 (including distribution of work, reductions of labour costs, and an alternative scheme for the financing of social security), demonstrating that at least in Flanders such a consensus existed. Within the SERV, an agreement was also reached regarding a reduction of labour costs in exchange for job creation. The so-called Leuven charter provoked angry reactions among Francophone trade unionists, especially because it can be interpreted as a nucleus of a Flemish collective agreement, but also because by its content the Flemish negotiators - who, incidentally, included the secretary general of the FGTB (and president of the Flemish interregional organisation) Mia De Vits and Miet Smet, the Federal (also Dutch-speaking) Minister of Employment - exceeded their powers, anticipating a further regionalisation of social and economic policies and even of social security (Krzeslo, 1998, 54; EIRO, 1997). Nevertheless, a similar Walloon charter seems to be in the making.

In 1999/2000, the current distribution mechanism for financing the regions and communities will expire and become subject to a re-evaluation. New negotiations between the regions, communities and the federal government are to be expected. Very likely, the recent socio-economic developments will come up, and the outcome certainly will have some effects on the trade unions as well. However, the latter do not seem to be anticipating this development, although union structures are currently on the move. Mainly because of changes in industrial patterns and of the necessity to rationalise, a new centralisation process has started, leading to fusions of affiliated national unions and local union structures (*Financieel-Economische Tijd*, 27 October 1998). However, the opportunity to establish new regional bodies at professional level has not been grasped.

Things are a bit different, however, for the public sector. Education and large parts of the public administration have completely been regionalised; in the federal administration the labour markets are largely segregated as well because of the existing unilingual language frames. Moreover, in the public sector, a different organisational and trade union culture in Flanders, Brussels and Wallonia can be observed, especially regarding strikes which in Belgium are permitted in almost every public administration. The christian and socialist unions for teachers fell apart, but the other public sector unions remained federal, even if a certain internal regionalisation was implemented. Recently, voices raise within these unions for a regional split and a regionalisation of federal public enterprises such as the national railway company.[9]

Conclusion

At the end of this overview, we have to conclude that, contrary to what is often easily assumed, the regional dimension has had a considerable impact on the labour movement in Belgium, and its impact is even likely to increase.

Flanders and Wallonia - internally quite divergent, however - followed very different courses from the start of industrialisation, and this deeply influenced the trade union landscape as well. The economic, political and religious geography contributed largely to the development of competing trade union movements: the socialist, christian and liberal trade unions,[10] with a particular working class culture and differing features and strengths (cf. Pasture, 1996). However, as a result of the different industrial structures of Flanders and Wallonia - as well as because of mutual competition, which forces the unions to act in similar ways - the outlook of the different trade union movements within each region is, in fact, quite similar. The Walloon trade unionists, for example, in the CSC just as in the FGTB, react more militantly than their Flemish comrades. Obviously, as we have seen on several occasions, this has often been a source of frustration for them and has contributed largely to the formation of the MPW of André Renard and to the internal regionalisation of the FGTB. This more militant charac-

---

[9] E.g. Jonny Van den Rijse, president of the Railways' section of the socialist union for the public sector (CCOD-Spoor/CGSP-cheminots) in *Knack*, 10 February 1999, p. 12-5.

[10] Although the regional membership distribution for the liberal union is not available, one can easily assume that the stronghold of the CGSLB is in Brussels. See Annex 2.

ter also appears in the strike patterns, which are quite different in Wallonia and Flanders.

Since 1963, the number of strikes in Wallonia has always been considerably higher than in the North. However, the difference in number of lost working days is lower, which indicates that strikes are usually shorter in Wallonia and last longer in the North. Vilrokx and Van Leemput attribute this difference mainly to divergent economic conditions and industrial relations: in Wallonia, workers and employers live more closely - physically, psychologically and socially - together at the level of the companies, while in Flanders (with its many multinational enterprises) employers are more distant, even physically (Vilrokx and Van Leemput, 1989). As we mentioned at the beginning of this analysis, social stratification too is different in both regions. In the industrial basins, the industrial working class has cherished the idea of class struggle, which has affected the whole political culture of the region - which is, among other things, reflected in the strong position of the Socialist Party in Wallonia. In a more stratified Flanders, the interclass Christian Democratic Party dominates. Obviously, pressure on wages and unemployment play their role too. On the basis of a detailed analysis of the strike pays of the CSC central strike fund since 1945 (which are indicative of the general trend as well: Martens, 1991, 276-7), Albert Martens demonstrated that between 1945 and 1957 - years of high unemployment and low wages in Flanders - the Flemings received relatively more strike benefits than their Walloon comrades; while, since 1957, the balance was the other way round. The difference was particularly high in the years 1978 to 1987, a period of more general and political strikes, especially in the public sector. In the 1990s, the strike patterns in the three regions dropped and tended to converge (Martens, 1991; forthcoming; comp. Vilrokx and Van Leemput, 1998).

As a result (or, perhaps, rather as an expression) of its gradual integration in the Belgian state through its struggles and successes, and notwithstanding an internationalist discourse that rejects any form of 'nationalism', the socialist labour movement developed a strong 'Belgicist' collective identity. It made it in general underestimate the importance of the Flemish question, which may well have hampered its growth in Flanders. This constituted a difference with the christian labour movement that allied itself with the Flemish movement, of which it was even a spearhead in the 1920s and 1930s.

Due to the dramatic decline of the Walloon industrial basins, in the socialist labour movement a strong Walloon identification took root, which surpassed the anti-Flemish resentments of the original Walloon movement, even if these at times do resurface. This Walloon orientation was combined with a more militant outlook, a contemporary echo of the anarcho-syndicalist tradition that was present in the Walloon heavy industries since the very formation of the labour movement, but resulting also from the economic conditions of the 'workers' aristocracy' in the large coal-mines and steel plants. Many Walloon socialists since the 1960s promoted the regionalisation of Belgian economic policy as well as of their own trade union structures as a prerequisite for structural reforms. Nevertheless, they continued to situate themselves within a Belgian perspective and certainly rejected any 'nationalist' connotation. Therefore, they defend the unitary character of social security, referring to 'national solidarity', an idea which appeals very strongly (but significantly also only implicitly) to the socialist ideal of the unitary working class - although if the advocates of regionalisation of social security are correct and Wallonia benefits most from social security finance, there may be some self-interest in the argument as well. Also, when political (in particular Flemish) nationalism is denounced, there is apparently some ambiguity in the discourse, especially when combined with threats about a possible 'reattachment' of Wallonia to France, even if this seems not to be a real option.[11]

It is paradoxical that the labour union with the strongest regional outlook from the outset, the CSC, was the most reluctant to accept internal regionalisation. This can mainly be attributed to the regional (lack of) balance in the union, where, given their overwhelming numbers, the Flemings did not need a separate organisation to have their views heard. The Francophones were relatively over-represented in the leading bodies but were nevertheless still too small to provoke an internal federalisation. In the socialist movement the difference was much smaller, and also even if the Flemings in the FGTB held a majority, this was not perceived as such because of the weight of the most important affiliated national unions, such as the metalworkers and miners unions, which were predominantly Francophone. But in the meantime things have changed and it seems that the regional and community perspective in the CSC has become stronger than in the FGTB. The latter shows a visceral aversion of Flemish nationalist aspirations and strongly insists on the need for national solidarity. However, it is also crystal clear that within the socialist trade union movement strong tensions exist between Flemish unionists and the traditional leadership of some affiliated national unions with their power basis in a more militant Wallonia.

---

[11] The theme of a possible attachment of Wallonia to France is a recurrent one in the Walloon movement. At its 'Walloon National Congress' of 1945 a majority of the participants, including some national (French-speaking) ministers, even voted for an attachment of Wallonia to France. Also recently some socialist politicians did plead for it, although it seems today a rhetorical threat rather than real politics.

Incidentally, the splitting of political parties and the different political orientations in the three regions has had some consequences for the political alliances of the unions as well, in particular in French-speaking Belgium. We mentioned the MPW, which grew out of Walloon trade union circles and paved the way for the development of French language parties; however, the socialist union movement remained closely tied to the Socialist Party (SP). After the split of the Christian Democratic Party (CVP), however, many Francophone christian trade unionists broke with the organised christian democracy and supported the new French language parties (noteworthily not the PS). In Flanders, the christian labour movement continued to cherish its 'special relationship' with the CVP, even if this was regularly questioned and became less exclusive.

Given the divergent socio-economic conditions and developments between the regions, one may rather wonder why the unions were so late in applying a regional logic at all. In fact, since the 1970s, they count among the more 'conservative', 'Belgicist' forces in Belgium. One can only observe that ever since the difficult coming together of different unions from Flanders and Wallonia within a national confederation during their formative years, both unions, the socialist labour movement just as much in the CSC, strongly emphasised the importance of national solidarity. Surely ideological motivations were important in this fundamental orientation, in particular for the socialist unions. But strategic factors played a crucial role too: the regional imbalances both within and among the unions were such that national unity was an important element of strength for defending the economic and political interests of the affiliates. In a regionalised socio-economic environment though, the weight of this calculus evaporates.

Sometimes, European integration is presented as an argument against the relevance of regionalism or nationalism. The analysis above rather provides evidence to support the opposite view. Even if the national economies in Europe tend to converge, European integration has reinforced regional diversities. However, the EC has also developed regional initiatives to limit these differences which constitute a threat towards further integration, such as the associated structural funds (Descamps, 1998; Hooghe, 1995; Cheshire, 1995; Mazey, 1995). European organisations - the EC but occasionally also the OECD - provide impetus towards the development of some interests which in Belgium are regionalised matters such as environmental protection, technology, research and development, social policy, education and culture (Hooghe, 1995).[12] Also this has increased the powers of the regional trade union bodies or has at least strengthened their position.

On the other hand, the regionalisation of their structures may increase even further the difficulties the unions face in organising at the European level. The ETUC, for example, does not take into account the regional dimension, and it will certainly not do so in the near future either: from its first days, the European trade union structures often constituted a way for the confederations to 'emancipate' themselves from the affiliated national unions, and, given the reluctance of the confederations to concede to internal regionalisation, it is likely that they will continue to follow this logic at the ETUC-level at the expense of the regional bodies. Sooner or later, this will create a new ground for tensions in the European labour movement and one more impediment to an effective workers' response towards European and global developments.

Abbreviations

CERW	*Conseil Économique Régional Wallon* (Walloon Regional Economic Council)
CESRW	*Conseil Économique et Social Régional Wallon* (Economic and Social Council for the Walloon Region)
CGSLB	*Confédération Générale des Syndicats Libéraux de Begique/ Algemeen Verbond van Liberale Vakbonden van België* (Confederation of Liberal Trade Unions)
CSC	*Confédération des Syndicats Chrétiens/Algemeen Christelijk Vakverbond* (Christian Trade Union Confederation)
CVP/PSC	*Christelijke Volkspartij/Parti Social Chrétien* (Christian Democratic Party)
ETUC	European Trade Union Confederation
FEB	*Fédération des Entreprises Belges/Verbond van Belgische Ondernemingen* (Federation of Belgian Enterprises)
FGTB	*Fédération Générale des Travailleurs de Belgique/Algemeen Belgisch Vakverbond* (General Trade Union Confederation)
SERV	*Sociaal-Economische Raad van Vlaanderen* (Social-Economic Council for Flanders)
SP	Socialist Party

---

[12] In her insightful analysis of Belgian federalism and the EC, Liesbeth Hooghe observed that EC institutions sometimes bypass not only the federal but also the regional state institutions to directly deal with other public authorities or private bodies. Among the latter we find trade unions as well. Obviously it is the regional trade union authorities that are involved in these contacts.

VESOC   *Vlaams Economisch en Sociaal Overleg Comité* (Flemish Social and Economic Consultation Committee)
VEV   *Vlaams Economisch Verbond* (Flemish Economic Association)

References

* This list does not contain references to union activity reports or newspapers.

ACV (1994), *Voor een sociaal Vlaanderen. Wegwijs in de Vlaamse instellingen*, ACV, Brussel.
Arcq, E. (1980), 'Évolution des structures internes de la FGTB et de la CSC', *Courrier hebdomadaire du CRISP*, No. 866, CRISP, Bruxelles.
Arcq, E. (1997), 'Collective Labour Relations and Social Pacts in Belgium', in G. Fajertag and P. Pochet (eds), *Social Pacts in Europe*, ETUI, Brussels, p. 97-102.
Beaufays, J. (1985), 'Le socialisme et les problèmes communautaires', in Institut Emile Vandervelde, *1885/1985: du Parti Ouvrier Belge au Parti Socialiste*, Labor, Bruxelles, p. 255-78.
Billiet, J. (ed) (1988), *Tussen bescherming en verovering. Sociologen en historici over zuilvorming*, KADOC-Studies 6, Leuven University Press.
Bismans, F. (1998), 'Croissances et convergences régionales en Belgique. Une approche macroéconomique et historique', in Congrès des économistes belges de la langue française, 13e, Charleroi, 26-27 novembre 1998, *Wallonnie et Bruxelles: évolutions et perspectives, 2: Localisation des activités économiques: efficacité versus équité*, Centre interuniversitaire de formations permanente, Charleroi, p. 63-78.
Blaise, P. (1996), 'Les élections sociales', *L'année sociale*, No. 95, ULB, Bruxelles, p. 47-9.
Bundervoet, J. (1973), 'Het doorstromingsprobleem in de hedendaagse vakbeweging: kritische literatuurstudie en verkenningen in de Belgische vakbonden', Unpublished PhD thesis, Katholieke Universiteit Leuven.
Buyst, E. (1993), 'The Decline and Rise of a Small Open Economy: the Case of Belgium', in E. Aerts et al (eds), *Studia Historica Economica: Liber Amicorum Herman Van der Wee*, University Press, Leuven, p. 71-81.
Capron, M. (1987), 'The State, the Regions and Industrial Development: the Challenge of the Belgian Steel Crisis', in Y. Mény and V. Wright (eds), *The Politics of Steel: Western Europe and the Steel Industry in the Crisis Years (1974-84)*, Walter De Gruyter, Berlin/New York.
Cassiers, I, De Villé, Ph. and Solar, P. (1994), *Economic Growth in Post-War Belgium*, Discussion Paper 986, Centre for Economic Policy Research, London.
Cheshire, P.C. (1995), 'European Integration and Regional Responses', in M. Rhodes (ed), *The Regions and the New Europe. Patterns in Core and Periphery Development*, European Policy Research Unit Series, Manchester University Press, Manchester/New York, p. 27-52.
Cheshire, P.C. and Gordon, I.R. (eds) (1995), *Territorial Competition in an Integrating Europe*, Perspectives on Europe. Contemporary Interdisciplinary Research, Avebury, Aldershot.
De Brabander, G.L. (1988), 'Economische transitie', in R. Gobyn and H. Gaus, *De fifties in België*, ASLK, Brussel, p. 104-21.
De Grauwe, P. (1993), 'Symptoms of an Overvalued Currency: the Case of the Belgian Franc', in M. De Cecco (ed), *International Economic Adjustment*, Oxford, p. 99-116.

Deprez, K. and Vos, L. (eds) (1998), *Nationalism in Belgium: Shifting Identities, 1780-1995*, Macmillan, Houndmills.
Descamps, E. (1998), 'Verslag over de economische en sociale convergentie tussen de regio's', *Nieuw tijdschrift voor politiek*, No. 2.
Destatte, Ph. (1995), 'Du rêve autonomiste à la souverainité internationale', in F. Joris, N. Archambeau and R. Collignon, *Wallonie. Atouts et références d'une région*, Gouvernement wallon, s.l., p. 59-84.
Destatte, Ph. (1997), *L'identité wallonne. Essai sur l'affirmation politique de la Wallonie (XIXe-XXe siècles)*, Institut Jules Destrée, Charleroi.
De Wever, B. (1995), *Greep naar de macht. Vlaams-nationalisme en nieuwe orde. Het VNV 1933-45*, Lannoo/Perspectief Uitgaven, Tielt/Gent.
Dryon, Ph. and Krzeslo, E (1997), *Setback for New National Social Pact*, http//eiro.eurofound.ie/.../be9710117f, October.
EIRO (1997), 'Focus on Employment Creation', http//eiro.eurofound.ie/.../be9707214n, July.
Falter, R. (1998), 'Belgium's Peculiar Way to Federalism', in K. Deprez and L. Vos (eds), *Nationalism in Belgium: Shifting Identities, 1780-1995*, Macmillan, Houndmills, p. 177-97.
Fitzmaurice, J. (1996), *The Politics of Belgium: a Unique Federalism*, Hurst, London.
Forman, M. (1998), *Nationalism and the International Labour Movement: the Idea of the Nation in Socialist and Anarchist Theory*, Pennsylvania State University Press, University Park (Pa.).
Francq, B. (1990), 'Les luttes sociales et la conscience de classe: les années Renard', *Socialisme*, Vol. XXXVII, No. 217/218, p. 71-83.
Galissot, R. (1989), 'La patrie des prolétaires', *Le mouvement social*, No. 147 (April-June), p. 11-25.
Galissot, R., Paris, R. and Weill, Cl. (1989), 'L'internationale et la guerre: le partage d'août 1914', *Le mouvement social*, No. 147 (April-June), p. 3-10.
Gerard, E. (1994a), 'L'épanouissement du mouvement ouvrier chrétien (1904-1921)', in E. Gerard and P. Wynants (eds), *Histoire du mouvement ouvrier chrétien en Belgique*, Kadoc-Studies 16, University Press, Leuven, Vol. I, p. 114-73.
Gerard, E. (1994b), 'Adaptation en temps de crise (1921-1944)', in E. Gerard and P. Wynants (eds), *Histoire du mouvement ouvrier chrétien en Belgique*, Kadoc-Studies 16, University Press, Leuven, Vol. I, p. 174-245.
Gerard, E. (1994c), 'Le MOC-ACW', in E. Gerard and P. Wynants (eds), *Histoire du mouvement ouvrier chrétien en Belgique*, Kadoc-Studies 16, University Press, Leuven, Vol. II, p. 565-631.
Gerard, E. (1998), 'The Christian Workers' Movement as a Mass Foundation of the Flemish Movement', in K. Deprez and L. Vos (eds), *Nationalism in Belgium: Shifting Identities, 1780-1995*, Macmillan, Houndmills, p. 127-38.
Hainsworth, P. (ed) (1992), *The Extreme Right in Europe and the USA*, Themes in right-wing ideology and politics series, Pinter, London.
Hellemans, S. (1990), *Strijd om de moderniteit. Sociale bewegingen en verzuiling in Europa sinds 1800*, KADOC-Studies, University Press, Leuven.
Heylen, F. and Van Gompel, J. (1992), 'De ontwikkeling van de werkloosheid en de inactiviteit in België (1970-1990)', *Maandschrift economie*, No. LVI, p. 162-86.
Hogg, R.L. (1986), *Structural Rigidities and Policy Inertia in Interwar Belgium*, Verhandelingen van de Koninklijke Academie voor Wetenschappen, Letteren en Schone Kunsten van België, Klasse der Letteren, 118, Brussel.

Hooghe, L. (1995), 'Belgian Federalism and the European Community', in B. Jones and M. Keating (eds), *The European Union and the Regions*, Clarendon Press, Oxford, p. 135-66.
Husbands, C.T. (1992), 'Belgium: Flemish Legions on the March', in P. Hainsworth (ed), *The Extreme Right in Europe and the USA*, Themes in right-wing ideology and politics series, Pinter, London, p. 126-50.
ILO (1997), *World Labour Report: Industrial Relations, Democracy and Social Stability*, ILO, Geneva.
Joye, P. and Lewin, R. (1967), *L'Eglise et le mouvement ouvrier en Belgique*, Société Populaire d'Edition, Bruxelles.
Kesteloot, C. (1988), 'Le mouvement populaire wallon et la prise de conscience du mouvement wallon (1961-1965), *Cahiers marxistes*, No. 157-158, p. 54-67.
Kesteloot, C. (1993), 'Mouvement wallon et identité nationale', *Courrier hebdomadaire du CRISP*, No. 1392, CRISP, Bruxelles.
Kesteloot, C. (1997), 'Être ou vouloir être. Le cheminement difficile de l'identité wallonne', *Cahiers d'histoire du temps présent*, No. 3, p. 181-201.
Kesteloot, C. (1998), 'The Growth of the Walloon Movement', in K. Deprez and L. Vos (eds), *Nationalism in Belgium: Shifting Identities, 1780-1995*, Macmillan, Houndmills, p. 139-52.
Krzeslo, E. (1998) 'L'encadrement de la négociation collective interprofessionnelle par le gouvernement avance à grands pas: le modèle belge s'enraye et les positions se tranchent', in *L'année sociale 1997*, ULB, Institut de Sociologie, Bruxelles, p. 49-58.
Kumps, A.-M. and Witterwulghe, R. (1981), 'Industrie: l'effrittement de la prépondérance wallonne', in H. Hasquin (dir.), *La Wallonnie. Le pays et les hommes*, La renaissance du livre, Bruxelles, Vol. 4, p. 213-30.
Lijphart, A. (ed) (1981), *Conflict and Coexistence in Belgium: the Dynamics of a Culturally Divided Society*, University of California, Institute of International Studies, Berkeley.
Lipset, S. and Rokkan, S. (1967), 'Cleavage Structures, Party Systems and Voter Alignments: an Introduction', in S. Lipset and S. Rokkan (eds), *Party Systems and Voter Alignments: Cross-National Perspectives*, Free Press, New York, p. 1-64.
Luyten, D. (1995), *Sociaal-economisch overleg in België*, VUB-Press, Brussel.
Mampuys, J. (1994), 'Le syndicalisme chrétien', in E. Gerard and P. Wynants (eds), *Histoire du mouvement ouvrier chrétien en Belgique*, Kadoc-Studies 16, University Press, Leuven, Vol. II, p. 151-277.
Martens, A. (1991), 'Is Mattheüs ook de rentmeester van de stakingskas? Kwantitatieve analyse van de stakingsvergoedingen die door de ACV-Centrale Weerstandskas werden uitbetaald (1948-1988)', in F. Lammertyn and J. Verhoeven (eds), *Tussen sociologie en beleid: vriendenboek prof. dr. E.J. Leemans*, Acco, Leuven/Amersfoort, p. 255-79.
Martens, A. (forthcoming), 'Het arbeidersprotest ingebreideld? Kwantitatieve analyse van de stakingsvergoedingen uitbetaald door de ACV-Centrale Weerstandskas tijdens de periode 1948-1997 (een halve eeuw Centrale Weerstandskas)', *Tijdschrift voor sociologie*.
Mazey, S. (1995), 'Regional Lobbying in the New Europe', in M. Rhodes (ed), *The Regions and the New Europe. Patterns in Core and Periphery Development*, European Policy Research Unit Series, Manchester University Press, Manchester/New York, p. 78-102.
McRae, K.D. (1986), *Conflict and Compromise in Multilingual Societies: Belgium*, The Politics of Cultural Diversity 2, Wilfrid Laurier University Press, Waterloo (Ont.).
Messiaen, J.-J. (1997), 'De intergewestelijken', in L. Peiren and J.J. Messiaen (dir.), *Een eeuw solidariteit. Geschiedenis van de socialistische vakbeweging*, ABVV/Ludion/AMSAB/IEV, Brussel/Gent, p. 129-38.
Mommen, A. (1994), *The Belgian Economy in the Twentieth Century*, Routledge, London.

Monfort, Ph., Thomas, I. and Wunsch, P. (1998), 'Disparités régionales et particularismes nationaux: la Belgique dans l'Europe', in Congrès des économistes belges de la langue française, 13e, Charleroi, 26-27 novembre 1998, *Wallonnie et Bruxelles: évolutions et perspectives, 2: Localisation des activités économiques: efficacité versus équité*, Centre interuniversitaire de formations permanente, Charleroi, p. 39-62.

Moreau, R. (1984), *Combat syndical et conscience wallonne. Du syndicalisme clandestin au Mouvement Populaire Wallon (1943-1963)*, Fondation A. Renard/Vie Ouvrière/Institut Jules Destrée, Liège/Bruxelles/Mt.-S.-Marchienne.

Muelenaer, G. (1997), 'Vlaamse CAO's. Doornroosje en het monster van Loch Ness', in J. Gavel (ed), *Naar een nieuw millennium, Personeel en organisatie. Jaarboek 1997*, Ced. samson, Diegem, p. 49-54.

Neuville, J. (1959), 'Recherches sur le taux de la syndicalisation en 1910', *Courrier hebdomadaire du CRISP*, No. 18, CRISP, Bruxelles.

Neuville, J. (1973), 'Le taux de syndicalisation en Belgique en 1971', *Courrier hebdomadaire du CRISP*, No. 607, CRISP, Bruxelles.

Neuville, J. and Yerna, J. (1990), *Le choc de l'hiver 1960-1961. Les grèves contre la loi unique*, Pol-His 3, De Boeck, Bruxelles.

Pasture, P. (1992), *Kerk, politiek en sociale actie. De unieke positie van de christelijke arbeidersbeweging in België (1944-73)*, Garant, Leuven/Apeldoorn.

Pasture, P. (1993), 'The April 1944 'Social Pact' in Belgium and its Significance for the Post-war Welfare State', *Journal of Contemporary History*, Vol. XXVIII, No. 3 (October), p. 695-714.

Pasture, P. (1996), 'Belgium: Pragmatism in Pluralism', in P. Pasture, J. Verberckmoes and H. De Witte (eds), *The Lost Perspective? Trade Unions between Ideology and Social Action in the New Europe*, Vol. 1, Avebury, Aldershot, p. 91-135.

Pasture, P. (1998), 'The Temptations of Nationalism: Regionalist Orientations in the Christian Labour Movement in Belgium', in P. Pasture and J. Verberckmoes (eds), *Working-Class Internationalism and the Appeal of National Identity: Historical Dilemmas and Current Debates in Western Europe*, Berg, Oxford/New York, p. 107-50.

Pasture, P. and Mampuys, P. (1990), *In de ban van het getal. Ledenanalyse van het ACV 1900-90*, HIVA, Leuven.

Pench, L.R., Sestino, P. and Frontini, E. (1999), *Some unpleasant arithmetics of regional unemployment in the EU. Are there any lessons for EMU?*, Economic Papers 134, European Commission, Brussels, April (PDF file, http://europa.eu.int/comm/dg02/document/ecopap/ecp134en/htm).

Pletinckx, A. (1985), 'Van relatieve eenheid naar scheiding: het Vlaams-Waals probleem', in J. Brepoels et al, *Eeuwige dilemma's. Honderd jaar Socialistische partij*, Kritak, Leuven, p. 96-126.

Quévit, M. (1978), *Les causes du déclin wallon. L'influence du pouvoir politique sur le développement régional*, Vie ouvrière, Bruxelles.

Saey, P., Kesteloot, C. and Vandermotten C. (1998), 'Unequal Economic Development at the Origin of the Federalisation Process', in K. Deprez and L. Vos (eds), *Nationalism in Belgium: Shifting Identities, 1780-1995*, Macmillan, Houndmills, p. 165-76.

Schreiber, J.-P. (1995), 'Jules Destrée entre séparatisme et nationalisme', in A. Morelli (dir.), *Les grands mythes de l'histoire de Belgique, de Flandre et de Wallonie*, EVO, Bruxelles.

Schwarzmantel, J. (1991), *Socialism and the Idea of the Nation*, Harvester Wheatsheaf, New York.

Seiler, D.L. (1975), *Le déclin du cléricalisme. Structure et comportement politique du monde catholique wallon*, Institut Belge de Science Politique, Bruxelles.

Serroyen, C. and Delcroix, J.P. (1997), 'Belgium', in G. Fajertag (ed), *Collective Bargaining in Western Europe 1995-1996*, ETUI, Brussels, p. 33-56.
Spineux, A. (1981), *Forces et stratégies syndicales*, Unpublished PhD thesis, Université Catholique de Louvain-la-Neuve
Spineux, A. (1990), 'Trade Unionism in Belgium: the Difficulties of a Major Renovation', in G. Baglioni and C. Crouch (eds), *European Industrial Relations: the Challenge of Flexibility*, Sage, London, p. 42-69.
Spruyt, M. (1995), *Grove borstels. Stel dat het Vlaams Blok morgen zijn programma realiseert, hoe zou Vlaanderen er dan uitzien?*, Van Halewijck, Leuven.
Steunpunt WAV (1998), *Higher Council for Employment issues controversial report*, http//eiro.eurofound.ie/.../be9803230f, March.
Streeck, W. (1992), 'Training and the New Industrial Relations: a Strategic Role for Unions?', in M. Regini (ed), *The Future of Labour Movements*, Sage, London, p. 250-69.
Strikwerda, C. (1997), *A House Divided: Catholics, Socialists, and Flemish Nationalists in Nineteenth Century Belgium*, Rowman and Littlefield, Lanham.
Tyssens, G. (1997), *Guerre et paix scolaires 1950-1958*, Pol-His 22, De Boeck, Bruxelles.
Van der Linden, M. (1988), 'The National Integration of European Working Classes. Explaining the Causal Configuration', *International Review of Social History*, No. XXXIII, p. 285-311.
Vandermotten, C. (1990), 'Tweehonderd jaar verschuivingen in de industriële geografie van België', in Mort Subite (coll.), *Barsten in België. Een geografie van de Belgische maatschappij*, Epo, Berchem, p. 77-1C8.
Vandermotten, C., Saey, P. and Kesteloot C. (1990), 'België in stukken: bestaan Vlaanderen en Wallonië echt?', in Mort Subite (coll.), *Barsten in België. Een geografie van de Belgische maatschappij*, Epo, Berchem, p. 11-65.
Van Gyes, G. and De Witte, H. (forthcoming), 'Belgian Trade Unions in the 1990s: Means Strong, Strong in the Future?', To be published in E. Gabaglio and R. Hoffman (eds), *Modernisation of Trade Unions*, ETUI, Brussels.
Vanschoenbeek, G. (1997), 'Socialisten: gezellen zonder Vaderland? De Belgische Werkliedenpartij en haar verhouding tot het 'vaderland België', 1885-1940', *Bijdragen tot de eigentijdse geschiedenis*, No. 3, p. 237-55.
Vanthemsche, G. (1989), *Le chômage en Belgique de 1929 à 1940. Son histoire, son actualité*, Archives du futur/Histoire, Labor, Bruxelles.
Veraghtert, K. (1981), 'Van Waalse industriële revoluitie tot Vlaamse heropstanding', in H. Daems et al, *De Belgische industrie: een profielbeeld*, De Nederlandse Boekhandel, Antwerpen/Amsterdam.
Vilrokx, J. and Van Leemput, J. (1989), 'De evolutie van stakingen en bezettingen sinds de jaren '60' in T. Beaupain et al, *50 jaar arbeidsverhoudingen*, Die Keure/Belgische Vereniging voor Arbeidsverhoudingen, Brugge, p. 279-313.
Vilrokx, J. and Van Leemput, J. (1992), 'Belgium: a New Stability in Industrial Relations?', in A. Ferner and R. Hyman (eds), *Industrial Relations in the New Europe*, Blackwell, Oxford/Cambridge (Mass.), p. 355-92.
Vilrokx, J. and Van Leemput, J. (1998), 'Belgium: the Great Transformation', in A. Ferner and R. Hyman (eds), *Industrial Relations in the New Europe*, Blackwell, Oxford/Cambridge (Mass.), 2nd edition, p. 315-47.
Visser, J. (1991), 'Trends in Union Membership', *OECD-Employment Outlook 1991*, OECD, Paris.
Vos, L. (1993), 'Shifting nationalism: Belgians, Flemings and Walloons', in M. Teich and R. Porter (eds), *The National Question in Europe in Historical Context*, Cambridge University Press, Cambridge, p. 128-46.

Vos, L. (1996), 'Nationalism, Democracy and the Belgian State', in R. Caplan and J. Feffer (eds), *Europe's New Nationalism. States and Minorities in Conflict*, Oxford University Press, Oxford/New York, p. 85-100.
Wils, L. (1986), 'De historische verstrengeling tussen de christelijke arbeidersbeweging en de Vlaamse beweging', in E. Gerard and J. Mampuys (eds), *Voor Kerk en werk. Opstellen over de geschiedenis van de christelijke arbeidersbeweging 1886-1986*, Kadoc Jaarboek 1985, University Press, Leuven, p. 15-40.
Wils, L. (1992), *Histoire des nations belges*, Quorum, Ottignies (LLN).
Witte, E., Craeybeckx, J. and Meynen, A. (1990), *Politieke geschiedenis van België van 1830 tot heden*, Standaard, Antwerpen.

Appendix 2.1: Trade Union Membership per Region, 1910-95

	1910	1930	1947	1956	1966	1976	1986	1995
FGTB								
Brussels	8,381	39,261	39,754	63,775	80,760	142,790	117,619	120,344
Flanders	41,663	214,134	221,515	288,207	292,011	378,095	374,997	445,187
Wallonia	36,788	204,597	192,726	132,316	261,926	378,129	370,741	415,053
Total	86,832	457,992	453,995	484,298	634,697	899,014	863,357	980,584
CSC								
Brussels	5,181	8,780	19,071	36,819	55,340	112,432	139,017	153,073
Flanders	32,283	184,735	268,395	434,815	521,955	719,854	825,022	919,586
Wallonia	12,014	19,584	48,865	76,651	133,048	195,930	237,002	302,572
Total	49,478	213,099	336,330	548,285	710,343	1,028,217	1,201,040	1,375,231

Source: CSC and FGTB; 1947-95 corrected by the author (following Pasture and Mampuys, 1990: FGTB: -20%; CSC: -25%/-15%). For the CGSLB, no regional distribution of membership is available. In Brussels, the majority of the CSC members are undoubtedly Dutch-speaking.

Appendix 2.2: Regional Distribution of Votes for the Workplace Health and Safety Committees, 1995 (in per cent)

	FGTB			CSC			CGSLB		
	Profit	Non-profit	Total	Profit	Non-profit	Total	Profit	Non-profit	Total
Brussels	41.4	35.4	40.6	45.3	51.5	46.1	13.3	13.1	13.3
Wallonia	53.9	25.0	46.7	41.0	70.1	48.3	5.0	4.9	5.0
Flanders	35.7	16.0	32.7	54.4	78.3	58.0	9.9	5.7	9.3
Belgium	40.9	22.1	37.7	49.5	71.3	53.3	9.6	6.6	9.0

Source: Blaise, 1996, 49.

3 The Italian Trade Unions and the Local Challenge

GIAMPIERO BIANCHI

Introduction: Characteristics and Limits of the Research

This article deals with the meaning and the effective significance of today's regionalism for the Italian trade unions, not only with regard to the great national confederations but also with regard to the few local experiences of regionalist and autonomist trade unions. Given the lack in Italy of a specific literature on this theme, especially concerning the most ethnic and cultural aspects, our research is mainly based on internal trade union sources and on direct witnesses of the protagonists - both at the national and the local levels - involved in the most recent events.[1]

These events, even if studied with historical method and therefore examined in the context of a wider perspective, relate in particular to the last few years, when the first debate over the issue of 'internal federalism' emerged among the Italian trade unions, which are traditionally very centralised and oriented towards the national level. The debate relates in par-

---

[1] This research has been possible thanks to some trade unionists from the various areas of Italy, who helped me to collect most of the trade union's printed internal material and offered their advise and comments during several interviews and conversations. I want to thank Francesco Corna (from Bergamo), Othman Lindner and Pino Giordano (from Alto Adige-South Tyrol), Gisella (National FIM-CISL), Geremia Gomboso (from Friuli), Italo Marguerettaz (from Val d'Aosta), Giulio Mauri (from Lombardy) and Mariano Murtas (from Sardinia).
On the absence in Italy of research on the regional dimension for trade unions and trade unions as a social force important in the development of local societies see Saba (1993). Santi (1983) attributes that this lack in the trade unions historiography to the exaggerated attention of Italian scholars toward the 'economic cycle' and to the 'cycle of the national party'.

ticular to the importance of the growing regional or local dimension of trade union action and its necessary consequences for the future of the trade union organisation moving in the direction of decentralisation. This essay intends to show how Italian trade unionism, starting from a tradition of centralism and national orientation (which is in fact the case for the three major confederations), has been forced to deal with this issue. Even if in past years it was already steadily gaining in importance for concrete trade union action, in very recent years, the regional question has 'erupted' in all its significance. However, this 'eruption' has turned out not to be so violent as it first appeared, and has resulted in the great confederations slowly adapting to these transformations. As for the (few) more autonomous and local organisations: for the time being they do not seem to be moving beyond certain very well delineated organisational limits.

Historical analyses of the Italian trade union movement never have paid much attention to the local specificities.[2] The historical divisions between North and South, have never been examined from the perspective of the cultural or socio-economic 'differences' between the various trade unionisms (for instance the trade unionism in the North and the trade unionism in the South), even though, as everyone knew, these differences existed and were important.[3] These differences, however, were often considered to be an 'internal problem' of the trade unions, a problem which needed to be solved in order finally to realise the desired national union of the workers - and of the trade unions themselves. The ideal of unity prevailed largely over the actual differences, which could not be considered as a base to build the trade union organisation upon.

The research shows that the trade union reality is changing slowly but steadily, and that today it is much more diversified at the local level than it was in the past, especially if we look at the specific aspects of trade unionism: (a) collective bargaining, for decades strictly national and centralised,

---

[2] For a list of most recent local history of the CISL, see Bianchi (1993); for a general survey of the local history of the workers movement in Italy, see Ganapini (1990).
Most of the historical publications of local trade unions are celebratory and, in any case, point at the microhistory in the social and trade unions context without, however, having the ambition of discussing the classic schemes and thus the 'national' schemes, of the history of the trade unions in Italy.

[3] There is a stream of trade union documents on the development of the South: for a useful general survey until the 1970s see Bartolozzi Batignani (1981). On the differences between the trade unions of the North and the trade unions of the North there is only Manghi (1983). These essays have to be interpreted in the light of the tradition of the CISL of the 1950s which looked at the peculiarities of the South, and promoted a trade union action which would provide an incentive for the 'individual factors of development' ('Relazione al consiglio generale sull'azione CISL nell'ambiente meridionale, Roma luglio 1954', in Ciampani (1992)).

more and more takes local differences into consideration; (b) development policies (thanks to European incentives to recognise local differences)[4] are pushing the Italian trade unions to play a stronger and stronger role in the local communities; and finally, (c) the trade unions' internal organisation, although with a lot of caution, is responding to the growth of the demand for a major decentralisation. Of course, it remains to be seen whether a new kind of trade unionism based on the regional identities will have the upper hand, or whether that of the provinces (much more Italian) or even that of the small centres will prevail. At the same time, it will be necessary to verify the actual relationship of the new localism with the new international dimension of trade union action. Finally, we should not forget the resistance of the central Italian organisations, which grew disproportionately during the 1970s and the 1980s, and which at the current time are certainly unwilling to reduce their own power. The main trend, nonetheless, is toward decentralisation.

A National Trade Unionism

In so far the three great trade union confederations have monopolised the representation of the workers: the CGIL, traditionally a 'class' and 'general' trade union, most of whose members vote for the two parties that developed out of the communist tradition (PDS and RC); the CISL, the 'free' trade union of the trades, most of whose members at least until recently voted for the DC; and the UIL, the smallest of the three of republican and socialist inspiration.

Traditionally, trade unionism has had a very strong presence in Italy, especially compared to similar situations in France and Spain: the three confederations, CGIL, CISL and UIL, together still had a total of 10,500,000 members in 1996, which represented about 37 per cent of all employees, even though they were undergoing a period of minor crisis at the time (the CGIL has about 5,200,000 members, the CISL 3,700,000 and the UIL 1,500,000). This crisis was in part a result of the high number of retiring workers, but the above numbers still reflect a strong adherence to trade unionism, despite the fact that the two great parties which were ideologically closest to the members of the CISL and UIL - the Democrazia Cristiana (the christian democrats, DC) and the Partito Socialista (Socialist Party) - recently disappeared. Trade unionism, therefore, is still strongly

---

[4] It seems that the expectations of the European Commission of a greater uniformity of the 'Latin' models to the local and regional development actually proved to be true (cf. Commission européenne, 1996).

rooted in the country, including the areas with the strongest regionalist and autonomist tendencies, such as the various regions of the north of Italy and Sardinia, where the local parties and trade unions compete overtly with the national trade unions.[5]

The Choice of 'Centralisation'

Such a presence in the country is deeply rooted in the history of the Italian nation and it reflects all those problems which have never been solved: such as the issue of the failed decentralisation of the Italian state and therefore its long-standing distance and impermeability to associative autonomies and local authorities. The decision taken during the 19th century to opt for the uniform and centralising state seemed obligatory to the ruling liberal class, especially in view of the problems in the South, which in fact were intensified by the overly hasty unification (Romanelli, 1995, 133-5). For them, what was missing - especially in the South - was the proper social web for self-management (this opinion was particularly strong among the Democrats of the South) and centralisation seemed to be the only path to modernisation for the country. On the other hand, they refused decisively every 'regionalism' or 'federalism' which would remind them of the old Italian divisions. To go back to the problem of the regions: it was not until the postwar period that the regions were mentioned in the Constitution (1948), even though nothing was done at the time. Regional governments were formed only in 1970. These governments missed many real powers, especially the financial. They were often nothing more than the arithmetic sum of the individual local and municipal authorities, even though the deep cultural differences between them were obvious (Romanelli, 1995, 175; on the differences of the Italian regional institutions, due to different civic traditions, see Putnam, 1993).

This was the Italian paradox: on the one hand, the problems of the South were considered responsible for the great national 'break' which prevented the actual economic unification of the country; on the other hand, there was the illusion (cultivated for years) that the simple unification of the Italian regions under the same legislative and administrative system was a way of overcoming the old economic and social unbalances between the different parts of the country. There were several 'special'

---

[5] The CISL sees a light decrease of membership among blue-collar workers in the industry, a stronger decrease among the agricultural workers and the public employees and an increase in the tertiary sector. The CGIL, on the other hand, sees a decrease in all sectors and an increase among the retired workers. The same applies for the UIL: 'Conquiste del lavoro', January 1997 e 'Nuova rassegna sindacale', November 1996. Important the results of the regions where the autonomist tendencies are stronger.

government interventions aimed at remedying the individual 'deficiencies' found in the various governments, until finally, in 1950, the 'dualistic' aspect of Italian development came to be accepted and a new organic and unitary (thus national) program of development for the South was launched: the so-called *Cassa per il Mezzogiorno* (Fund for the South of Italy), a system which, alternating periods or real reform and innovation with periods of simple management, has survived up to the present time (Marongiu, 1994, 385 ff.; for a bibliographical survey see De Bernardi and Ganapini, 1996, 222-6).

The problems of the South of Italy, therefore, are part of the history of Italy and represent a constant, laudable point of engagement for intellectuals, politicians and economists working to realise the true unity: it is not, however, an acknowledgement of the regional and local diversities which divide the Southern society, like the rest of the country (Marongiu, 1994, 407 ff.; for a history of the South of Italy, see Bevilacqua, 1993).

To understand why trade unions have always considered the regionalist or autonomist tendencies a danger to be avoided, they must be viewed within the context of Italian national history. Their collective bargaining, their political action and their organisational structure have always been strongly oriented toward the national offices, with very little functional autonomy, either in the confederations or in the national unions. Moreover, their ideologies have also played an important role: the left wing, the communists and the social-reformers, have always viewed the autonomist local tendencies as dangerous 'breaches' into class unity and a source of weakness and political uncertainty. The catholics, on the other hand, were not against decentralisation in theory. However, worried about the remnants of nineteenth century polemics, they did not wanted to be accused of being against the unity of the workers movement or against the unity of the country. Finally, they too felt the need of strong, centralised structures.

Italian Development: the Unexpected 'Local' Resource

Paradoxically, the success of the Italian economy - observed with amazement by other countries[6] - has demonstrated both the great peculiarities of Italian development and its permanent internal diversity. As for the peculiarities, it is necessary to recall the very high percentage of independent workers (36.8 per cent), the small amount of heavy industry (no more than the 5 per cent of the employees) and the great web of small and medium-sized modern and export companies (57 per cent of the workers are em-

---

[6] In the introduction of the Italian edition Van der Wee (1989) describes the 1980s as a series of 'miracles'.

ployed in factories with less than 100 workers), interconnected with one another by local chains of solidarity and co-operation which have transformed several territorial Italian systems (known as 'industrial districts') into centres of flourishing local development. This is a development which, by unanimous agreement, finds its own terrain in the local cultures and traditions. As for the differences, there has been a high level of general development in the country as a whole, including the South. The differences remained, however: in 1969 the internal gross product in the South was 69 per cent of the gross product in the Centre and in the North, as it was still in 1989.

In short, we can say that the characteristics of the great, unexpected, Italian development, based upon the small and medium-sized enterprises and on the vitality of the local economies, brought to the fore in radical terms the issue of the regions and the problem of a different organisation of the institutions which would strengthen and promote the successes already obtained (Bagnasco, 1996). The country's recent political and institutional crisis may have grown out of the issues mentioned above. The trade unions have been necessarily affected by these issues and for this reason, there has been slow progress from the central cultural positions toward the valorisation of the areas of autonomy and of the autonomies and diversities.

The Slow Appearance of Diversities

Transformations in Trade Union Action

The structure of the collective agreements inherited from the fascist system of corporations was very centralised. The underlying philosophy as well as the existing practice were continued after the war by trade unions and industrialists alike, although sectoral collective agreements (on a national level) were concluded as well. The unions emphasised, however, that the confederations - and not the national unions - were in fact the contracting parties: no other type of negotiation was admitted. The systems of calculation were national and automatic; also the mechanism which established the minimum wages - which, however, were adjusted according to the different areas of the country (the 'wage cages') - was always decided at the centre. The reasons for this choice must be sought in the economic difficulties of the postwar period and in the reciprocal interests of the unions and employers. In this way the trade unions managed to catch up with inflation and the industrialists managed to stop all those local claims that were viewed as potential disorder (Valcavi, 1976; Saba, 1981, 333-444).

After the secession (1948), the CISL tried to introduce strong innovations (plant-level bargaining, productivity, the new industrial relations in the workplace, etc.) for the decentralisation and the progressive reduction of the wage automatisms, but they were rejected everywhere. With the economic development, however, all the faults of the old system came to the surface and, in fact, during the 1960s the collective agreements of the sectoral organisations became more substantial, which ushered in a period of modest agreements with the companies. In 1968-69 a new period of central bargaining took off. The reasons for this return were strictly 'ideological' and 'social', such as, for instance, the myth of equality and the struggle against discrimination (Accornero, 1992). Not only were the 'wage cages' abolished, but also new salary increases were promoted, with an indexation mechanism which is equal for everyone (*scala mobile*).[7] During the 1980s the trade unions were at a turning point. There was conflict among the various trade unions regarding the reduction of inflation and the end of the *scala mobile* (1992). The transformations took place within a strictly centralist perspective, with major agreements between the government and the social partners. In the meantime, however, collective bargaining inside the factories became more common, though it was not officially recognised.

The general picture was clarified with the agreement of July 1993, when the two levels of industrial relations were finally acknowledged, one taking place at a national level and the other at the factory level or at a 'territorial' level. This was a historical turning point in the direction of decentralisation, though not yet sufficient in a country characterised by small enterprises, 'industrial districts' and great territorial differences. The debate today is still very lively. Some intellectuals and industrialists in the metallurgic industry have called for the abolition of the national agreements. Some industries, such as the textile and the agricultural industries, are already negotiating at the territorial level. The CGIL, even though it is against the concept of 'territory', has acknowledged that only 30 per cent of the firms have negotiated national collective agreements, while the CISL has presented a system of differentiated minimum wages to help the development of the regions in the South. During the last negotiations for a new general agreement (Patti di Natale, December 1998), the CISL, with the support for the employers, has demanded a stronger decentralisation of national collective bargaining, but this proposition did not find the necessary support from the CGIL, which - influenced by its left wing - refused to take any decision in the matter and postponed it to a later date.

---

[7] Scholars criticised the 'cages' because they did not protect everyone and because they favoured illegal jobs: e.g. Palmerio and Valiani, 1978.

A parallel change toward the local dimension seems to be a reality even for the remaining areas of trade union action, ranging from the economic policies and the development of the labour policies, to the social and welfare policies. For years, the 'horizontal' structures of the trade unions have been the tool for the transmission at the local level of general and national mobilisations, which naturally were enriched by the contents typical of the local reality of labour. Now the 'horizontal' structures of the trade unions (regional, provincial, etc.) witness their own territorial activities grow, far beyond the traditional political action of 'general mobilisation' and of the co-ordination of local industrial trade unions. Some examples might be useful to better understand this point.

The first example regards the so called 'area agreements': these are local agreements reached in the areas affected by unemployment, where the social forces are engaged in projects for the creation of new employment, supported in this endeavour by government financial provisions, fiscal benefits and various incentives.[8] The 'territorial agreements' promoted by the National Board of Economy and Labour constitute a second example: local agreements, of various extent, promoted by the social forces for the economic and social development of a specific area. The aim of this experiment - created just after the agreement in 1991 dealing with the development of the South, and then extended to the entire country - is the mobilisation of endogenous resources, human and material, of a given territory for the purposes of development. As of November 1996, the trade unions were actively involved in 95 territories (Cnel, 1996b). Even the role played by the programs of the European Community relating to local and especially rural development is interesting: these programs are not very widespread, but they are forcing the trade unions to change their mentality. They certainly have made some regional unions of the CISL, for example, to experience the value of the rural territory for the purpose of promoting economic development and improving the quality of life of the workers, after years of industrialist myths and traditional trade union activity (USR-CISL, 1996). For their part, some regional trade unions of the 'classist' CGIL have discovered the central value of the small enterprise for the development of the Italian territory and are looking for the best way to support it (CGIL, 1994).

Transformations in the Trade Union Organisation

The rigid and centralised unitary model of the CGIL was established ever since its first Congress in 1947. All the internal life of the trade union was

---

8 'L'Accordo per il lavoro', *Industria e sindacato*, September 1996.

directed, and often managed, by the national centre, including the resources and the staff. With the appearance of the CISL, strong national unions entered the scene, provided with resources and the power to sign collective agreements. However, they were the smaller version of the same centralist model of the confederations. The existence of important internal cultural differences remained for many years a taboo: 'national' trade unionism could not admit that the same structures, run by the same written rules and belonging to the same organisation, in reality behaved in totally different ways. The divergent trade union practices did not only result from external factors (the employers, the government, the economy, etc.) but were the outcome of differences in culture and mentality. Bruno Manghi (1983) showed how these differences (especially between the trade unions of the North and those of the South) were a reality and how the new action for the South should start from them (table 3.1).

Table 3.1   Priorities of trade union action in the north and in the south of Italy

North	South
1. Plant-level bargaining	1. Individual protection
2. National collective bargaining	2. Welfare
3. Management of agreements	3. Public employment service
4. Industrial disputes	4. Industrial disputes
5. Individual grievances	5. Management of agreements
6. Welfare	6. National collective bargaining
7. Public employment service	7. Plant-level bargaining

Source: Manghi, 1983.

A few years later, after the explosion in the country of the 'federal' question, the debate over the real decentralisation in the territory, hidden for a long time by the rhetoric of the national trade union, burst out especially inside the CISL. The practically oriented central tendencies of the CISL did not have ideological motivations and, among the trade unions, the CISL was the most exposed to the 'wind of the Lega', especially since the CISL had the majority in the areas where the Lega was strong. The CISL of Lombardy, for example, asked to promote federalism and to apply it to the internal structure of the trade union, thus transforming the old regional bodies into true regional trade unions, then 'federated' among one another.[9] In the following months, after a meeting organised by some regional trade unions of the CISL, an internal debate on the possible 'subsidiarity' among the various structures was started up. Even if this debates continues up until today, so far, there have not been many changes implemented, except for an increase in the financial endowments of the regional federations.[10] The CGIL instead preferred only to discuss how, eventually, to conform its action, awaiting a new federal reform of the Italian State.[11]

Trade Union 'Regionalist' Experience

The compendium of the Italian trade unions would not be complete without relating some particular experiences of trade unionism concerning specific regional or ethnic matters. These relate to a number of circumscribed areas of the country, normally boundary territories, inhabited by populations characterised by a different language, history and identity, and tending to distance themselves from the rest of the Italian nation. These areas also exhibit a consolidated experience of regionalist and autochthonous trade unionism, which in some cases has existed for a long time already, and these unions are clearly in competition with the local organisations of the CGIL, CISL and UIL. Finally, we would like to relate the recent experience of the trade unions in the Po Valley, currently promoted by the Lega Nord, the party which in the last few years has been endorsing a policy of separation of the entire north of Italy (which they call 'Padania' or 'Po Valley region') from the rest of the country.

At first glance, all of these unions seem to follow one rule: they all support, more or less directly, the local 'autonomist party'. In this political support they in fact follow a tradition typical of Italian trade unionism.

Trade Unionism in Alto Adige

Alto Adige, or South Tyrol, is a small mountain province (the main town of the district is Bolzano), with vast and fertile internal valleys, located on the border with Austria and which since 1918 has been part of Italian territory. The majority of its population speaks German. During the years of

---

[9] 'Relazione al congresso USR-CISL Lombardia 1993', typescript.
[10] 'Convegno delle USR-CISL *Per una nuova identità nazionale, Il ruolo e le potenzialità delle regioni*', February 1994, typescript: 'il dibattito interno continua anche in vista del prossimo congresso CISL (giugno 1997) dove però non si prevedono consistenti cambiamenti organizzativi verso il decentramento' (Tesi confederali CISL, 2 November 1996).
[11] *XIII congresso nazionale CGIL. Documenti*, Roma, 1996.

the fascist regime, the province was subjected to a policy of forced 'italicisation', involving measures ranging from the prohibition of the public use of German to the support of the government and a massive immigration of workers and Italian families. Later on, during the war, it was annexed to Germany and finally in 1945 reintegrated into Italian territory. Since then it has enjoyed a special autonomous status (see the Austrian-Italian agreements of 1946 and of 1972), involving such special measures as bilingualism, and during the last few years it has witnessed alternating moments of 'tension' and 'relaxation' between the two communities - the Italian community and the German community - and between the local government, which is firmly controlled by the German-speaking party (SVP), and the government in Rome. This is the context in which particular experiences of trade unionism have originated and developed.

Traditionally agricultural and rural, through the years Alto Adige has undergone strong industrial development (first under fascism, later on during the 1960s, and finally at the current time) which created the conditions for a trade union. In 1945 the CGIL came into being, Italian-speaking and with a communist majority. In 1948 the catholic workers from both the ethnic groups created an experience of inter-ethnic and bilingual trade unionism, the so-called Libera-CGIL. In 1949, when some republican and social democrat workers joined the catholic workers, they formed the CISL. In 1964 part of the German workers of the CISL created the trade union ASGB which, according to the statutes, is supposed to be composed exclusively of German workers and supported by the SVP. The ethnic tensions, which had subsided during the 1970s, later led to a period of intense social disorders in whole Italy, and also in Alto Adige. They erupted again at the beginning of the 1980s. It was in this period that the general picture was formed and consolidated, which shows, on the one hand, great economic prosperity (the rate of unemployment is close to zero and the incomes are among the highest in Italy) and, on the other hand, the awakening of reciprocal fears and suspicions between the two communities. In the last few years, while the extreme right-wing party AN replaced the DC as the largest Italian party in the region, the ethnic rule of the SVP continued undisturbed in the local governments.

In the world of the working people and of the cities nowadays the workers of the two ethnic groups tend to mingle more and more regularly, even if differences remain. The trade union organisations are taking different approaches to the ethnic question. The CGIL, even though it had a dual name (CGIL-AGB: 26,700 official members in 1996, mostly Italians), has not substantially changed its old belief that the two national and ethnic identities are actually an obstacle on the way to the union of all the workers, and still believes that the unifying factor consists in their common working conditions. The same thing, substantially, applies to the small UIL. The ASGB is following its own particular course (it does not reveal the number of its members) and since the legislative acknowledgement obtained in 1978, it still continues to be, for its part, a trade union composed only of German-speaking people, careful about defending those rules and those proportional quotas - essential to maintain the ethnic status quo - in the workplace and in society which the German community sees as a necessary means for defending their ethnicity.[12]

The experience of the CISL-SGB is different from all the other unions (26,327 members in 1996, about 14,000 of which were German and 11,000 Italian, the rest being immigrants). It is the only trade union which has always been openly 'inter-ethnic' and which, after one period of 'relaxation' (during the 1970s) on the ethnic front, decided in 1979 to become the centre and the driving force of concord between the two communities in Alto Adige. In order to do so it asked and obtained a greater trade union autonomy from the national CISL, it strengthened its internal statutory rules as a guarantee for the two groups (with alternating appointments, bilingualism, collective decision making, etc.) and it engaged itself outside, in the world of the workers and in the society of South Tyrol, for the formal and substantial equality of the rights of all groups and individuals. In order to do so, it had to make use of a high degree of pragmatism in a situation in which the issues of labour (immigration, equal opportunities, etc.) and the social issues (housing, education, welfare, etc.) were the most problematic.[13]

Ethnic Trade Unionism in Val d'Aosta and in Sardinia

Val d'Aosta enjoys regional autonomy and has special statutes. It is a small Alpine valley at the border of France. The majority of its population speaks a French-Provencal dialect. Officially bilingual (Italian and French), Val d'Aosta has been run since 1945 by a local autonomist party, the Union Valdotaine (UV), first together with the DC and now with the PDS. Even though it is an essentially agricultural-rural-tourist area, its mineral wealth

---

[12] To complete the picture, we have to mention also the ACLI, pre-union association of catholic workers (very strong in a territory traditionally religious) where in the same organisation there are two different federations. Entrepreneurs, on the other hand, are even formally separated in two different associations, one Italian and the other German (in 'La politica interetnica della CISL-SGB, Relazioni al Seminario di studio', dicembre 1986, typescript).

[13] See Ghirigato, 1986; 1988; CISL-SGB, 'Il sindacato confederale e il confronto con le questioni economico-sociali in Alto Adige. Relazione al XII congresso', May 1993. Membership figures: local offices CISL and CGIL.

and its proximity to the great communication routes always favoured the presence of industries in the plains and therefore also of workers engaged in the trade unions.

In the postwar period, a unitary CGIL made its appearance in Val d'Aosta, with a communist majority, though with many minor internal factions, the most numerous being the autonomist faction. In 1948 when the catholics left the CGIL, in Val d'Aosta - just as in the rest of the country - the autonomists decided to stay, even though they were not getting along with the communists. The break between them and the CGIL happened afterwards, in 1952, when the autonomist syndicalists created the autonomous trade union of the Val d'Aosta of the workers SAVT. Later on, the SAVT federated with the UIL, until 1966, when the latter decided to found its own regional structure, in competition with the SAVT. During the 1970s, the three Italian trade unions and the autonomist trade union reached an agreement about a federation (which allowed the autonomist trade union to sign collective agreements). This lasted until 1984 when, just as in the rest of Italy, this agreement was dissolved because of irreconcilable internal disagreements. Ever since, the SAVT has represented the third trade union power in the region (with almost 6,000 members), behind the CGIL (about 10,000) and the CISL (about 6,500).

The SAVT has close contacts with numerous European trade unions 'of the ethnic communities of the Community', among which the ASGB from Alto Adige. Unlike the ASGB, however, the SAVT speaks in its statutes of defence of 'the workers of Val d'Aosta'. Nevertheless, at the current time many of its members do not originate from Val d'Aosta: they are migrants from elsewhere in Italy or from outside the European Community.[14] The Congress of 1993, even though it stressed the importance of the 'ideals of autonomy and federalism', would in fact like to see more collaboration among the social powers and more unity among all the workers of Val d'Aosta.[15]

The Sardinian trade union represents another case of regional trade unionism formally constituted. Sardinia is an island located in the centre of the western part of the Mediterranean Sea (with more then 1,650,000 inhabitants); the island is endowed with great natural beauty, though the economy is traditionally backward. It has always been characterised by a

---

[14] The statute talks of: 'defence and promotion of the economic, moral and cultural interests of the Valley region workers' and of supporting the 'local development' and the 'cultural, economic and political emancipation' in the Val d'Aosta community (in 'Statuto del SAVT', typescript, 6).

[15] For what concerns its identity, the SAVT indicated a 'cultural action to preserve the ethnic and linguistic specificities, granted in the special statutes of the Val d'Aosta' (in 'Motion Final du XI congres confederal du SAVT', typescript).

strong cultural-regional identity; it also has its own autochthonous language, Sardinian. Like Alto Adige and Val d'Aosta, Sardinia enjoys the privilege of a special statute granting strong political and legislative autonomy. Its week economy and long-standing social and civil backwardness make it one of the regions in Italy which are the source and focal point of the notorious 'Southern Issue'. It is for this reason that its recent history has witnessed numerous and expensive state interventions, the one following upon the other, each aiming to promote the region's development.

The Sardinian trade union Confederation (CSS) was founded on 19 January 1985, in a period of great, and for many reasons unexpected, electoral successes for what had always been a small political group of the left wing in the island: the Sardinian Party of Action (Partito Sardo d'Azione - PSD'AZ), the 'landmark' of the trade unionists of the CSS, most of coming from the CGIL. The aim of the new organisation was the 'protection of the rights and individual characteristics of all the Sardinian workers, employed and unemployed'.[16] This is a formulation very close to the 'general' trade union model of the CGIL, even though a model like this by the CSS has been applied only to the Sardinian situation.[17] Since the beginning, the CSS has tried to conjoin with various spontaneous forms of trade unionism as they arose from the workplace during the 1980s.

The CSS established strong links with the *comitate di base* (COBAS), a form of national interconnection of the spontaneous and local left wing unions (with two agreements, one in 1988 and one in 1992) (Malaberba, 1995). Contrary to all expectations, however, the anticipated growth of the CSS did not take place and, at the same time, after alternate successes, the electoral decline of the PSD'AZ set in. The last documents of the CSS also reveal a decreased focus on mere 'trade union' themes, such as the Sardinian collective national contract for each category, with a consistent preference for more generic themes and political issues such as the environment, social security and alternative industrial development, in addition, of course, to the defence of the Sardinian language and identity. This is a turning point which has led to some internal dissension.[18]

---

[16] 'The CSS wants to protect the interests and the rights of the Sardinian workers, employed and unemployed, and wants to defend the national rights to the full expression of their linguistic and cultural values, and it also wants to promote the development of the personality and professionality of the workers and to create a regional bargaining system in all sectors' ('statuti confederali', in CSS, 1966, 13).

[17] It in fact defines itself as a 'collective organism of economic decision, elaboration and proposal, a structure for realistic unitary politics of all the Sardinian workers, organisation of the employees, employed and unemployed, residents and aliens' (ibidem, 11).

[18] 'So far we have limited ourselves, on the one hand to trade union assistance... on the other to talk about Sardinian culture and language' (in 'III congresso nazionale della Css', ibidem, 69).

The Lega Nord and the Trade Unionism of the Po Valley

During the second half of the 1980s a new phenomenon made its appearance on the Italian political scene: the *leghismo* or affiliation to the Northern League. It consisted of local electoral lists, normally assembled on a regional basis (Liga Veneta, Nord Piemont, Lega Lombarda, etc.), with their programs focused on two main issues: (a) an indignant criticism of the 'Roman' parties, people of the centre, inefficient workers and squanderers of the national wealth (this was also the start of the violent anti-fiscal polemic); (b) the demand for stronger local autonomy and for a transformation of the Italian state into a federation of states or, if necessary, the complete independence of the northern regions (which also leads into the polemic against the south of Italy in general and its populations). The electoral successes of the *leghismo* are well known: first, some small local victories (1987-89), and then some sensational successes (20 per cent in Lombardy in 1990, the relative majority in Brescia in 1991) and, growing out of this, the success at the national level in the political elections of 1992 (roughly 18-20 per cent in the Northern areas), the last elections carried out on the basis of the proportional system. The new majoritarian electoral system transformed the Lega into a national protagonist, first allied with the centre and the right-wing, and then pushed off into a 'splendid isolation', which could not reverse its growing radicalisation in some areas of Northern Italy, usually in small population centres and in alpine valleys (political elections of 1996).

Lombardy, which was the cradle of the movement, is one of the richest regions of Europe, and has always been the driving force behind the nation's manufacturing (20 per cent of the national internal product, 30 per cent of the export) and the heart of its industrial production (760,000 firms and 3.1 million employees). In Lombardy itself, in Bergamo, on 31 May 1990 some representatives of the Lega founded the Lombard Autonomous Trade Union (SAL), which has two aims: preferential treatment for workers from the North, concerning both industrial relations and the welfare state, and a mixed solution - almost neo-corporative - for the problems of unemployment (employees and entrepreneurs together).[19] Another characteristic of the SAL was the strict relationship, mentioned in the statutes,

---

[19] 'The SAL aims at pursuing and protecting the legitimate interests of the dependent workers, and of the retired workers of the people of Lombardy, aiming at realising real solidarity and social justice among the Lombard people' (in 'Costituzione del Sal', Notarial act of 31 May 1990, Bergamo). 'The Lombard trade union organisations belong to the SAL, they gather employees and also the small entrepreneurs' (in 'Statuto del Sal', ibidem).

with the political party of the *Lega*[20] - a formula which caused a good deal of internal debate among the trade unionists of the Lega themselves.

After 1990, the representatives of the Lega created new trade unions even in other regions. Their first general congress took place in 1993 in Bergamo, with delegates representing 35,000 members. They gathered to elect the national executives and to define their objectives: (a) to promote trade unionism among the new workers who have never been in the trade unions before; (b) to strengthen the political ties with the party of the Lega; (c) to promote the creation of a regional wage system and a regional health system; (d) to implement major preferences for the workers from the north in state subsidised housing and in the recruitment for government appointments. On the Lega/SAL report at the congress, Senator Bossi declared: 'I am asking you *only to follow the political line of the Lega and I am asking you overtly*' (*L'Eco di Bergamo*, 3 May 1993). The official aim was to provoke the failure of the national parties and - after that - of the trade unions affiliated with them. It is noteworthy to observe that the electoral areas more subject to the Lega were those which traditionally had been under the influence of the CISL.

Actually, apart from the support of a few trade unionists - in particular those coming from the UIL - and apart from the election of a few general representatives in some factories, the frequent challenges coming from the Lega warning of the approaching end of confederate trade unionism, seem to have come to nothing, especially where they thought they would win: in the companies. In fact, between 1993 and 1996, apart from a few isolated victories in some small firms ('Il carroccio sfratta la CGIL dalla fabbrica', *Il giornale*, 21 January 1996), the failure of SAL seems even more evident, especially in those areas which were more subject to the Lega. A recent survey of the FIM-CISL (metalworkers' union) in Lombardy confirms that one-third of the members of the CISL declared that they were voting for the Lega and that a much greater number agreed with the Lega objectives of federalism and autonomy. This fact, however, does not seem to be the cause of any doubts on the part of the workers about their traditional mass support for national trade unionism and, in particular, for the CISL. And this is the case even in some industries, such as textiles, and in areas such as the Lombard valleys, where the Lega receives more than the 50 per cent of the votes.[21] Given these precedents, the strategy of the CGIL-CISL and

---

[20] 'The SAL organisations have to separate their responsibilities from those of the specific political organisation, to which they should however be able to adhere to create a relationship of reciprocal consultation' (ibidem).

[21] 'Sindacato, Lega e politica: quali relazioni? Alcune riflessioni sulle intenzioni di voto rilevate da indagini su iscritti FIM-CISL', CGIL Lombardia and CGIL-CISL-UIL Veneto, typescript, September 1996. See also Braun, 1998.

UIL is to avoid frontal clashes with the SAL and, if possible, to ignore it, emphasising the positive capacities of the confederal experience, responding properly to the needs of the workers and coping in a different way with the issues which are crucial for the workers (local autonomy, less state intervention, defence of professionalism, etc.). And this has proven to be a winning strategy so far. There is a fundamental difference, however, between the trade union experience of the Lega and the experience of those regional unions examined above. The fact is that there is no clearly defined cultural identity in the Po Valley or in Northern Italy as a whole; rather, there are many regional identities, which in turn are more the product of the ideals of nineteenth century intellectuals than a reality. The specific situation in the north of Italy, as Meriggi recently stated, is that of a 'long history, made up more of differences than of similarities, more of localisms than of regionalisms' (Meriggi, 1996). Yes, they are united, but more in terms of expressing their unease toward the central government than in terms of their own identities, which for the most part are linked to the small town or commune, to the love of one's birthplace and to local pride (Bagnasco, 1996).

The Trade Unions and the New Local Issues

Italian trade unionism seems today to be at a crossroads. It can carry on with the traditional centralising approach, perhaps with some tactical changes, and still continue to rely on the historical support of the affiliated parties, or it can respond in a serious manner to the challenge of the latest transformations and totally restructure every plan of action and organisation. Some fundamental issues, such as the new local dimension (parallel to the growing globalisation) and the current transformations of work and of the industries, show clearly that the traditional methods employed by the Italian trade unions in the 1970s and 1980s, such as centralised collective bargaining and decision making, have now become out-of-date.

Many Italian trade unionists, both in the North and in the South, are aware of this reality. The problem in these cases, however, arises from the need to provide solutions according to the different local contexts, as the CNEL (National Council of Economy and Work) demonstrated so clearly in one of its surveys about the end of the national agreements and about the new frontiers of labour representation (Cnel, 1996a). One leader of the CGIL from Veneto explained to us that in his view the crisis of industrial relations comes from the inability to understand the world of the workers any longer, much more differentiated now than in the past. He proposed renouncing the usual 'general' and generic mobilisations, and working instead for an effective process of territorial negotiation within the small and medium-sized enterprises and for better trade union policies, always paying careful attention to the increasingly evident regional and professional differences. One leader of the CISL in Lombardy, on the other hand, pointed out that the claims of the workers are no longer limited to the conditions regulating their work contract, but also involve the problems of social rights and the need for assistance and for legal advice (including financial advice), observing finally that the smaller the firm, the larger the role of the trade union could be in this respect. In another interview another executive, who saw in the elaboration of the regional politics of development arranged by the social partners the path to future local development, also discussed the regional dimension in Lombardy. As for the internal reform of the trade union organisation, everyone wanted less control from Rome and an increased presence in the workplace - an issue which lies at the centre of an intense debate in Italy. The 1991 compromise of the *Rappresentanze sindacali unitarie* (Plant-level Union Structures, RSU) makes everybody unhappy. The CISL asked for the presence of the trade unions in the firm, whereas the CGIL demanded the presence of the representatives of all the workers.

This small 'example' can perhaps give some idea of the various debates presently going on among the Italian trade unions. These unions are strong and firmly rooted in the country. However, they are now struggling with some crucial and historical 'knots' that must be untangled, and the new local dimension of trade union action is one of these knots.

Abbreviations

ACLI	Assoziazione Cristiani dei Lavoratori Italiani
AN	Alleanza Nazionale
ASGB	Autonome Südtirolische Gewerkschaftsbund
CGIL	Confederazione Generale del Lavoro
CISL	Confedarazione Italiana Sindacati Lavoratori
CNEL	Consiglio Nazionale Economia e Lavoro
COBAS	Comitate de Base
CSS	Confederazione Sindacale Sarda
DC	Democracia Cristiana
FIM	Federazione Italiana Metalmeccanici CISL
PDS	Partito Democratico della Sinistra
PSD'AZ	Partito Sardo d'Azione
RC	Rifondazione Comunista
SAL	Sindacato Autonomo Lombardo

SAVT   Sindacato Autonomo Valdostano dei Lavoratori
SVP   Südtirolische Volkspartei
UIL   Unione Italiana del Lavoro
USR   Unione Sindacale Regionale CISL

References

Accornero, A. (1992), *La parabola del sindacato*, Bologna.
Bagnasco, A. (1996), *L'Italia in tempi di cambiamento politico*, Bologna.
Bartolozzi Batignani, S. (1981), *Sindacato e Mezzogiorno (1945-72)*, Varese.
Bevilacqua, P. (1993), *Breve storia dell'Italia meridionale dall'800 ad oggi*, Roma.
Bianchi, G. (1993), 'Per una storia dell'USR-CISL del Lazio', in Aa. Vv., *L'unione sindacale regionale, un soggetto nella soria della regione Lazio*, Roma.
Braun, M. (1998), 'Regionalism Threatening Trade Unions in Northern Italy?', in P. Pasture and J. Verberckmoes (eds), *Working-Class Internationalism and the Appeal of National Identity. Historical Debates and Current Perspectives on Western Europe*, Berg, Oxford/ New York.
CGIL, Marche, Emilia Romagna, Toscana, Veneto, Friuli (1994), 'Piccole imprese, sistemi produttivi e movimento sindacale', *Nuova rassegna sindacale*, No. 9 (March).
Ciampani, A. (ed) (1992), 'Sindacato e società meridionale', *Opinioni*.
Cnel (1996a), *Laboratori territoriali. Le rappresentanze nella questione settentrionale*, Roma.
Cnel (1996b), *I patti territoriali dossier: lo stato di avanzamento delle proposte pervenute al Cnel*, Roma.
Commission européenne (1996), *Un nouveau champ d'activités syndicales. Agir dans les régions pour l'Europe des régions*, Luxembourg.
CSS (1966), *Sindacato etnico sardo*, Cagliari.
De Bernardi, A. and Ganapini, L. (1996), *Storia d'Italia, 1860-1995*, Milano.
Ganapini, L. (1990), 'Movimento operaio e sindacati in Italia. Una rassegna critica di studi', *Studi storici*, No. 1.
Ghirigato, I. (1986), *Sindacato e questione etnica*, Roma.
Ghirigato, I. (1988), *Ritrovare la memoria*, Bolzano.
Malabertba, G. (1995), *Dai Cobas al sindacato. Un percorso per ricostruire uni organizzazione di classe dei lavoratori*, Roma.
Manghi, B. (1983), 'Il lavoro sindacale nel Mezzogiorno, e Solidarietà difficile: il sindacato nel Sud', *Il progetto*, No. 14-15.
Meriggi, M. (1996), *Breve storia dell'Italia settentrionale dall'Ottocento ad oggi*, Roma.
Marongiu, G. (1994), *La democrazia come problema. Politica, società e Mezzogiorno*, Bologna.
Palmerio, G. and Valiani, R. (1978), *Alcuni effetti della scala mobile e della Cig sul divario Noed-Sud*, Milano.
Putnam, R. (1993), *La tradizione civica nelle regioni italiane*, Milano.
Romanelli, R. (ed) (1995), *Storia dello stato italiano dall'Unità ad oggi*, Roma.
Saba, V. (1981), 'Verso un nuovo sindacato (luglio 1948-55)', in S. Zaninelli (ed), *Il sindacato nuovo. Politica e organizzazione del movimento sindacale in Italia negli anni 1943-55*, Milano, p. 333-444.
Saba, V. (1993), 'Per un sindacalismo regionale', in Aa. Vv., *L'unione sindacale regionale, un soggetto nella soria della regione Lazio*, Roma.

Santi, E. (1983), 'Il territorio: uno spazio problematico per la presenza sindacale', in Cesos, *Itinerari sindacali*, Roma.

USR-CISL, Abruzzo, Lazio, Marche, Toscana, Umbria (1996), *La sfida della complessità. Agricoltura e sviluppo ruralenelle regioni dell'Italia centrale*, Roma.

Valcavi, D. (1976), 'Politica salariale ed azione contrattuale in Italia (1944-73)', in *Annali della Fondazione G. Pastore*, Roma.

Van der Wee, H. (1989), *L'economia mondiale tra crisi e benessere (1945-80)*, Milano.

4 Industrial Relations in Spain: Does Regional Diversity Awaken Union Tendencies to Divergence?

JACINT JORDANA

The Regions and Spanish Industrial Relations

Since the last decade, from many points of view, specialists in European politics have been insisting about the emergence of a regional space in Europe. Often politically underdeveloped, because of the persistent power of nation states in the European institutions, the regions appear to be the homogeneous economic and social areas across Europe that are working out strategies for their own progress and that are co-operating or competing among themselves to improve their attractiveness for private and public investment. In this paper we want to analyse a concrete case related to this broad and complex development in European politics. The case in point is that of the unions in the Spanish regions and their rise as actors belonging to significant regional arenas in the field of labour and industrial relations.

In the late 1970s, during the Spanish transition to democracy, when the new industrial relations framework was being constructed, the regions were given very little room in which to manoeuvre. All the main actors conceived of the Spanish labour market as a set of common institutions and statewide homogeneous conditions for workers and employers, and the structures they in fact established on the basis of these conceptions were implemented by means of centralised social pacts and state legislation. At the present time, however, the territorial picture of industrial relations in Spain is not so clear as it was thought to be twenty years ago, and the regions have gained their own place - with many differences from region to region - in the fabric of Spanish industrial relations, a place which is parallel to the remaining space controlled by the statewide actors. One hypothesis for explaining why these changes occurred so quickly could be the insufficient time available for the strengthening of the democratic institutions and actors at the state level in Spain, before the growth of European and regional pressures to obtain political space in this field. However, keeping this element in mind, we want to explore other aspects of the emergence of new regional industrial relations arenas in Spain, analysing the economic regional diversity and the existence of different identities. It is our aim to find out if these factors are also influential in the tendency of the trade unions to divergence.

Many comparative analysts of European industrial relations refer, to some extent, to the existence of similar aspects in the industrial relations of some European countries, aspects that are distributed homogeneously over great territorial areas of Europe and that can be observed as such. These observations suggest the possibility of thinking about something like different models or types of industrial relations in Europe. In his book 'Industrial Relations and European State Traditions' (1993), Colin Crouch presents many ideas tending in this direction, without offering a complete typology. Among many attempts of this type, we could also mention Hyman (1994), who refers to three western European models of industrial relations: the Nordic, the German and the Mediterranean. Other authors, such as Slomp (1992) and Wiarda (1982), have focused specifically on the analysis of the particulars of one specific area: Southern Europe.

Each of the models or typologies takes on a specific significance, depending on whether each author emphasises the institutional aspects (institutions of collective bargaining, informal rules or cultural attitudes) or the political and economic aspects (the union party relationship or the union's macroeconomic objectives). This chapter does not aim to develop a systematic analysis of the different attempts to establish conceptually systems or models of industrial relations in Europe. Rather it simply posits the existence of something like a set of common characteristics related to southern European industrial relations (in terms of structures, strategies and behavioural patterns), and to carry on in our work from this point of view. Summarising some discussions (Crouch, 1993; Slomp, 1990), it is possible to argue that the Spanish case presents most of the aspects that are typical of the Mediterranean or southern European model of industrial relations - in which we could include countries such France, Italy, Greece or Portugal. Thus, in brief, the central characteristics of industrial relations in Spain include the following specific points.

a) Historically, both workers' unions and employers' associations have had only weak organisational power, often being divided and badly coordinated. These organisations have usually been organised - and thus divided - along political lines, but frequently other forms of internal division have also appeared in the Spanish working class, such as cultural differences, nationalism and distributive conflicts. Also, due to the predominance of small and medium-sized firms in the Spanish economy, the presence of unions has traditionally been uneven and segmented throughout the different economic sectors (Jordana, 1994).

b) Both historically and at the present time, fully institutionalised and effective corporatism or neocorporatism has never really existed in Spain. Many times in the course of the 20th century, aided by different ideologies, there have been unsuccessful attempts to impose authoritarian corporatism (under the Franco dictatorship) or to introduce bargained corporatism (during the transition to democracy) as models of industrial relations between the actors of the Spanish industrial relations system (Martínez Alier and Roca, 1988). These attempts to develop corporatist arrangements, however, frequently degenerated into empty institutional structures, mainly because they lacked the mixture of political culture, formal rules and informal norms that in other countries guaranties continuously effective micro-adjustments among the actors of the industrial relations system.

c) As a consequence, we find few (and only weak) institutionalised patterns of behaviour associated with the relationships among social partners present in the arena of industrial relations, both at the national and the regional levels. Usually, labour institutions and formal collective agreements tend to be seen quite flexibly, sometimes becoming in fact just an instrument to aid the actors in renegotiating substantive issues. Often, agreements are not completely observed, excepting the issues in which there is a common knowledge that a strong coercion - by the state - certainly will be applied. The centrality of labour law and the predominance of statutory regulation of industrial relations probably is a by-product of this situation, as these are the only means to assure enforcement of the collective bargaining agreements in the Spanish case, and also to guarantee individual labour rights, in the absence of fully credible union commitments (Martínez Lucio, 1992).

d) It is possible to observe in the domain of Spanish industrial relations some aspects that traditionally have characterised the whole Spanish political system, such etatism and clientelist practices. Accordingly, what we see in the field of industrial relations is also the influence of a strong state tradition, in the sense of monitoring and regulating society (i.e. thinking that society is always unable to regulate itself). But paradoxically, on the other hand, there have always been attempts by individuals and organised interests to use the resources of the state for specific private purposes. Elitist networks of influence and mutual help inside the state apparatus - sometimes linked to interest groups - are quite common, and these configurations also exist within the networks of industrial relations (Subirats, 1992).

e) Despite their links with the elitist networks inside the state apparatus, interest groups in Spain - as formal bodies - do not play a very important political role. They are hardly considered to be subjects of public concern, and, in effect, policy conflicts are dominated by structures of political influence based on a system of elite connection and certain types of political patronage. These forms are often more permanent and influential in a given policy domain than the conventional type of formal organisations. In the public sphere of Spanish industrial relations, unions appear to be linked more to the political realm than the employers, but it is precisely because of the predominance of less visible mechanisms of representation of interests among the employers. Influenced by this difference in representation, there appear frequently problems in the integration of interests - especially within the employers' organisations - in the Spanish industrial relations system. Problems appear indistinctly across the territorial dimension, among sectors, and also hierarchically, between grassroots and top-level organisations. Often in the past, political co-ordination by parties or other authoritative bodies was the only possible means of establishing conclusive agreements.

Certainly these are not all the relevant aspects that characterise Spanish industrial relations (for a global analysis, see Fishman, 1990; Führer-Ries, 1991; Köhler, 1993). These five points are brought into the discussion only because of their relevance for the main objective of this paper: the analysis of union territorial divergences in Spain, a country with considerable regional differences. And what we have shown is that the formal organisational cohesion of unions across the territory is not very strong, and also that institutionalised rules in Spain for the purpose of articulating and mediating interests are not usually well adapted to the regional situation, thus leaving room for a considerable amount of uncertainty. Given these characteristics, we want to discuss the hypothesis that union confederations are realising regional politics from centre to periphery, in accordance with plans made during the years of transition to democracy (Alberts, 1993). To the contrary, in our opinion, since the 1980s the regions and their union regional affiliates - formally linked hierarchically to the centre - have been involved in arenas at the regional level, and frequently these have been just as important for them as the existing ones at the national level. In the following section we will present some recent trends within Spanish unions in the 1990s, followed by a discussion of the regional dimension of unionism in Spain.

Recent Tendencies of Spanish Trade Unions in the 1990s

First, it is important to remember the context and the legacies of the past decades. In comparison with many other European countries, for many years Spain experienced an economic underdevelopment linked to a prolonged authoritarian regime which continued until the 1970s (although during the 1960s the Spanish economy grew very rapidly). During the 1980s, after the process of transition to democracy (Franco died in 1975), Spain experienced a very dynamic process of economic growth linked to its integration into the European Union (1986). Parallel to the Europeanisation of the Spanish economy, the cultural habits and lifestyles of most of the population changed as well, and in most fields European standards progressively came to dominate Spanish society. At the present moment in Spain there are two main union confederations, CC.OO. (Comisiones Obreras) and UGT (Unión General de Trabajadores), with membership covering all sectors and territories, and also two quite small confederations, USO (Unión Sindical Obrera) and CGT (Confederación General del Trabajo), which are much less well extended. In addition, there are company or professional unions in some sectors, not linked to any confederation. Though relatively important in the public sector, in global terms these small unions represent or negotiate on behalf of less than 10 per cent of the total population of Spanish workers.

In this context, the political dimension of unions in Spain has been transformed during the 1990s. There has been a very notable reduction of the influence of leftist political parties in the union movement. The traditional relationship between UGT and PSOE (Partido Socialista Obrero Español, the socialist party), and CC.OO. and PCE (Partido Comunista de España, the communist party), which was maintained over a period of many decades, has broken up - a fact which implies the disappearance of a strong influence of the party over union strategies. In other words, the political parties have lost their capacity to act as authoritative co-ordination bodies for the unions. The break-up of the socialist family came first, in the years 1987-88 (Astudillo, 1996; Wozniak, 1993), and the split between the CC.OO. leaders and the party leaders of Izquierda Unida increased after 1993, a fact which implied the end of their relationship, as well. The political divisions between socialists and communists that dominated the union competitive arena during the 1970s, had lost most of its significance in the late 1980s after the end of the Cold War (Jordana, 1992). Since then, the two main union confederations in Spain, the UGT and the CC.OO., being free from political party dependencies, have tended to move into a close relationship, almost always acting together in their strategies vis-à-vis the government and employers. Moreover, union identity and union strategies have become more labour-centred and less hierarchical, though, in continuity with the preceding years, Spanish unions have also endeavoured to promote class-oriented inclusive policies, thus avoiding being organisations dedicated exclusively to the welfare of the union membership.

The evolution of union membership figures in Spain in the years after the transition to democracy has for some time been a very controversial question, the predominant view being that in general there had been a continuous decline since the early 1980s. However, new data clearly show the inaccuracy of the declining union thesis in the case of Spain. An analysis of available sources demonstrates a major increase in Spanish trade union membership beginning in the mid-1980s, and especially in the period 1988-93. Furthermore, the decline in union membership of 1979-80, which left Spanish unions with relatively low membership levels, has been placed in a new light: the maximum membership levels achieved in 1978 probably were not as high as was previously thought, and the recovery of union membership since 1985 has roughly doubled the figures at the low point in 1985. These data provide a basis for appreciating the ability of Spanish unions not only to mobilise workers but also to overcome some of the organisational difficulties which had produced the extremely low levels of membership (Jordana, 1996).

Since 1977, the social partners have from time to time attempted to provoke changes in the structure of collective bargaining (proposing a new relation between contents and territorial levels). However, the task of transforming the existing structures of collective bargaining proved to be extremely difficult, and only limited moves have succeeded in the course of the years. During the period up to 1986, the dynamics of collective bargaining was limited to national agreements between top-level organisations (at the state level), in which these organisations imposed the wage levels and other basic conditions on all their affiliate unions (Roca, 1987). But, on the other hand, its co-ordination was very chaotic, dominated in many cases by the legacies of the Francoist era, such as the predominance at the provincial level of sectorial bargaining (Aragón and Gutiérrez, 1996). Since those years, unions have always tried to centralise collective bargaining at upper levels with slow processes of reform, but in fact this aim has not been achieved, and in the 1990s the unions have failed to establish the main focus of bargaining at the national level, where they were relatively stronger in organisational terms. To overcome these difficulties, union confederations have tried to introduce more mechanisms of internal co-ordination within the industrial unions - including the ability of the national federations (statewide industrial unions) to control more union economic resources.

Table 4.1 Structure and levels of collective bargaining in Spain, 1988-94 (x 1,000 workers)

	1988 N	1988 %	1994 N	1994 %
Company agreements	1,070.4	15.59	1,022.7	13.63
Provincial level	478.8	6.97	462.1	6.16
Regional level	31.2	0.45	71.5	0.95
Interregional level	560.3	8.16	489.1	6.52
Agreements at any other level	5,794.3	84.41	6,479.4	86.37
Group of firms	12.1	0.18	30.2	0.40
Provincial level	4.3	0.06	11.8	0.16
Regional level	0.6	0.01	3.1	0.04
Interregional level	7.1	0.10	15.3	0.20
Local-county level	16.1	0.23	14.4	0.19
Provincial sector	3,761.4	54.79	4,105.9	54.73
Interprovincial sector	132.2	1.93	501.1	6.68
- Regional	110.5	1.61	306.9	4.09
- Interregional	21.7	0.32	194.1	2.59
National Sector	1,872.5	27.28	1,827.9	24.37
Total number of workers covered	6,864.7	100.00	7,502.1	100.00

Source: MTAS, *Anuario de Estadísticas Laborales*, 1989 and 1995.

In Spain, the 'formal' coverage of collective bargaining is relatively high, reaching a level similar to that of most European countries (Visser, 1996). From the end of the 1970s onward, the country very rapidly achieved coverage near 80 per cent of all wage earners, and since then this percentage has remained quite stable throughout the entire democratic period. Examining the territorial levels at which the agreements have been established, we see that the number of workers covered by national agreements (statewide) has also been stable - from the early 1980s through the mid-1990s. As we see for the year 1994 in table 4.1, about 26.7 per cent of all covered wage earners were covered in terms of collective bargaining by national or interregional sectorial agreements, and another 6.5 per cent by company agreements at the supraregional level. In the years 1995-96 the figures did not change very much (although we have only provisional data at our disposal), in spite of certain labour law reforms and the pressures to promote the establishment of some national agreements. In sum, wage and work conditions of nearly a third of covered workers (or a quarter of all wage earners) have been established at the statewide level, but for the rest of covered workers (two-thirds of the total), these conditions have been negotiated at the regional or lower levels.

Parallel to the development, extension and consolidation of sectorial collective bargaining, a second dimension of collective bargaining has taken on a place of its own in Spanish industrial relations. We are referring here to the company level, where in parallel to the sectorial level - and sometimes overlapping the sectorial agreements - there exists an intense process of bargaining on wage and work conditions, mostly in the larger firms. This dual approach to bargaining often implies that the sectorial collective bargaining is something like a ground level for wage and other conditions, and what is negotiated at the company level usually improves on the sectorial level agreements, when the unions are sufficiently strong. There are no complete statistics on company level bargaining, but this system is predominant among large and medium-sized firms from well-established sectors. To some extent, this implies a dualistic model of representation and negotiation, where the sectorial agreement represents a reference basis, especial for small and medium-sized firms. For the unions, the problem is their weak presence in many companies, which leads to great diversity in the agreements which in fact are reached: 'This could mean that the employers can dominate where the delegates or committees are weak - which is the case in the majority of situations - or they can confront the committees and the trade unions where the committees are strong' (Miguélez, 1995, 93).

As we mentioned before, from the mid-1980s to the mid-1990s, the labour market in Spain was highly dual, with a huge percentage of short-term contracts (nearly 35 per cent of the labour force), a core of workers who are well-protected by the labour laws and the unions and who have stable contracts, and a high percentage of unemployed (more than 20 per cent of the labour force). It is easy to think that most of the unionised workers in Spain still belong to the protected core group (Rebollo et al, 1993). In addition, the territorial and sectorial distribution of these labour market conditions are uneven, with great differences among regions. However, in 1997 a pact between CC.OO., UGT and CEOE (Confederación Española de Organizaciones Empresariales, the main employers association) made possible the introduction by the government of certain legal reforms that challenge this labour market configuration, favouring the use of stable contracts for stable jobs.

The worsened conditions of the labour market, the forms of collective bargaining (issue contents, formal coverage, etc.), the predominance of the regional and provincial bargaining levels, the role of the company bargaining level as the second milestone of a dualistic structure of collective bargaining - all these factors have conditioned the possible moves of the actors in the Spanish industrial relations domain. By way of summary, as in other countries, it is possible to observe that the patterns of labour market and collective bargaining influence heavily the form and the roles that union organisations have taken on. In this sense, we could remember that the unions that emerged after the transition attempted to become quite centralised and symmetrically organised, but their objectives were not actually realised. In fact, the affiliate regional organisations - the territorial level of unions - has developed an organisational diversity and also gained more and more internal political influence at the confederal level since the 1980s. Meanwhile, during the 1980s the industrial (sectorial) organisations operating at the national level - called federations - did not obtain an important role in the operations of the trade union confederations as a whole (CC.OO. or UGT). In the next decade, the 1990s, however, after several important mergers, the remaining sectorial organisations reinforced their strength within the union confederation, and in some cases they also promoted nationwide sectorial policies in dialogue with state agencies and employers.

Unions and Regions in Spain: Economic Differences and Cultural Diversity

We have seen in brief some characteristics of southern European industrial relations as reflected in the Spanish situation, and we have also pointed out some of the recent trends in the development of trade unions and industrial relations in Spain. Now we have the conceptual elements to begin the discussion about the challenge of the regions for the dominant encompassing unions in the Spain (UGT, CC.OO.). In this sense, we argue that the internal differences within the unions across territorial borders are very important, considering the differences between the Spanish regions. It is another question, however, as to whether these differences lead to regional confrontation or not. It will be necessary to identify and justify the most important dimensions for the comparison, related to the logics of identity and interests present in the Spanish unions. Afterwards, we will examine some paths of conflict and co-operation in the case of Spanish industrial relations, in which the territorial issue plays a central role.

Before beginning this discussion, we want to examine the institutional development of union participation in regional politics and administration in Spain. If new arenas of industrial relations are emerging at the regional level, they need to construct their institutional settings and to determine the significant issues that concern them. After the transition to democracy and ratification of the new democratic constitution (1978), Spain was newly divided into seventeen regions, and autonomous governments were progressively constituted in each of these regions, with varying levels of political autonomy. Among the new institutions constituted at the regional level, many regions have built up organisations devoted to the management of certain aspects of industrial relations relegated by the central government to the regions, such as ministerial labour departments. Also, in the years after their constitution, many regional governments defined and created new institutions for the improvement of relationships among the social partners, such as specific socio-economic councils to promote the dialogue between labour and capital (Lopez, 1993), or the establishment of voluntary courts to solve labour conflicts through the mediation of the public administration (García Roca, 1996).

Labour legislation in Spain is quite centralist, which protects the homogeneity of the Spanish labour market. However, during the 1980s a great deal of space has been developed for regional industrial relations. In the Basque country, where nationalist unions have been dominant, the actors have effectively imposed their own regional framework of industrial relations, legislating extensively on many matters. This has taken place in parallel with the extensive use of the mechanism of collective bargaining in the same sense, as well. Other regions with nationalists in government, such as Catalonia, have been more moderate in this sense. Nevertheless, activities and meetings between administration, unions and employers in order to bring about the possibility of promoting social dialogue and of enabling industrial pacts, occupational agreements, vocational programs, etc. have been very common during the last years in many Spanish regions, regardless of their nationalist aspirations. The existence of institutionalised frameworks to promote social dialogue has facilitated the formation of these pacts and to some extent has given an impulse to active labour market policies at the local and regional levels, with the participation of the unions (Harmes-Liedtke, 1996; Jordana, 1998). In addition, the disappearance of the mutual social consultation at the level of the central government since 1986, the growing capacity of regional administrations in Spain, and the maintenance of decentralised collective bargaining, have aided the opening of these new spaces for discussion and decision making in the field of regional labour politics (Lopez, 1993; Miguélez, 1995).

To consider the importance of the differences between the Spanish regions, there are certain well-known variables that introduce major divisions, such as the predominance of certain economic sectors in specific regions (linked to significant economic indicators, such as unemployment or public investments). However, there are also other known variables that we want to explore, such as the political nationalism present in certain parts of Spain. Among the variables used to discuss the internal differences within labour organisations at the regional level, we have the number of union organisations themselves (depending especially on the nationalist division) and the level of membership fragmentation, the differences in union density, and the coverage and structure of collective bargaining in each region.

During the last decades there has been a significant process of convergence among the Spanish regions in terms of GNP per capita. However, in more recent years this process has been decelerating, despite the existence of strong redistributive policies among the regions, and the heterogeneous composition of the economic sectors has not changed significantly since the early 1980s (Marimon, 1996, 197-8). The economic structure of Spain is quite polarised. Data from the *Encuesta de Coyuntura Laboral* (see appendix 4.1) shows us that significant concentrations of industrial workers exist only in Catalonia (around half a million), Madrid and Valencia (around a quarter million each city). Andalucia, the Basque Country, Galicia and Castilla-Leon also have sizeable communities of industrial workers (more than a hundred thousand each), though they are smaller. Activities are very diverse (the chemical, automotive and food industries are predominant, though not exclusive), and the firms are not very large in size. No more than roughly 25 per cent of wage earners are employed in firms with more than 250 workers (Asturias and Madrid are the only significant exemptions, with more than 35 per cent). Other regions do not have great concentrations of industrial workers, though there is the case of Asturias, a northern region of Spain with a strong cool industry, and Navarra, which are not very crowded but which have high concentrations of specific industrial activities. Services are dispersed in a more balanced form throughout the different Spanish regions, although some regions concentrate a huge proportion of wage earner workers in this sector. This is the case for Andalucia (65.4 per cent), Canarias (77.9 per cent), Baleares (74.4 per cent), Extremadura (62.3 per cent) and Madrid (65.9 per cent). Tourism activities are the key to explaining these percentages, except for Madrid (where white-collar jobs are dominant) and Extremadura (with no totally clear explanation). Analysis of public investment in Spain during the 1980s shows that it was greater (per capita) in the poorest regions of Spain: Extremadura, Castilla-La Mancha and Andalucia, and this produced the redistributive effect already mentioned. However, positive effects were also observed, in particular the creation of jobs in the sectors of construction, energy and public services, though not in private services and industry (Marimon, 1996, 248).

Table 4.2 Percentage of wage earners with temporary contracts and unemployed workers in relation to the active population, 1995 (in per cent)

	Temporary contracts	Unemployment rate
Andalucia	38.3	33.9
Aragon	27.6	15.9
Asturias	25.3	20.2
Baleares	32.4	14.3
Canarias	42.0	23.7
Cantabria	30.5	22.3
Castilla-La Mancha	39.5	20.2
Castilla-Leon	29.8	20.5
Cataluña	29.4	19.9
Comunidad Valenciana	34.9	22.4
Extremadura	43.1	30.6
Galicia	33.8	17.6
Madrid	27.2	20.9
Murcia	33.5	23.7
Navarra	29.8	12.9
Pais Vasco	23.3	23.0
La Rioja	30.6	16.1
Ceuta/Melilla		30.3
Spain	31.5	22.9

Sources: Temporary contracts: INE, *Encuesta de Coyuntura Laboral*, 1995.
Unemployment rate: INE, *Encuesta de Población activa*, 1995 (annual average).

In comparison to European figures, the unemployment rate is very high in Spain. There is much disagreement on the explanations for this fact and we are not going to discuss them here (Toharia and Jimeno, 1994). We only wish to show that, although unemployment is a big problem in all the regions of Spain, some regions are more intensely affected than others. This has an effect on union behaviour, especially in relation to the firms of the most predominant size and on the type of contract which is more often used (short-term versus long-term). As we see in table 4.2, two regions, Andalucia and Extremadura, have very high unemployment rates (more than 30 per cent, which combined constitute a quarter of the total Spanish unemployment figures). Others, such as Murcia, Basque Country, Cantabria, the two Canarias and Valencia, have rates of between 22 per cent and 30 per cent, which are quite significant rates in Spanish terms. Other regions, such as Baleares, Navarra and Galicia (and others), have unemployment rates which are lower than the Spanish average. And Madrid, Asturias and Catalonia are near this average, circa. 22 per cent in 1995 (Caravaca and Sánchez, 1995). If we examine the other side - the formation of new jobs - we see that Andalucia, Extremadura and Castilla-La Mancha are especially active only in creating jobs in public services and construction. Murcia and Baleares create intensely jobs in all sectors, and Basque Country, Asturias and Cantabria present a very negative situation in terms of job losses in industry and private services (Marimon, 1996, 232-3).

Respect to the huge proportion of wage earners with short-term contracts, another specific characteristic of the Spanish political economy, there exists also significant regional differences. On the basis of data from 1995, about 35 per cent of Spanish workers have temporal contracts and 65 per cent have long-term contracts. This proportion has remained more or less stable the last four or five years. The regions where the proportion of temporal contracts are higher are Andalucia (38.3 per cent), Canarias (42 per cent), Castilla-La Mancha (39.5 per cent) and Extremadura (43.1 per cent). However, with the exception of the Basque Country and Asturias, all the other regions have percentages ranging up to 25 per cent. The other variables that have a stronger influence on the predominance of temporary contracts are the type of economic activity (e.g. tourism, temporary services) and the pressure of unemployment rates (there is a clear relationship - as shown by the negative C.Correl. of -0.51 - between the proportion of stable contracts and the unemployment rate). It would be interesting to explore the question as to whether there is a possible relationship between these figures and the presence of trade unions and their strength in each region. In this sense, for the year 1993 we found an interesting positive C.Correl. of 0.54 between the percentage of stable contracts in a region and the percentage rate of union membership in the region, examining all seventeen regions of Spain. It is also possible to see an unclear negative relationship between the regional unemployment rate and the regional percentage rate of union membership (in the years 1990-93 there was no relation; then in 1994-95 the relationship appeared again, though it was not a very strong correlation (-0.15)).

From this economic analysis, we see that the intensity of economic and labour problems is very diverse, varying in many cases from region to region. Thus, the existence of different configurations could necessitate the configuration of regional union preferences not always coincident at the state level. This is usually a matter for the internal politics of unions at the level of statewide confederations - in the sense of building coalitions for the support of union strategies that could be acceptable for most regions and sectors; but the increasing differences - or divergent problems - complicate this task enormously. However, our question is whether economic regional differences are the only important reason for the tendency of unions to diverge, or are there other factors which lead to differences.

With respect to the unions and the nationalist political divisions, the first aspect that should be noted for our analysis is that there are some important nationalist confederations that cover all sectors in their respective regions: the CIG (Confederación Intersindical Galega) in Galicia, and ELA (Eusko Langillen Alkartasuna) and LAB (Langille Abertzale Batzordeak) in the Basque Country. These three nationalist confederations are quite closely linked to nationalist parties in their respective regions and have traditionally obtained support from them. This is also the case in Galicia, where the nationalist parties have always been in the opposition (Beramendi and Núñez, 1995). As in the Basque Country the nationalist unions have the majority of union delegates in many sectors, (and the collaboration of a considerable share of the employers, as well), they have been jointly developing many aspects of an autonomous system of industrial relations since the early 1980s that only shares the basic laws with the Spanish system (Casas Baamonde, 1985; Mees, 1998). For this and many other reasons, the Basque case is by far the clearest example of the union tendency toward divergence that we have noted from among the Spanish regions. But in no other region with nationalist movements is there a similar situation, either in Galicia or in Catalonia, for example. However, the question remains open as to why in Catalonia - with a nationalist party in the government - the Basque approach did not work, and also why there is not a strong nationalist union confederation, in spite of the efforts made (Jordana and Nagel, 1998).

One important institutional aspect is the fact that only the two main confederations, the UGT and the CC.OO., are present in all of the processes of collective bargaining at all levels, because they are the only organisations that obtain more than 10 per cent of the representatives in the worker councils at the firm level throughout the whole of Spain; (this is a law enacted to prevent the fragmentation of union bodies). What is remarkable, however, is that in the last worker councils elections, the three nationalist union confederations obtained a sufficient number of worker representatives, thus gaining the right to be present, according to the law, in all the processes of collective bargaining in which they were affected, including the state level (contributing more than 15 per cent of the representatives in their region). With this 15 per cent barrier, set up in 1980 by the Spanish parliament as an article of the basic labour law (the Estatuto de los Trabajadores), the former ruling party UCD (Unión del Centro Democrático) was trying to integrate moderate Basque nationalism into statewide structures (they had in mind the case of ELA, which in 1980 was the only important nationalist union), and, at the same time, to impede the emergence of new nationalist unions, from the Basque Country or from other regions. This mechanism was leaving other unions with figures below these barriers without any formal capability of representation. Nevertheless, radical nationalist movements in the Basque Country and Galicia grew in strength during the 1980s, and their new confederations surpassed the 15 per cent barrier in the early 1990s. By way of summary, in Spain there is now one region, the Basque Country, with four well established union confederations (all of them able to be active in all sectors and levels), one other region, Galicia, with three union confederations, and the other fifteen regions with only two well-established union confederations. Examining appendix 4.3, however, we do not see an increase in the fragmentation of Spanish unionism during the period 1985 to 1995. The percentage of unionised workers belonging to unions other than CC.OO. and UGT remains more or less equal, although there have been some regional shifts.

There is significant variance in union density from region to region. Due to the dynamics of union growth during the 1980s and 1990s, it is now possible to observe the existence in Spain of three different territorial types of union implantation, with significant differences among them. We have the Mediterranean regions (Catalonia, Valencia, Baleares), characterised by the dominance of small-sized firms and industrial districts, in which union density is very low (between 10 per cent and 15 per cent in 1990), and in which membership has increased moderately in the period from 1985 to the present. Secondly, we have the south of Spain - including a part of the centre, with the capital, Madrid - where union density is not very great (between 15 per cent and 20 per cent) but where membership rose significantly during the years 1989 to 1992. The importance of services in these regions and the relative absence of industry (despite the presence of many factories in Madrid itself) could help to explain this trend, (along with the growth of the public sector in Spain during the late 1980s).

Third, there are the northern regions of Spain, which have the highest density rates in Spain (more than 20 per cent), and which also increased their total membership by up to 100 per cent between 1985 and 1995. The predominance of medium-sized enterprises, the extension of services, and the presence of large firms and a traditional industrial nucleus (in the process of being reconverted) combine to explain this differential. Nevertheless, we have special cases within this third type. One is the Basque Country, where strong political mobilisation and nationalist competition introduce specific variables into the workers' movement. Another case is Asturias and Cantabria, where the general northern trend differs: these two regions have the highest union density rates (in accordance with their historical development), but they are experiencing a much lower increase in total membership. The dominance of industrial restructuring and a major loss of employment serve to explain this specific situation (Vega García, 1995).

By way of summary, with only a few exceptions (such as Asturias and Cantabria), since the mid-1980s we have observed growing divergence. Regions with higher union density are experiencing a greater increase in their membership growth, while regions with lower union density, are experiencing a much more moderate increase. This situation is undoubtedly also producing changes in the internal politics of the unions. For many years now, certain regions have been continuously losing their power quotas in the union confederations, while other regions have been gaining more and more influence thanks to their increasing number of delegates in the congresses and other union decision making bodies at the state level. The question remains as to the political consequences of these changes: whether or not they increase the internal union conflicts because of the possible non-acceptance, in some cases, of the new balance of power. One clear example is that of Madrid and Catalonia, which during the First Congress in 1978 provided 19.2 per cent and 27.1 per cent of the entire CC.OO. union membership, respectively, while in 1994 these figures had fallen to only 14.4 per cent for Madrid and 17.3 per cent for Catalonia.

Just as with the distribution of the different economic activities in Spain in general, the metal workers' unions of the CC.OO. and the UGT are extremely concentrated in certain regions. For UGT Metal (see the regional figures presented in in appendix 4.2), 62 per cent of the total union membership in 1995 was concentrated in just five regions (Catalonia, Basque Country, Valence, Madrid and Asturias). At the current time, the metal unions are still the most powerful unions in Spain (though their membership has been declining each year since 1992), and this means that there is also a concentration of regional power within the broad confederation. However, for many years now already, it is in the services that the unions have really been expanding. In contemporary Spain, three type of unions are quite powerful in the services sector: banking, transport and communications, and the public services (including public health, education and public administration). The first two are concentrated in the big cities (especially Madrid and Barcelona), though the public services unions are the largest and most widely distributed all over the country. In the case of the UGT, the FSP (Federación de Servicios Públicos) concentrates roughly 20 per cent of its total membership. This union is heavily present in three

Spanish regions, with more than 50 per cent of its membership in them (Andalucia, 22.4 per cent; Madrid, 13.7 per cent; Valencia, 14.3 per cent).

Since the early 1980s, stability has been the main characteristic of the territorial levels in the collective bargaining structure. The most important level of collective bargaining in Spain since the 1960s has surely been the 'province' level (an administrative division smaller than the regions). This is a legacy of Francoism, since the province was the traditional level of bargaining imposed by the official union OSE (Organización Sindical Española) when collective bargaining was re-established in Spain beginning in 1958. The importance of this level has continued up to the present. For example, in 1990, 57 per cent of all workers covered by collective bargaining were included in agreements at this level. The figure for 1994 was similar (55 per cent). The third level, in terms of the number of workers covered, is the company level. Nearly 14 per cent of workers covered by collective bargaining are related to this level, frequently being employed in large companies with long-standing traditions of union presence and bargaining within the firm.

Despite several union attempts to introduce the regional level of bargaining, with less than 4 per cent of covered workers, the regional level remains marginal when we consider its role at the territorial level in collective bargaining, and it is concentrated only in Catalonia and Valencia. The emergence of 'regions' as administrative and political bodies during the 1980s, after the transition to democracy in Spain, and also many years after the configuration of the levels of collective bargaining, could be (*a la* Clegg) a clear cause of the minor importance of this level for collective bargaining in Spain. In this sense, the regional public sector is probably one of the few places in which there are collective pacts at the regional level - in part because it corresponds to a new administration, established after the restoration of democracy.

Table 4.3 gives the percentage, region by region, of wage earners that are covered by processes of collective bargaining at the regional level or below, irrespective of whether this relates to sectorial or company-based agreements. At the bottom of the table are the figures showing the number of workers covered by supra-regional agreements, again irrespective of whether it relates to sectorial or company-based agreements. Comparing the figures of 1988 with those of 1994, we see that the percentages for the most part remain stable (with only small variations). However, in the cases in which there is a significant shift (i.e. of more than ten points, such as for Andalucia, Asturias, Canarias, Valencia, Extermadura and Galicia), this shift is always in the direction of increasing the percentage of workers covered by regional or infra-regional collective bargaining. Nevertheless, we should point out that there are certain statistical problems in this table, because we are not capable of distinguishing in each region between the workers who are covered by supra-regional collective bargaining and the workers who are not covered at all (because they are public servants or because there is no collective bargaining in a specific sector of a given province).

Table 4.3   Coverage of collective bargaining at the regional or infra-regional level, 1988-94 (x 1,000 workers)

	1988			1994		
	Covered workers	Wage earners	%	Covered workers	Wage earners	%
Andalucia	755.8	1,235.3	61.18	906.1	1,219.9	74.28
Aragon	169.4	266.3	63.61	172.5	279.1	61.81
Asturias	78.5	212.8	36.89	144.2	208.3	69.23
Baleares	131.6	173.4	75.89	141.5	176.4	80.22
Canarias	154.2	342.6	45.01	213.9	354.4	60.36
Cantabria	44.2	99	44.65	49.2	105.7	46.55
Castilla-La Mancha	196.1	317.7	61.72	187.4	318.5	58.84
Castilla-Leon	189.4	454.6	41.66	210.1	493.1	42.61
Cataluña	800.1	1515.5	52.79	850.9	1,603.4	53.07
Comunidad Valenciana	506.5	861.4	58.80	607.9	895.8	67.86
Extremadura	109.5	175.2	62.50	150.2	185.5	80.97
Galicia	196.8	509.6	38.62	248.5	507.2	48.99
Madrid	562.2	1,269.8	44.27	562.3	1,334.3	42.14
Murcia	115.4	224.0	51.52	123.3	224.3	54.97
Navarra	64.3	119.6	53.76	75.8	131.7	57.56
Pais Vasco	301.7	500.5	60.28	292.2	506.7	57.67
La Rioja	20.9	56.1	37.25	30.2	57.8	52.25
Ceuta/Melilla		18.1			24.1	
Interregional agreements	2,461.6			2,526.6		
Spain	6,858.2	8,351.5	82.12	7,492.8	8,626.2	86.86

Source: MTAS, *Anuario de Estadísticas Laborales*, 1995.

What it is possible to suggest, however, is that only Madrid and few other regions show percentages of infra-regional collective bargaining under 50 per cent. For the rest of regions, it is possible to affirm that they control - in terms of numbers of workers - the majority of processes of collective bargaining. This means that possibilities exist for strategic moves of the regional unions in this field, and, in the absence of strong internal coercion or changes in the bargaining structure, only co-ordinating policies between the centre and the peripheries could sustain nationwide union strategies. However, in the case where there is co-ordination among the various province and firm level processes of sectorial collective bargaining possible, which is the best co-ordinating 'locus'? Is it the region or the state? Is a clear answer to this question even possible?

Some Thoughts on Regional Differences, Union Cultures and the Dimensions of Spanish Industrial Relations

After this analysis of the main differences - economic, political and institutional - existing in the regional dimension in Spain, it is easy to conclude that there are some important divisions within the broader context of important socio-economic difficulties. Apart from the Basque Country and its system of autonomous industrial relations with nationalist unions, there are important differences between the Spanish unions at the regional level, and these differences have either grown or at least remained stable over the past ten years, as we have already seen. However, the most characteristic trend in Spain within the context of the European Union is not its internal regional differences, as significant as these may be (surely as significant as those in Italy or Germany), but rather the huge rate of unemployment and the enormous numbers of temporary contracts in the Spanish job market. The impact of these variables - which have remained quite constant over many years - on Spanish society is more important than the good news that some economic indicators seem to be announcing (e.g. that inflation is getting under control and the continuous increase in the GNP. One of the focal points of the new tensions provoked by the precarious conditions in the labour market could be an exacerbated competition between the regions.

In this sense, the key question to ask is whether in the Spanish case the capability of inter-regional co-ordination both within a given union confederation and between the different industrial unions, is sufficiently strong and flexible to resist the tensions growing out of the extremely precarious conditions in the labour market. Such conditions create many incentives for unions to compete with one another (e.g. in terms of wages, controls, etc.), and - leaving the issue of competition aside - they force them simply to struggle to survive as organisations in each region. Theoretically, these difficult economic conditions plus the previously analysed regional divergences could easily lead to a growing inequality (if this is the case), exacerbated competition (Scharpf, 1996), or political opportunism (linked to ethnic or cultural elements), between different Spanish regions challenging the nationwide encompassing policies carried on by the UGT and the CC.OO.

Specifically, the question is how the pressures for homogeneity versus the pressures for diversity affect internal labour market conditions in Spain. An important related question is whether or not in Spain the homogeneity necessarily has to be linked with the tendencies toward centralisation and symmetry (as it is in Germany). Alternatively, homogeneity - but not symmetry - could also be understood in the sense that all regional unions are practising 'encompassing' policies at the regional level, as well as establishing certain informal pacts between them that ensure the maintenance of fair play in order to avoid an exacerbated competence among the regions.

To fully answer this question we would need to observe two new dimensions: first, the formal and informal mechanisms of internal union co-ordination between regions (decision rules, forms of co-optation, veto powers, circulation of information, control of monetary funds, the role of focal points in non-hierarchical bargaining, the appointments, etc., including the exercise of self restraint, when necessary). This is necessary because of the importance of these mechanisms in the effort to avoid conflicts by viewing the tensions from a different perspective and/or by spreading out the problem-solving process over time. The second dimension relates to the substantive magnitude of differences between regions, the form and frequency of co-operative moments and the traditions of cultural differences as opposed to the objectives of cultural homogeneity. In other words, in the case of Spain there is a historically created divergence. We have a tradition of industrial relations imposed by the Spanish state which continues to survive alongside the emergent (and more competitive) traditions of bargaining within regional labour communities: traditions whose roots sometimes lie in popular identities and sometimes in nationalist ideologies - and that sometimes are quite new.

In the absence of more thoroughgoing research on the above-stated questions, we can only point out that, for the moment, the existence of territorial tensions in Spain does not necessarily lead to visible competition among the unions from the point of view of the other actors in the industrial relations arena. Regional diversity in Spain does not inevitably lead to union divergence, although this tendency does exist in Spanish unionism. However, regional diversity complicates union policies and internal union politics; it necessitates the implementation of several different forms of coordination, and it produces different levels of independence with respect to the confederation. In short, the regional branches of the major Spanish unions do indeed experience disputes and contradictions (the core issue being increased regional autonomy versus centralisation), but they discuss the differences internally and they develop a variety of coalitions. This struggle is sometimes clearly visible - usually during the trade union congresses. It is also linked to political-partisan divisions: the combining of new alliances of sectors and regions (which normally change by periods and confederations) is increasingly emerging. These alliances, however, do not display an organised and permanent front between different groups of regions (i.e. North-South, Atlantic-Mediterranean, Center-Periphery, etc.).

In sum, if we assume that there will always be a degree of conflict between the regional unions and the central confederation, then the danger of a major divergence within the unions in Spain based on territorial differences does not appear to be greater than the sectorial or professional differences that also affect union encompassing policies. Only nationalist ideologies or major institutional changes (i.e. the regionalisation of European industrial relations) could induce a substantially new framework in the Spanish industrial relations. However, to maintain the current situation stable, the homogeneity of trade unions in Spain has to be compatible with two issues: the existing regional diversity and also with the different paths of adjustment to the changing conditions of regional labour markets and economies.

References

Aguilar, S. (1985), 'El asociacionismo empresarial en la transción postfranquista', *Papers*, No. 24, p. 53-84.
Alberts, D. (Comp.) (1993), *La política regional de los sindicatos europeos. Un análisis comparativo*, MTSS, Madrid.
Aragón, J. and Gutiérrez, E. (1996), 'Salarios y negociación colectiva', *Cuadernos de Relaciones Laborales*, No. 9, p. 77-93.
Astudillo, J. (1996), 'The Transformation of Social Democracy: the Decomposition of Party Union Ties in Socialist Spain', Paper presented at the *10th International Conference of Europeanists*, Chicago.
Beramendi, J. and Núñez X. (1995), *O Nacionalismo Galego*, Promocións Culturais Galegas, Vigo.
Caravaca, I. and Sánchez, P. (1995), 'Cambios socioeconómicos, desempleo y desequilibrios territoriales en España', *Estudios Regionales*, No. 42, p. 15-52.
Casas Baamonde, M.E. (1985), 'Relaciones laborales y autonomías territoriales: nuevas perspectivas', *Relaciones Laborales*, No. 14, p. 1-8.
Crouch, C. (1993), *Industrial Relations and European State Traditions*, Clarendon Press, Oxford.

Fishman, R. (1990), *Working-Class Organization and the Return to Democracy in Spain*, Cornell University Press, Ithaca.
Fishman, R. (1992), 'Divergent Paths: Labor Politics in Barcelona and Madrid', in R. Gunther (ed), *Politics, Society and Democracy*, Westview Press, Boulder.
Führer-Ries, I. (1991), *Gewerkschaften in Spanien*, Nomos, Frankfurt a.M.
García Roca, J. (1996), 'Estado Social y marcos autonómicos para la solución extrajudiacial de conflictos laborales', *Revista Internacional de Ciencias Socialess*, No. 94, p. 7-46.
Harmes-Liedtke, U. (1996), 'El sindicalisme de les autonomies a Espanya', *Anuari sociolaboral de Catalunya 1995*, Publicacions de la Universitat de Barcelona, Barcelona.
Hyman, R. (1994), 'Industrial Relations in Western Europe: an Era of Ambiguity?', *British Journal of Industrial Relations*, Vol. 33, No. 1, p. 1-24.
Jordana, J. (1992), 'The shaping of a competitive trade union arena in Spain', Paper presented at the *Joint Sessions of ECPR*, Limerick.
Jordana, J. (1994), 'Sindicatos y política en España', *Revista Internacional de Sociologia*, No. 8-9, p. 137-86.
Jordana, J. (1996), 'Reconsidering union membership in Spain, 1977-94', *Industrial Relations Journal*, Vol. 27, No. 3, p. 211-24.
Jordana, J. (1998), 'Les Organizacions Sindicals a Catalunya', in S. Giner (ed), *La Societat Catalana*, Institut d'Estadística de Catalunya, Barcelona.
Jordana, J. and Nagel, K.-J. (1998), 'Trade Unionism in Catalonia: Have Unions Joined Nationalism?', in P. Pasture and J. Verberckmoes (eds), *Working-Class Internationalism and the Appeal of National Identity*, Berg, Oxford/New York.
Köhler, H.-D. (1993), *Spaniens Gewerkschaftbewegung*, Westfälishes Dampfboot, Munster.
Lopez, J. (1993), *Marcos autonómicos de relaciones laborales y de protección social*, Marcial Pons, Madrid.
Marimon, R. (1996), *La economía española: una visión diferente*, Bosch, Barcelona.
Martínez Alier, J. and Roca, J. (1988), 'Spain after Franco. From Corporatist Ideology to Corporatist Reality', *International Journal of Political Economy*, Vol. 17, No. 4, p. 56-97.
Martínez Lucio, M. (1992), 'Spain: Constructing Institutions and Actors in a Context of Change', in A. Ferner and R. Hyman (eds), *Industrial Relations in the New Europe*, Basil Blackwell, Oxford.
Mees, L. (1998), 'Social Solidarity and National Identity in the Basque Country: the Case of the Nationalist Trade Union ELA/STV', in P. Pasture and J. Verberckmoes (eds), *Working-Class Internationalism and the Appeal of National Identity. Historical Dilemmas and Current Debates on Western Europe*, Berg, Oxford/New York.
Miguélez, F. (1995), 'Modernisation of Trade Unions in Spain', *Transfer*, Vol. 1, No. 1, p. 80-97.
Rebollo, O, Marín, A. and Miguélez, F. (1993), *El sindicalismo a través de sus protagonistas*, CONC-CERES, Barcelona.
Roca, J. (1987), 'Neocorporatism in Post-Franco Spain', in I. Scholten (ed), *Political Stability and Neocorporatism*, Sage, London.
Scharpf, F. (1996), *Economic Integration, Democracy and the Welfare State*, Max-Plank-Institut fur Gesselschaftforschung, Working Paper 96/2.
Slomp, H. (1990), *Labour Relations in Europe. A History of Issues and Developments*, Greenwood, Westport.
Slomp, H. (1992), 'Trade Unions and Politics: the Mediterranean Model', Nijmegen, Political Science Reports 18.
Subirats, J. (1992), *Un problema de Estilo. La formación de políticas públicas en España*, Centro de Estudios Constitucionales, Madrid.

Toharia, L. and Jimeno, J.F. (1994), 'Los hechos básicos del paro', in O. Blanchart and J.F. Jimeno (eds), *El Paro en España*, CEPR, Madrid.
Vega García, Rubén (1995), *Comisiones Obreras de Asturias en la transición y la democracia*, Unión regional de CC.OO. de Asturias, Oviedo.
Visser, J. (1996), 'Traditions and transitions in industrial relations: a European view', in J. van Ruysseveldt and J. Visser (eds), *Industrial Relations in Europe*, Sage, London.
Wiarda, H. (1982), 'From corporatism to neosyndicalism: the State, organized labor, and the changing industrial relations systems of Southern Europe', *Comparative Social Research*, No. 5, p. 3-57.
Wozniak, L. (1993), 'The Dissolution of Party-Union Relations in Spain', *International Journal of Political Economy*, Vol. 22, No. 4, p. 73-90.

Appendix 4.1: Wage Earners: Regions, Sectors and Company Size, 1995 (x 1,000 Workers)

Region	Sectors				Company size		
	Industry	Construction	Services	Total	6-50	51-250	Above 250
Andalucia	159.3	79.1	451.5	689.9	346.3	162.9	180.7
Aragon	80.7	15.9	89.6	186.2	93.4	42.3	50.5
Asturias	59.5	17.3	66.8	143.6	60.8	31.4	51.5
Baleares	23.1	13.7	106.7	143.5	75.3	37.8	30.4
Canarias	29.1	26.7	196.8	252.6	124.3	70.5	57.7
Cantabria	27.1	8.4	35.4	70.9	34.6	15.9	20.3
Castilla-La Mancha	66.4	25.8	101.6	193.8	114.0	50.3	29.6
Castilla-Leon	113.4	26.8	161.9	302.1	153.1	71.4	77.7
Cataluña	492.0	92.8	694.3	1,279.1	618.0	316.6	344.5
Comunidad Valenciana	244.9	54.4	292.5	591.8	332.0	149.3	110.3
Extremadura	13.9	15.0	47.8	76.7	46.4	19.3	10.9
Galicia	107.0	40.8	162.8	310.6	160.2	74.1	76.3
Madrid	280.8	98.4	735.2	1,114.4	422.0	264.6	427.8
Murcia	47.7	10.7	85.0	143.4	72.3	34.3	36.8
Navarra	52.4	8.7	47.7	108.8	46.1	30.1	32.6
Pais Vasco	159.0	31.3	184.6	374.9	165.2	106.8	103.0
La Rioja	21.2	3.2	17.1	41.5	24.6	10.8	6.2
Ceuta/Melilla							
Spain	1,977.5	569.0	3,477.3	6,023.8	2,888.6	1,488.4	1,646.8

Source: INE, Encuesta de Coyuntura Laboral, 1995.

Appendix 4.2: Metal and Public Services Membership in the UGT by Regions, 1995 (x 1,000 Workers)

Region	Membership UGT Metalworkers Union			Membership UGT Public Services Union		
	Members	Regional %	Union %	Members	Regional %	Union %
Andalucia	7.13	7.00	7.08	29.94	29.41	22.94
Aragon	5.31	18.28	5.27	5.50	18.93	4.21
Asturias	9.62	23.19	9.55	4.96	11.96	3.80
Baleares	0.58	4.33	0.58	2.40	17.91	1.84
Canarias	1.10	6.29	1.09	3.85	22.01	2.95
Cantabria	3.19	23.97	3.17	2.09	15.70	1.60
Castilla-La Mancha	1.55	5.84	1.54	4.93	18.58	3.78
Castilla-Leon	6.15	11.89	6.11	9.42	18.21	7.22
Cataluña	17.94	25.14	17.81	9.83	13.78	7.53
Comunidad Valenciana	10.57	14.02	10.49	19.13	25.38	14.66
Extremadura	0.82	3.76	0.81	4.37	20.03	3.35
Galicia	5.70	15.44	5.66	5.48	14.84	4.20
Madrid	10.03	15.30	9.96	18.31	27.93	14.03
Murcia	1.43	9.20	1.42	4.42	28.44	3.39
Navarra	4.87	36.98	4.84	1.06	8.05	0.81
Pais Vasco	13.50	36.98	13.40	3.64	9.97	2.79
La Rioja	1.23	14.25	1.22	1.17	13.56	0.90
Ceuta/Melilla	0.04	1.30	0.04	2.45	79.80	1.88
Spain	100.72	15.67	100.00	130.50	20.30	100.00

Note: Non-adjusted date. Unemployed, retired and self-employed members included.

Source: UGT-Sec. organización, *Datos de afiliación y elecciones sindicales*, 1997.

116 *Cultural Diversity in Trade Unions*

Appendix 4.3: Estimated Total Membership and Union Density by Regions, 1985-90-95 (x 1,000 Members)

Region	1985 Total union members	1985 Non-UGT/CC.OO. members (%)	1985 Net density rate (employed only) (%)	1990 Total union members	1990 Non-UGT/CC.OO. members (%)	1990 Net density (employed only) (%)	1995 Total union members	1995 Non-UGT/CC.OO. members (%)	1995 Net density (employed only) (%)
Andalucia	128.5	11.05	12.28	211.1	12.46	16.04	289.8	14.87	22.65
Aragon	27.6	27.17	12.04	54.1	24.40	18.51	73.9	20.84	26.28
Asturias	81.8	5.87	38.19	101.3	9.38	43.03	96.7	7.14	43.82
Baleares	22.9	17.03	15.65	38.8	18.04	20.69	44.9	29.62	22.15
Canarias	32.2	33.85	11.68	57.0	34.39	15.86	72.1	35.37	19.22
Cantabria	21.9	33.33	21.99	33.0	22.12	29.23	35.1	20.51	32.14
Castilla-La Mancha	47.9	15.03	17.34	63.0	14.76	18.10	87.8	14.01	27.56
Castilla-Leon	48.2	31.74	11.59	100.8	28.08	19.73	131.6	21.50	26.56
Catalunya	166.5	24.20	12.80	217.7	17.04	13.10	266.9	18.58	16.34
Ceuta/Melilla	1.4			4.4			8.8	7.95	34.78
Euskadi	123.6	49.84	25.61	187.6	60.71	33.69	185.4	50.43	36.42
Extremadura	15.7	19.75	11.03	27.0	27.41	13.66	46.3	13.61	25.04
Galicia	59.3	38.79	12.81	104.9	46.71	18.98	127.6	41.54	24.40
Madrid	138.1	21.72	12.36	217.3	18.32	15.29	247.3	22.08	17.70
Murcia	25.2	23.41	13.05	36.7	27.52	15.29	46.6	21.46	19.77

Region	1985				1990				1995			
	Total union members	Non-UGT/CC.OO. members (%)	Net density rate (employed only) (%)	Total union members	Non-UGT/CC.OO. members (%)	Net density (employed only) (%)		Total union members	Non-UGT/CC.OO. members (%)	Net density (employed only) (%)		
Navarra	11.4	*	10.17	30.8	*	23.04		33.9	*	25.47		
Rioja	8.4	44.05	17.32	14.6	34.93	23.86		20.1	25.87	33.50		
Valencia	142.9	12.74	19.17	192.5	15.79	20.01		225.6	16.05	23.52		
Spain	1,103.2	23.69	15.09	1,697.0	25.44	18.30		2,040.4	23.50	22.82		

* The CC.OO. members are included in Euskadi.
Note: For the methodological aspects of this estimation, see the discussion in Jordana (1996).

Source: Data provided directly by the CC.OO. and UGT confederations.

5 Industrial Relations and Trade Unions in Economic and Social Transformation in East Germany

VOLKMAR KREIßIG

The System of Industrial Relations in the Federal Republic of Germany under Pressure to Reform and Adapt

In essence, the (West) German system of industrial relations consists, at institutional level, of two principal components.

a) Collaboration between sectoral trade unions and employers' associations at national level. This is expressed in the conclusion of time limited collective wage agreements that are binding on both sides. When in force, collective wage agreements contractually regulate wages, holidays and various other working conditions and both sides are obliged to abide by the agreement. Collective bargaining and wage negotiations take place after the expiry of agreements and before their renewal. The achievement of union demands after the expiry of an agreement (during which there is an obligation to avoid conflict) can be effected by various forms of pressure, down to sectoral or regional strikes. However, strikes can only be used as a last resort for achieving union demands. 'Wildcat' and 'political' strikes, as well as the threat or use of force, are inadmissible. The employers have corresponding weapons at their disposal during wage disputes, such as lockouts (i.e. the temporary exclusion of a large number of employees from work).

b) The institution of company codetermination by elected works councils, whose members are released exclusively for this role in companies above a certain size. Works councils enjoy protection from dismissal. They can conclude company agreements concerning working hours regulations, technological changes, protection against rationalisation and other personal and social issues with the company heads (the management or the company owners). Company codetermination is also observed by union representatives on the supervisory boards of limited liability companies and other large concerns which have similar control facilities. This form of codetermination extends to the joint occupation of supervisory boards by employers' and employees' representatives in companies in the coal and steel industry - what is known as coal and steel codetermination. This is connected with the establishment of the function of director of industrial relations in companies with this kind of codetermination, whose appointment is partially influenced by the unions.

Where the employer is not a member of relevant associations which conduct wage negotiations by means of general wage level agreements, employers and works councils can also conclude internal company wage agreements. This also applies to the conclusion of wage agreements which exceed the wage and other standards of the general wage levels.

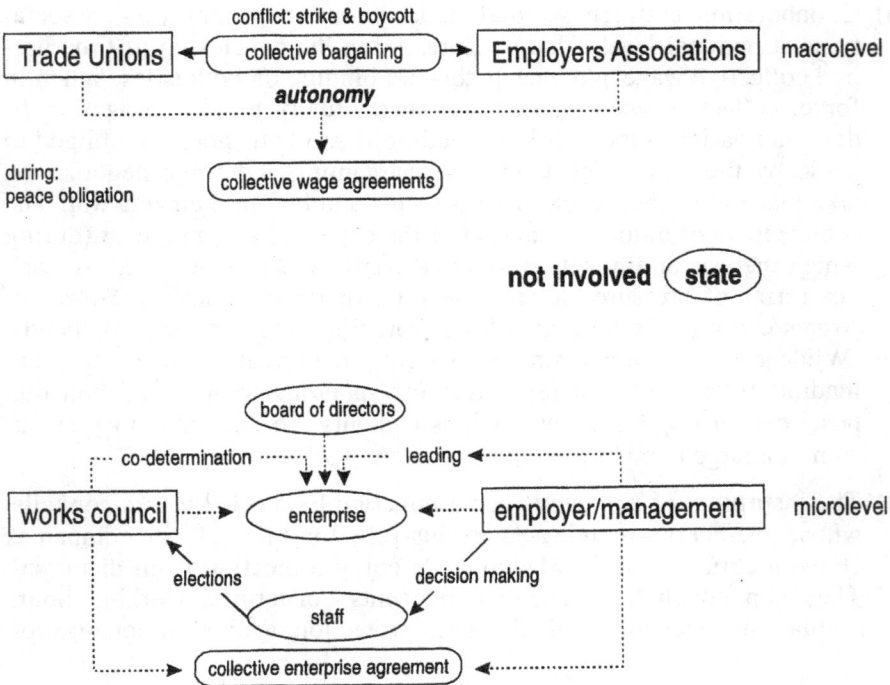

Figure 5.1 The German system of industrial relations

The (West) German system of industrial relations, as a result of employment law and wage legislation as well as the Industrial Constitution Law, is thus an extensively controlled, standardised and regulated system of relations between the various actors (employers, employees, executives, works councils) at shop-floor and at company level, as well as at sectoral and national levels (unions and employers' associations). It covers the identification and resolution of conflicts, and contains among other things, rules for relations, negotiation mechanisms and conflict resolution models between employers, managers and employees. This system is to a large extent based on consensus within the company and within society and thereby contributes to the stability of businesses as well as the avoidance of broad-based, socio-political conflicts. For this reason, it is not a system with three equal players, in which the state plays a regulatory role. Wages are negotiated between the parties directly affected - the unions and the employers' associations - independently of the state. A state of mutual independence exists between the contractual partners. There is no state-established legal minimum wage, only minimum entitlements to state-guaranteed employers' contributions as well as entitlements to unemployment insurance in the event of job loss; this is organised at state level and managed by the corresponding administrative bodies.

Among other things, industrial relations govern the pattern of working hours and the distribution of the profits. Sometimes efficiency models and job protection measures are also agreed contractually. Likewise, rules and mechanisms also exist for the settlement of wage disputes at different levels. Industrial relations thus include all regional, sectoral and national regulations, which provide the framework for these relations as an internal company relationship.

The German system of industrial relations was conceived in the wake of the Second World War. It is based on the historical experiences of the Weimar Republic. Another contributory factor was also the fact that in the former Federal Republic, during a time of economic prosperity and high levels of employment, a relatively high standard of living was achieved for employees and that, until now, only a few long-term comprehensive disputes concerning wages and other issues between employers and employees. This creates a decisive, advantageous location factor for the German economy.

The system of industrial relations in the Federal Republic works together with the state welfare institutions and the institutions of the labour market as well as this market's regulatory mechanisms and institutions. A functioning state welfare system as well as a current and essentially efficient labour market with its regulatory mechanisms are thus both the result of politically effective action by the actors in industrial relations, as well as being a condition for the functioning of industrial relations on different levels.

The social security systems which exists in the Federal Republic are centred around equal financing by employers and employees. Equally, they include codetermination mechanisms and are thus closely interrelated to the system of industrial relations. The following figure shows how they interact.

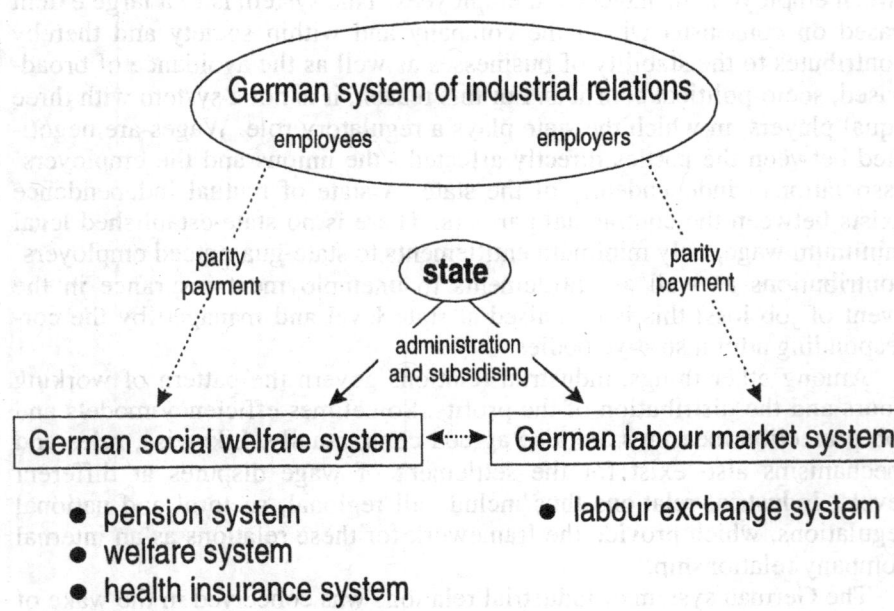

Figure 5.2 Interaction of industrial relations, the welfare system and the labour market

This institutional system of industrial relations, which thus regulates and standardises relations between employers and employees to a significant extent, was already under pressure to reform and adapt in the Federal Republic at the time of German unification. Debates about reform had begun which, however, have yet to achieve any binding results. Among other subjects, academic discussions have been held about the pros and cons of a possible transformation into a matter for individual companies (Müller-Jentsch, 1995), or Japanisation (Altmann, 1992) of the German system of industrial relations.

The economic and social situation in the Federal Republic had substantially changed during the 1970s and 1980s. Certain crisis-linked phenomena produced a situation whereby the proceeds of strong economic growth and profits could no longer be relatively simply distributed between employers and employees, as they had been in the past. At the same time, the conditions for applying the system of industrial relations which had hitherto existed were called into question. Also, a basic underlying level of mass unemployment had arisen which could no longer be eradicated. The funding of unemployment, sickness and pension insurance became increasingly problematic. It is currently causing particularly serious problems. Politicians and employers are attempting to reduce the role of the latter in the joint funding of contributions, which is apparently damaging for the Federal Republic's economic position. Disputes about the distribution of wealth no longer took place exclusively between employers and employees: new kinds of conflict arose concerning the apportionment of society's wealth between the socially needy and the sick on the one hand and the healthy and fit on the other hand, between those with and those without work, between the young and the old and, after German unification, between the East and the West in particular.

Relations between the German system of industrial relations, the welfare system and the labour market system had shifted. Welfare state facilities, the system of income support and of sickness and pension insurance came under financial pressure as a result of decreasing contributions and the refusal of employers to continue to pay on an equal footing. Municipal finances were overstretched as a result of increasing expenditure on welfare benefits and simultaneously falling tax receipts. The labour market and employment services became overburdened as a result of the mass unemployment which was beginning to look like a permanent phenomenon. Their regulatory mechanisms were increasingly incapable of handling the constantly high base level of unemployment, let alone reducing it. As a result, by the 1980s, the system of industrial relations of the old Federal Republic had itself fallen prey to other burdens and its stability was being put to the test. In particular, questions were and continue to be asked about whether it is in a position to guarantee social harmony at company level and throughout the area of working life, to identify, resolve and regulate conflicts in good time.

The Starting Position in East Germany and the Transfer of the West German Institutional System

When the former German Democratic Republic joined the Federal Republic on a constitutional basis, membership of the European Community followed automatically. The economic and monetary union between East and West Germany, which had been completed three months previously, was constitutionally enshrined.

As a result of this unification, the efficiency of the East German national economy which was taken over had often been subject to contradictory estimates. Widely varying opinions existed and still do exist concerning its actual efficiency. In 1978, the German Institute for Economic Research (Deutsche Institut für Wirtschaftsforschung) concluded that national product was growing at the same rate in East and West Germany and that East Germany was only lagging behind by one fifth. In 1987, the same Institute determined that productivity in East Germany was 50 per cent behind that of West Germany. In 1990, the productivity level in the East was only 20 to 30 per cent of that in the West (*Freie Presse*, 4 May 1997).

At the same time as German unification, the West German institutional system was constitutionally transferred into the East German economic and social setting. In this way, the objective of the Federal Government, as well as of the majority of East Germans, was pursued, i.e. to adapt East German conditions to those of West Germany and to resolve the profound structural and adaptation crisis of the East German economy and society. The West's social security systems, such as the unemployment insurance system, as well as the highly legalistic (West German) system of industrial relations, were also transferred to the East. Trade unions in East Germany were taken over and restructured by West German sister organisations and employers' associations were reconstructed with West German help, following the West German model. The system of industrial and welfare tribunals was also set up according to the West German model. At company level, legal rules governing industrial relations were introduced and works councils took over leadership of the former state socialist company trade unions.

At the same time, during the emerging system transformation, a completely different kind of East German cultural context, with more than 40 years of distinct socialisation patterns for employees and managers, as well as with a different understanding of the role of the trade unions, was coming up against and having to deal with a new political, economic and social situation (Kreißig, 1992). This new situation had to be intellectually embraced and handled by the various parties involved in industrial relations (employers, unionists, works councils, East German employers' representatives, new business owners and managers) who had grown up in the former state socialist system. Old patterns of behaviour could no longer be successfully applied by the various parties. The enforced political conformity and subjugation in the state socialism of the former GDR had gone, along with almost total job security. New freedoms were now being paid for with increasing social insecurity of employees and managers, of the former opposition as well as the former holders of political power and of union officials. The East Germans (as well as the West Germans) were deeply uncertain about how to assess the new situation and how to handle it from now on, at the levels of business management, the national economy, politics and society. Employees had now to put aside the critical remarks which they had often previously made very openly about defective work organisation in companies, or they would to face warnings or even disciplinary action. Rapidly rising unemployment became a tough disciplinary measure for the occasionally very critical workforces in companies. Former 'socialist leaders', such as foremen and other executives, now either became new managers equipped with considerable disciplinary resources, or new business owners, having taken over companies through management buy-outs or with Western capitalists as their partners. At the same time, despite changes in ownership, the socialisation pattern that had existed in the GDR in many cases continued to operate.

Many former GDR citizens - employees, executives and union representatives - originally seized upon renewed political conformity as the best means of controlling the changing system. At first, they did not imagine that they would have to deal with the ways and functions of a completely new system and develop appropriate and completely different patterns of behaviour. Old forces of conformity, which essentially have little in common with the present ones, were replaced with new ones. On the other hand, even today there are constraints. A tactful silence must be maintained in certain places in companies, while the expression of political opinions which were previously suppressed is now permitted in public.

The particularly high expectations of internal company participation and democracy in the production process were not fulfilled. Codetermination exists only in a limited sphere of application. Moreover, it is delegated by individual employees to the works council.

Originally, the overwhelming majority of East German employees did not believe that mass unemployment could befall them. This is revealed by a company survey carried out by the author in 1990 in an industrial company in Chemnitz, as well as by observations made during the mass demonstrations and political discussions of 1989/90. 'Anyone who really wants a job in the West gets one', was the central theme of visitors from the former Federal Republic who, in many cases, had previously left East Germany.

The coming mass dequalification and payment of wages below the agreed rate were matters which were scarcely discussed. The concept of rationalisation was in general positively received in East German companies. To many employees, this concept meant a welcome change to a style of work which was leisurely and often characterised by involuntary stoppages due to shortages of materials. This idea was not yet associated with unemployment. The majority of East German employees did not believe that, with foreign capital investment, at least some of their salary would be paid in convertible currency i.e. in West German Marks (DM). Company closures in the course of privatisation seemed to be ruled out. With the introduction of new western managers in East German companies, employees and executives generally hoped for the introduction of new, more promising production concepts and more modern and attractive products.

However, privatisation and company take-overs by western companies were to bring repeated staff cutbacks. Furthermore, company closures by the Trustee Institution responsible for privatisation led to completely unexpected mass unemployment, averaging 15-25 per cent. Employees were overtaken by social insecurity, something previously unheard of. In the opinions of many, this cannot be compensated for by the civil liberties which had been gained.

In the short transition period during which the old regime collapsed or imploded peacefully and almost without resistance, the sense of freedom and sheer joy in going out into the streets in peace and, for the first time, being able to articulate the most diverse political and social demands, was unbounded for the activists of radical political change and German unification. Subsequently, most East German actors in working life felt a great deal of insecurity about how they could now deal with the new demands of capitalist production and work.

To some extent, during this transition period, independent works councils had spontaneously been formed as counterparts to the former company trade unions which had been loyal to state and party. This was partly with their support and under their control, since critical forces had often been represented in the company trade union leadership. They had for the most part been established in order politically to oppose the leaders who were still active and had formerly received state support. In many cases, the latter were regarded by some of the workforce as no longer morally tolerable or as incompetent. The new independent works councils severely criticised the old leaders, but were for the most part unable to offer any economic alternatives, at internal company and national levels, which could be used to reconquer the markets in the East and in East Germany itself (which had collapsed after monetary union), and to open up new markets in the West.

Economic Transformation in East Germany

After economic and monetary union, described as 'economically insane... primarily inspired by vote-winning motives' and not by 'responsible unification policy' (Vilmar and Dümcke, 1996), sales by the East German economy fell rapidly. Existing over-capacities expanded and new ones arose. Traditional exports to the East stagnated and fell dramatically. The former East German internal markets were increasingly lost to large Western suppliers. These possessed more marketing experience, to some extent better products and more capital and power, with the result that they were able to engage in destructive competition with their East German competitors. West German over-capacities, for example in the automotive industry, could be reduced by East German purchasing power, which had grown considerably after monetary union. The savings of East Germans, now held in Deutschmarks, were initially invested by many in a new or used car as a symbol of general German prosperity. For example, between 1990 and 1994, about 3.4 million new private cars were registered in East Germany. Among the big names, Volkswagen, Opel and Ford-Europa developed into market leaders in East Germany. As a result of this, German producers did not experience the general recession in this sector until some two or three years later.

In the East, in contrast to the economic situation created in the West German by unification, production capacity was increasingly closed down in most sectors (Kreißig, 1996a; 1996b).

The result of this 'restructuring' of the East German economy in the interests of improved opportunities for profit for the dominant economy in the old federal states is that 'a de-industrialised GDR whose state controlled sales outlets were taken over by West German individuals and stocked almost exclusively with Western goods could be transformed into one big "market" which contributed to special conditions in the West German economy lasting many years' (Vilmar and Dümcke, 1996, 39-40).

Employment levels in the East German clothing and textiles industry fell from approximately 320,000 employees in 1989 to approximately 23,000 in 1996 (*Freie Presse*, 27 December 1996). Likewise, in the chemicals industry, employment fell between 1989 and 1996 to about 10 per cent, in other words from about 300,000 to about 30,000 employees. The East German automotive and supply industries, which were substantially modernised using western investment, employed only approximately 28,000 by 1996, compared to 300,000-350,000 previously in this sector (Kreißig, 1996a).

Originally, East German employees and West German managers and economists usually held the inadequate state socialist leadership responsible for this, or simply the state socialist planned economy system. Against this planned economy model, the economically more effective and socially more secure West German state, economic and social systems were put forward as supposedly the best and only alternatives. The East Germans were of course conditioned by their lack of knowledge (and had turned away from the Marxist analysis of the capitalist system, which in this case was to an extent justified), and therefore did not see the need for reform which already existed in the area of industrial relations and in the trade union organisation process (cf. Martens, 1989) and which was further exacerbated by the political, economic and social problems of unification. Both before and after the collapse of the Wall, East Germans who had emigrated from the East to the West, during their visits back to the East, reported for the most part only about their successes and their good impressions of the social security system in the West, rather than about its problems. Special credits which East German settlers in the former Federal Republic received by way of launching aid, confirmed still further their impression of the unlimited possibilities of the market economy and of the West German welfare state. More realistic portrayals of the situation in the West, depicting the many problems, were virtually non-existent or, as the case may be, they were consciously ignored in the East or only believed by a few East Germans.

The Start of the Transfer of the West German System of Industrial Relations to the East. Legitimacy of Capitalist Institutions or an Attempt to Help Fashion Social, Economic and Political Change?

With German unification, many other people besides trade unionists and business owners ready to make investments came from the West to the East. Former landowners could assert claims for the return of their property. A total of 13,200 businesses had to be privatised by sale or by return to former owners. In return for this, most East Germans hoped to receive help, especially from entrepreneurial know-how and capital and particularly from West Germany.

West German 'advisers and aid workers' of all different shapes and sizes turned up in the East after the opening of the border and unification of the two states, having absorbed the wisdom of market economic processes with their mother's milk. On several occasions, such 'aid workers' were shown up as charlatans and unscrupulous profiteers with no sense of social responsibility.

For state socialist managers, whose businesses had been subject to privatisation or liquidation by the Trustee Institution, West German business consultants offered legitimacy for their new market economy-oriented actions, including matters concerning employees. The business consultant from the West said so, therefore the company had to be restructured in this and in no other way, so many employees had to be dismissed and certain lines of production had to be stopped and new ones started up. Western business consultants, who were often later exposed as 'spies' for interested Western competitors and who returned to their cosy homeland after carrying through these actions, satisfied with all the details about the businesses which they had gleaned, slowly took over the function of legitimisation of the former state-appointed leaders from the former party secretary. Similar functions were occupied by various employees of the 'Trustee Institution' privatisation agency, which represented the interests of East German businesses' main competitors and broke up efficient East German businesses. Of course there was no need to ruin already ailing businesses. Since the Trustee Institution very quickly redefined its role from its original one as protector of state and national property from speculation and abuse into that of privatisation agency which, within five years, had to privatise the aforementioned 13,200 businesses as quickly as possible, the East German de-industrialisation process was preprogrammed. Just some of the causes of East German industrial and economic decline include the almost complete initial lack of control of the privatisation process; the dearth of sanctions for non-compliance with business concepts and for further reduction of secure jobs which should have been kept, as well as other forms of corruption and scandal during the sale of healthy and viable businesses. Dümcke and Vilmar estimate that in the medium and long term, some 70 per cent of former GDR businesses could have been restored to profitability if a more reasonable policy had been implemented, rather than the 'overhasty introduction of the DM' and the 'strategy of exclusive privatisation of all former so-called nationally owned businesses by the Trustee Institution' (Dümcke and Vilmar, 1996, 15). The former head of the Trustee Institution and the politicians responsible at the time still continue to deny that the structural organisation of this process of privatisation was misconceived, rather than just a few formal aspects. Monetary union immediately made East German products approximately 300 per cent more expensive and led to the conquering of East German markets and their customers by West German businesses who, in 1991, were able to increase their turnover by over 50 per cent more than predicted growth (Dümcke and Vilmar, 1996, 15).

For works councils and employee representatives, experienced union members from the West served as counsellors and helped legitimise the process. With their help, it seemed that rapid wage increases up to Western levels were possible and, as a result of union action, the creation of more jobs. West German trade union officials who, it must be said, liked to flex their muscles and who reported their successes more often than their failures, also conveyed the impression that strong Western unions could achieve virtually anything. The need for reform, weaknesses in bargaining and structural defects were often not mentioned in these East-West encounters or not understood as such by the East Germans. Works councils from West German showpiece companies also frequently painted a picture of wonderful and complete codetermination, a picture which, for example, overlooked the fact that many businesses do not belong to associations and have no works councils at all and that many company wage contracts in the West operate at a level clearly below that of the general wage agreement. As a result of a partial political power vacuum in East German companies during the transition period, the idea also arose that it was now possible to set up a virtually unlimited production democracy whose guarantors would be the West German works councils and trade unions. The former state socialist leaders were also looking for new legitimacy and possibilities for support for their power position. They thought they could see this guaranteed in the industrial peace obligation in the Industrial Constitution Law, to which they referred in discussions with employees. In various cases, however, they also took pains to ensure good collaboration with the works councils.

The East German economy, which now found itself in a difficult position, was given an additional adaptation shock with economic and monetary union, when it switched to West German currency and was very soon cut off from its traditional East European external markets. Likewise, the East German internal market, which had been protected by a non-convertible domestic currency and was run on highly regulated planned economy lines, was directly exposed to the shock of major competition, especially from West Germany. Representatives of large firms had an informal head start in market economy operations. They were very quickly able to obtain positions of economic and political power in the newly formed institutional structures of the new federal states. Thus, their lobbyists were not only represented in the Trustee Institution which was responsible for privatisation: in the regional governments and municipalities, lobbyists from the major West German and European firms showed up just as quickly, helping them obtain public and private commissions in the building sector, which was generously supported by state funds and financing from the European Community, from the infrastructural investment plans and other means of support planned by the East German economy. For example, the subsidised redevelopment of the East German shipyards and of the chemical industry, as well as new investment in the East German car industry, brought numerous good orders. Additional investment and numerous tax breaks also gave

West German firms a significant incentive to buy up East German companies as subsidiaries and to invest in them - of course the purpose was also to maintain East German jobs. The take-over of East German rival companies and the desire to be better informed about East German and East European markets were also reasons for the privatisation of companies which was ultimately the biggest factor in the creation in the new federal states of a dependency economy reliant on the West (Grabher, 1996, 30 ff.). However, the lack of modernisation in the East German planned economy was not made up for by this process. Rather, it was simply used by the political and economic authorities of the united Federal Republic as a cut-price ideological self-justification in order to argue that the East German economy had been rotten, after the catastrophic collapse of a large part of this economy (Vilmar and Dümcke, 1996, 40).

Small and medium-sized East German companies, which came into being either through management buy-outs or through reprivatisation and were not directly taken over by large Western companies, found it very difficult to maintain their old internal market position against the Western businesses, equipped as they were with informal and power advantages, slowly to rebuild traditional relations with the East which had been cut off and which represented an East German strength, or indeed to gain a position in the strongly contested European market (Hennersdorf, 1996, 60 ff.; Wenzel, 1996, 88 ff.). Furthermore, a whole series of East German businesses were of course hopelessly out of date and were manufacturing under untenable ecological conditions. Occasionally, the closure of such companies was thus unavoidable and reorganisation on economic grounds was out of the question in such cases. However, the technologically well-equipped businesses also had to struggle hard against strong competitors from the West. The latter particularly turned power and information advantages to their benefit. Mismanaged privatisations through which damaged businesses had the added effect of destroying jobs in East Germany. After the spectacular collapse of the Vulkan shipyard in Bremen, in which some 750 million DM of subsidies, provided to modernise and secure jobs in the East German shipyards, was transferred to a West German business which was going bankrupt, the European Commissioner for competition intervened. He used this as an opportunity to examine subsidy policy in the East from the point of view of competitive equality with other structurally weak European regions.

The particularly weak capital resources of East German companies, as well as the lack of experience in crisis management, further weakened their position ('Schubkraft im Aufschwung Ost läßt deutlich nach' [Thrust of Recovery in the East Tails Off], *Freie Presse*, 21 January 1997). The capital problem was primarily conditioned by old debts which, in the case of management buy-out solutions, were normally not resolved by a release from indebtedness. Business owners and trade unions in East Germany, surprisingly enough, agree completely on this point ('Nur 20 Prozent der Metallbetriebe im Verband' [only 20 per cent of metal companies in associations], *Freie Presse*, 16 January 1997).

The Transfer of the West German System of Industrial Relations as the Start of a Solution (or the Substitute for a Solution?) for the Political and Social Problems of Mismanaged Privatisation?

Along with the institutional system of the former Federal Republic, the system of industrial relations was also transferred to East Germany, along with the complex system of special institutions for regulating the economy and the labour market.

It must be said that this transfer in many respects took place in a formal fashion which paid too little attention to the transition process in East Germany.

As we have already established, at the time of German unification, this institutional system was already under considerable pressure to reform and adapt. Reform debates had been set in motion, but conclusive results are still lacking to date. The central point of these discussions concerned the possible transfer into a matter for individual companies (Müller-Jentsch, 1995) or Japanisation (Altmann, 1992) of the German system of industrial relations together with the corresponding pros and cons of doing so.

Reform of this system, made all the more urgent by falling membership of unions and employers' associations, as well as by new challenges in general, was discussed in the West during the 1980s, but not initiated to the extent that was necessary. Thus, in 1990, a West German system which itself was under pressure to adapt, was transferred to the East for want of a system better suited to the case of the transition of an economy from a centralised state planned model to a capitalist market one. Lengthy reform dates in Germany as a whole had scarcely been possible as a result of increasing economic collapse and political instability in the East. The opportunity for such a debate was also passed up because it was not desired by the ruling political class. Political pressure from the East German masses for unity was growing constantly. This would not have been appeased by lengthy national debates about reform and discussion about the modalities of the transfer of institutions, or through long-term preparations for unification.

The question was subsequently raised of how the West German institutional system could manage to cope with the massive structural and adaptational crisis of its transfer to the East. For the purposes of this presentation, we wish to consider the East as a region which bears the hallmarks of an alternative cultural context which lasted some forty years, that of state socialist development, which was strongly influenced by the Russian model of state socialism. The structural crisis which had already developed under state socialist conditions was heightened and triggered by the shock therapy of economic and monetary union. The progenitors of this therapy, advocates of a neoliberal fundamental viewpoint, were of the opinion that this aggravation of the crisis would soon lead to rapid economic recovery. This economic recovery was supposed to be quickly achieved by the privatisation of the economy and by the transfer of funding from the West, leading to an improvement in the East German infrastructure and an increase in investment. Facilities for financial transfers were made available by the federal German central state within the framework of the collective initiative for the recovery of the East, as well as by the European Commission. Financial transfers already amounted 139 billion DM in 1991 and had risen, by 1994, to 174 billion DM. In 1991, 21.4 billion DM was transferred to finance the labour market policy alone. This sum had already grown by 1994 to 35 billion DM (Kreißig, 1996b). These sums of money, contributed by German tax payers, did prevent millions of unemployed people as well as institutions and municipalities from sinking into total poverty and were used to improve the infrastructure. On top of these, transfers came from the European Union. However, they did not lead to investments suitable for an economically sustainable recovery (Vilmar and Dümcke, 1996, 42). The new federal states were included in Target Zone 1 of the European Community - a zone which can count on special aid measures - together with the particularly economically problematic regions of Portugal, Spain, Ireland, Greece, etc.

The question now being asked about the West German institutional system, including the industrial relations system, was whether it could help cushion the economic decline and create the impetus for reform on different levels, or whether it could contribute to sparking off a general German institutional crisis process which would have an effect on European development as a whole.

Today it is clear from the facts that the transfer of this institutional system could not compensate for the destruction of economic structures through 'economic colonialism' and the burdening of the East German economy with fictitious debts as a result of the conversion method of monetary union, as well as through the original property reservation policy which established the return of former property in return for compensation in the Unification Treaty (Vilmar and Dümcke, 1996, 42). As a result, investments were particularly risky for a long time, due to unresolved questions of ownership and negotiations were long and drawn out since they could only be achieved by reference to the 'Investment Priority Law' which gives investors priority over people simply claiming back their own property or that of their ancestors. Financial manipulations, property speculation and criminal activities were helped still further, as has already been mentioned, by a lack of controls, lack of expertise and corrupt officials both in the Trustee Institution and in the newly evolving administrative bodies and institutions.

Until the point where the pan-German economic and institutional system was transferred, an institutional vacuum existed, which all too often gave more room for manoeuvre to corrupt profiteers than to those few honest reconstruction workers who really wanted to achieve something new. Once the institutions had been transferred, their room for manoeuvre was also hampered by the traditional bureaucratic and tedious operational procedures of German administration, which tends to put the brakes on rapid reconstruction work. The (West) German institutional system, particularly that of the labour market and the welfare state, is today under considerable pressure in both the East and the West. This pressure will supposedly be met from now on by reforms to the tax and welfare system and the system of labour relations, mainly by reducing current regulations. The privatisation of enterprises which have so far remained public, services and welfare state functions is regarded as one of the cornerstones of the reforms. It is therefore envisaged that a policy which, from the liberalist viewpoint, has already failed in the East German economy, will be continued. It is a policy which also led to de-industrialisation, so that only some 4-7 per cent of German industrial production originates in the East, while approximately 20 per cent of the German population live there. The erroneous privatisation policy of the Trustee Institution often led, as has already been mentioned, to the rapid selling-off of East German businesses and hence to a situation where West German businesses could get rid of troublesome competition through cheap purchases, or to a situation where speculators could strip healthy firms of their finances and bring them to ruin. This is in contrast to the Institution's legal task of rehabilitating East German businesses and then privatising them.

Today, therefore, when such a form of privatisation of public businesses is once again favoured because it will supposedly lead to greater efficiency, but where its consequences can certainly not be estimated neither from a national economic nor from a social point of view, real doubts must be raised regarding the success of the future course of reform.

It remains uncertain whether, through privatisation and the outsourcing of previously public functions, a more effective system of public services is ultimately produced, one which permits greater economic power to be unleashed in the triad and can thus again produce social welfare on the basis of increasing economic dynamism, while guaranteeing environmental standards. The answer to this question will depend in particular on the form and on the conditions of future privatisations. The author doubts, however, whether a continuation of the existing privatisation policy, which has destroyed 4 million out of a former total of 10 million jobs in East Germany and has led to mass dequalification, will usher in greater efficiency and at the same time higher quality in the formerly public services, rather than leading to further mass job losses and renewed problems on the labour market. French and British experiences of business privatisation reveal a very diversified picture, which must be thoroughly scrutinised in the specific case of any public enterprise, both with respect to the techniques used and in terms of the professed aims and the conditions (21).

Demonstrations by miners in Bonn and construction workers in Berlin in March 1997 point to the increasing frequency of conflicts, rather than to economically effective welfare state developments creating a political consensus, which are linked to the current reforms of the institutional framework of the Federal Republic in the field of economic and social policy.

It is to be concluded that the transfer of an institutional system which is itself in need of reform can scarcely make up for a flawed economic and privatisation policy. Until the alleviation of certain social hardships, it has scarcely had any further creative possibilities, or has as yet failed to produce any.

On the Transfer of the System of Industrial Relations and on the Development of Trade Unions after Unification

The former system of industrial relations was also considerably damaged after its transfer to East Germany.

Naturally, the level of trade union organisation in West Germany, which had gradually been falling, was at first reversed after the amalgamation of trade unions through the recruitment of East German trade unionists (the East had previously had approximately 9-10 million members - in other words over 90 per cent of the 10 million East German employees were members of a trade union). All the single-industry trade unions were considerably strengthened in terms of membership.

Originally, the precise form of the transfer or accession of the East German unions was undecided. Trade union organisations in the East were not only characterised by a different approach to trade unionism and organisation (the trade union as the vehicle for welfare state institutions such as social security and as organiser of social policy for companies), but

East German trade unions still had an outdated mechanism which was linked to a system which had been rejected by the majority of employees. The transfer of this mechanism posed a considerable problem of political legitimacy and, as a result, most unionist organisations decided to dissociate themselves from the East German mechanism and move to a new organisational structure.

On the fringes of the classical West German sphere of organisation, the industry-based union, which was formally characterised by individual industry and sectoral unions, in the same way as the West German system, displayed organisational and classification differences with the West German sectoral unions. Transfer or accession brought competition for members. This competition affected, among others, not only the ÖTV union in the public sector and the German civil service union which did not belong to the DGB (German Trade Union Federation), but also industrial trade unions such as those in the chemicals, metal and textile sectors, etc.

At the same time, the East German trade union uniform organisation was linked in a centralised fashion to its leadership in Berlin, which dissolved itself by resolution as the trade union umbrella organisation. At this point, no regional or Länder organisations existed, as in the West. New organisational structures had to be created as a result of the changing political, administration and regional structure - five new Länder had been created and East and West Berlin had been united - and the structural transformation of the economy. The main problem was the fact that in the 'new' Federal Republic, with its rapidly growing infrastructure and population, two distinct wage zones existed in the medium term. The unions, for the most part, clamoured for the rapid equalisation of wage levels so as to avoid further exacerbation of the fault lines in the labour market and competition for jobs within Germany as a result of heavy migration pressure from the East.

There were also considerable problems with the new trade union structures in the East. New officials who were not politically compromised were lacking, as were effective organisational structures, precisely at a time when mass employee cutbacks were already underway and employees' needs for protection from their trade union organisation were growing strongly. The West German unions had enormous problems with reorganisation. New organisational structures were to be created with East German members and a body of officials who had been to a greater or lesser extent politically compromised by the previous system had to be reformed or newly recruited. This took place partly from the ranks of the former democratic opposition, partly through the West-East transfer of young trade union members, partly through the fresh recruitment of officials from that part of the political system which was sympathetic to the unions and partly through taking on less compromised East German officials from the lower and middle organisational levels. New officials would also soon be employed and taken on from the ranks of the newly elected works councils.

As a result of the start of mass employee cutbacks, employees now had a particular need for protection precisely at a time when the reconstruction of unions in the East was still underway. Even the works councils originally had no experience in dealing with the Industrial Constitution Law, with regulations concerning protection against wrongful dismissal or with the drawing up of welfare plans for inevitable mass redundancies.

East German officials very quickly had to learn how to deal with the conditions of the capitalist system, which were new to them. East and West German union members had to learn how to communicate with one another, given that they came from different backgrounds and had different experiences.

A particular role was played in this phase by the unions' industrial legal protection scheme, which was granted to members free of charge. Where redundancies are threatened, this documents the protective function of the union and is keenly observed. It was built up very quickly and was strong in the area of personnel.

The body of officials embarked upon a very steep learning curve, a curve which was also connected with the considerable loss of members as a result of mass redundancies. For example, even the regional associations of IG Metall in Saxony and Brandenburg, which could scarcely be said to have been newly founded and were strong in terms of membership, had to amalgamate with the Saxony-Brandenburg association in order to counter the reduction in number of members it faced as an organisation.

New, independent unions were created under the influence of and with the personal, political and, subsequently, financial support of the West. They also arose under the condition that East German employees originally had no experience of the West German capitalist system. Furthermore, these new unions developed in an unusual political and economic situation of the transformation of economic structures. This placed all sorts of demands on them and posed a considerable challenge to their flexibility and openness to reform.

As we have already pointed out, the belief was widely held in the West, for example, that the transition could pass off without loss of jobs, or with only temporary and short-term unemployment, even for that minority of employees who were overwhelmingly seen as workshy.

Unions were regarded by employees as important guarantees that unemployment would be avoided. They were also regarded by many employees as important institutions which could guarantee rapid prosperity. Their legitimacy grew out of these expectations. It was precisely for this that the trade unions in the West had acted for forty years with successes and failures, with victories and defeats, but they had never yet had to act under such conditions of deep crisis as those of East Germany or in the face of such widespread company closures. The problems of organisational reconstructing were added to this.

As a consequence of this structural crisis and of the mismanaged privatisations, from a statistical point of view every citizen in the East of Germany had to change job at least twice between 1989 and 1995 in order to have one job for which he was usually over-qualified. The transfer of trade union organisation spheres from industry into the service sectors was generally connected with this fact. Sectoral transfer, however, often causes a decline in members for the unions. The service sector is also generally less well-organised than the industrial sector because it includes more small businesses with greater organisational problems than major industry. Unemployment further decimated the number of trade union members.

The unemployment rate in East Germany, as has been mentioned, stood at between 15 and 25 per cent, a figure which does not include people over 55 taking early retirement or employees in job creation schemes and re-training. In 1996, in Chemnitz, a city with about 280,000 inhabitants, approximately 2-3 per cent of the inhabitants applied to receive social welfare.

The scale of the social restructuring process in the labour market connected with this huge structural transformation is shown by the following figures: in the federal state of Saxony in the southern part of East Germany, previously a mostly industrialised area with the highest union organisation in the industrial field, each of the 3,016 million employees was unemployed at least once or twice in five years, or had been long-term unemployed, or had fallen into a welfare benefit situation, through unemployment benefit. Seven out of ten people changed their job at least once or twice (22). Connected with this was a dramatic restructuring of employment from the industrial sector into the service sector. The only industrial sector which showed growth in employment was the building industry, which was especially supported by the state in the areas of housing, road construction and modernisation of the infrastructure. This sector, which had accounted for 6 per cent of employees and was somewhat underdeveloped in the GDR, increased to approximately 12-15 per cent and became top-heavy; growth in employment depends directly upon continued state support. In this instance, a economic slump and a decline in employment levels during 1996-97, which was also seasonally determined by the winter, was soon also noted. The abolition of bad weather pay is likewise having a notable effect on the strongly seasonal employment pattern in this sector. Over and above wage negotiations, many employees were particularly aware of the effects of the unions in free legal representation, which was often first encountered in protection against wrongful dismissal actions. The negotiation by works councils of severance pay in the case of mass redundancies, whereby the councils produced welfare plans and developed particular professional expertise in this matter, was an important but not in fact an especially typical task for the unions. Originally, unions such as IG Metall, for example, were even able to achieve successes such as a time-restricted six month protection against wrongful dismissal, with zero employment at an additional agreed payment rate - although this was something which to some extent had a negative effect on the mobility of the labour market and reduced the opportunities for finding a new job. In the automotive supply sector, around the new Volkswagen works in Mosel bei Zwickau where the famous 'Trabbis' had previously been produced, a whole series of new jobs was created. While metalworkers persisted in the dead end of short-time working, instead of applying for jobs in the new supply companies, many women from the textiles industry who had been made redundant earlier found work in assembly line jobs which were better paid than their previous jobs and which also suited them better from an organisational point of view.

At the same time, with the restructuring process through privatisation, many smaller companies were set up, often as branches of larger Western enterprises. For the most part, however, these were seen as less organisation-friendly. The East had few large companies like the main factories in the automotive sector or in the metal and chemical industries. Amongst these, Volkswagen in Saxony, with about 2,500 employees, counts as one of the largest.

Following privatisation, frequently only a small proportion of employees was taken on under the same conditions when the transition occurred, retaining their rights as long-standing employees, in accordance with section 613a of the Civil Law Code. Other employees in established companies lost their rights as long-standing employees, for example, higher levels of redundancy payment and greater job security. They were also generally incorporated into lower wage scales. The Trustee Division Law was especially created for this purpose, in that it permitted the dividing up of subsectors during privatisation and the transition to new wage scales. The unions were unable to prevent this.

Thus for example, at the former car factory in Chemnitz, which was privatised by Volkswagen after several intermediate stages, only 400 employees at most out of a previous total of 4,000 were taken on with all rights. A further 1,600 who were employed in hived off businesses and who even worked partly under the conditions of a divided factory, in other words, who were working for foreign companies with different wage rates and work contracts within the same business, had to conclude new employment contracts and accept different, usually poorer conditions. The aforementioned Trustee Division Law, which permitted the individual privatisation of different sections of a business, created the legal basis for this. For example, the employees of Volkswagen Saxony, which functions as an autonomous business formally independent of the company, do not get the Volkswagen company wage rate, which is one of the highest in Germany. Here, in 1995, 84 per cent of the Bavarian Umbrella Agreement wage was being paid, which is itself is clearly lower than the Volkswagen rate. Although the highest productivity and quality levels in the whole of the VW group are achieved here, the employees of Volkswagen Saxony clearly work longer hours and for less money than those in the main works, where redundancies were avoided by reducing working hours. Despite this, the employees in this factory are content. Compared with other local people, they receive a good wage.

The supply companies in the vicinity Volkswagen Saxony, which for example often depend directly on its work rhythm because they use the just in time supply methods, are often paid using a different scale despite the fact that, increasingly, entire modules and structural elements are assembled there. These are activities which, conventionally, used to be carried out within the final assembly process in the factory but which are now contracted out to other firms. As a result, the production work undertaken in the parent company has fallen to only about 25 per cent of overall manufacturing and wage costs have been further reduced. Approximately 0.46 million employees (approximately 15 per cent) in Saxony were involved in a job creation scheme at least once between 1990 and 1995 and 0.765 million, or one in four employees, were in further training paid for by the job centre at least once, in other words, they were virtually unemployed during this period (Lubk, 1995). As a rule, labour was therefore transferred from East to West and from more highly-qualified industrial jobs to less industrialised service sector work, with lower or completely different qualification requirements.

The unions, such as IG Metall for example, originally worked to organise their members into so-called ABSs (Arbeits-, Beschäftigungs- und Strukturentwicklungsgesellschaften - work, employment and structural development societies) and, here too, they tried to implement appropriate wage conditions. With the introduction of section 249h of the Labour Promotion Law, under which unemployed people can be put to work especially in measures to clean up the environment, a particularly high number of women became employed in physically heavy work outdoors, simply in order to obtain temporary work for another year. However, as finances grew scarcer, increasing cutbacks had to be made in wage payments in the

ABSs also, and in this respect the year 1997 has been a year of particular cuts in this kind of employment.

For these reasons, the fall in membership in East Germany was particularly pronounced. Thus, the number of members in the DGB unions fell in 1996 by 11.6 per cent, down to about 2.09 million (*Freie Presse*, 30 January 1997). The number of employees in Germany organised into DGB member unions fell between 1991 and 1996 from about 11.8 million to 9 million; here, the decline through de-industrialisation in East Germany is the most obvious cause. In 1996 alone, membership levels fell still further as a result of redundancies by 3.8 per cent, or 349,000 (*Freie Presse*, 30 January 1997). Nonetheless, considering that East Germany accounts for only about 16 million of the approximately 84 million inhabitants of Germany, in other words only some 19 per cent of the population, 2.09 out of 9 million represents 23 per cent of overall trade union members. In other words, despite extensive unemployment and the structural collapse that has taken place, the degree of organisation here is higher, while the proportions of pensioners and unemployed people are greater than in the Western federal states.

With the amalgamation of unions (in the form of collective affiliation or the individual affiliation of members, as well as through the transfer of officials from West to East), the additional problem arose that the spheres of organisation were not identical. This meant that on the margins of the ÖTV (Öffentliche Dienst, Transport und Verkehr - public services and transport union), IGBE (Industriegewerkschaft Bergbau und Energie - mining and power workers' union), and of IG Metall and IG Chemie, among other single-industry unions, membership overlapped and competition existed for members. The DAG, which did not belong to the DGB, and the ÖTV posed particular problems. Occasionally, a friendly exchange of organisational fields took place, but there was also stiff competition.

Expectations were also high on the part of the employees who were organised into unions, as has been mentioned, concerning the trade union system, which they regarded as guaranteeing rapid adaptation of East German working and living conditions to levels in the West. Hopes were also high for the system of works councils. This was supposed to replace the company trade union leadership, which had been thoroughly discredited through its collaboration with and subordination to the company SED party leaders and it was regarded as an internal company guarantee for efficiency, better working conditions and greater democracy, for instance. There was no recognition that the unions could not keep uncompetitive jobs open during the structural transformations and that for the most part they possessed only the traditional means of wage policy.

The self-presentation of unions as political organisations tended to be rejected in the East. This was connected with a general disenchantment with politics and was also the result of particular East German reluctance to engage in politics after an excessively political atmosphere which had persisted for over forty years. Unions are regarded in the East rather as professional organisations which are responsible for protection against wrongful dismissal and for employees' wage problems. For example, East German unions often rejected political training in the history of the German labour movement, because every employee in the East had had to learn about it over many years in further education programmes.

To redetermine the role of the trade unions in the structural transformation is therefore also an existential question for the unions as member organisations, not only in East Germany. Incidentally, it is known that membership numbers have always declined during structural crises throughout the history of the unions. It is nothing unusual. It has contributed to the particularly rapid process of making normal working conditions in the East more flexible. This is especially true for the public services and for the individualisation and decline in solidarity as a result of teleworking, etc. This fact raises further organisational problems. Since, particularly in the East, the transfer of jobs to other East European countries, for example in the textiles and clothing industries, is progressing particularly rapidly, it is immediately obvious that rising nationalism, even in trade union circles, is increasingly becoming a problem.

The Europeanisation of social problems as a result of the principle of labour mobility is an additional factor and can foster primitive regionalism.

A Glance at Further Problems of Trade Union Organisation in the East

Since the process of structural transformation in the East was accompanied by the Industrial Constitution Law, this guaranteed a certain degree of internal company security. Social plans and the creation of rescue companies served as important areas for the practice of codetermination. Rescue companies provided limited training for people who had lost their jobs or equipped them for a successful return to their original labour market, or often, in fact, 'maintained' them. Unfortunately, the problem of privatisation was largely kept out of codetermination schemes. At best, influence could have been exercised over the question of membership of union delegates on the supervisory boards, but the union members represented on these boards often came from the West and therefore had virtually no corporate knowledge. The East German representatives, on the other hand, had no experience of the work of the supervisory boards. They were therefore scarcely able to assert rights to codetermination and information where privatisation took place. In addition, privatisation was not handled within the companies, but was decided externally. The Trustee Institution did not implement codetermination and participation rules. The only body on which the unions had seats and votes was the chemical industry steering committee, which was consulted and was to reach a decision about the reorganisation and privatisation of chemical companies.

The Trustee Law retrospectively envisaged codetermination only in the case of management buy-out privatisation, where works councils could rule out a privatisation conducted by former socialist leaders. However, works councils had no decision-making powers and did not even have to be informed about sales to ailing companies such as the Bremen Vulkan shipyard or the Munich Hurth Gruppe. As a result, relatively healthy East German companies suffered because the support granted by the European Commission for their reorganisation and stabilisation flowed into economically ailing West German parent companies. In the case of the Vulkan shipyard, as has been mentioned, some 750 million DM intended for the reorganisation of East German shipyards was transferred to the West in order to make the parent company temporarily solvent. The ultimately inevitable bankruptcy of the parent company destroyed further jobs in East Germany and weakened union organisation, without the trade unions or works councils being able to exert any influence on this damaging privatisation policy. Of course, the exertion of influence of this kind always raises a question of specialist competence and the resolution of such a problem would have placed excessive demands on union organisations as a result of the demand for far-reaching economic codetermination. In many respects, the works councils held out exaggerated hopes for privatisation by large companies, from whom they were expecting to gain capital, know-how and competence. The purpose of such privatisation, however, was often to wipe out East German competition, or simply to gain information about rival companies in order then to go on to buy them at an advantageous price. Internal and Eastern market share was of especial interest to privatisers, as well as distribution channels to the East, which the corresponding East German companies possessed. The primary purpose of privatisation was not to maintain jobs or to create new ones. In fact, property speculation played a role here which should not be underestimated. The Trustee Institution was often unable and unwilling to prevent this. Works councils were also scarcely able to recognise, evaluate or prevent such wheeling and dealing in the privatisation process and, besides, they had no legal standing in this area.

On condition that unions in the East adopt the West German system in parallel, that they go along with and shape the structural transformations, build up new organisations, replace discredited officials and apply Western unionist experience to the structural transformation, they did succeed in what experts in the field had expected of them and, indeed, to some extent they surpassed those expectations. If in the end they did not prevent mass redundancies and confined themselves to traditional lines of action, this was not surprising. In addition, at the same time they had to cope with their internal organisational problems between the umbrella association and the single-industry unions, as well as the merging and restructuring of single-industry unions and the problem of the Europeanisation of industrial relations. In this respect, adaptation to the model of other European states played as much of a role as the setting up of European works councils. In this respect, the German unions are now confronted by major additional challenges which overlap with those created by unification.

However, the same is also true for their counterparts, the employers' associations, who have similar if not greater organisational problems and must redefine their tasks in order either to maintain the system of industrial relations as a contradictory system for dealing with and resolving disputes or to adapt it to the new demands of European integration and to modernise it. Here, it is also a question of observing and adapting social and welfare state regulations to avoid falling back to the level of a third world country or turning into a Latin American-type country or allowing American relations to be introduced into Europe.

Thus, the system of industrial relations from the West, through the corporate centralisation of codetermination helped to transform conflicts at company level and to dismantle and regulate these conflicts at this level. Unions and works councils also strengthened their position as co-managers with conceptual approaches and alternative plans for initiatives in political structure. Through trade union collaboration and initiatives, new institutions were also created in the labour market, such as the work, employment and structural development associations or the 'Innovation and Work in Saxony' foundation, which followed on from an innovation and labour market offensive and represents a regional alliance for labour.

Through pressure from the unions and works councils as well as through the effect of publicity, mismanaged privatisations could also sometimes be revised and corrected. Occasionally, employee-owned companies were created as a last resort escape from mismanaged privatisation.

In general, however, this system, which has been devised to deal with wage negotiations and the form of company and sectoral working conditions, has been unable to prevent economic and industrial decline in the East, which is to be attributed on the one hand to the legacy of the state planned economy and, on the other hand, to mismanaged privatisations and lack of structural policy. The structural policy continually reiterated by the unions was implemented hesitantly, often after delays and when basic industrial structures had already been destroyed. Sometimes it was not implemented at all. The economic power difference between West and East could not be removed by simple admonitions. To some extent, the unions also gave in to pressure from the majority of their members to defend their strong position in the West and were inclined to give up their weaker position in the East, even as far as company trade union positions were concerned. The geographical debate now being pursued at European level, of German jobs versus jobs in other countries, had its precursor in the domestic German context.

As a result, it was possible to practise something in the East which had hitherto seemed impossible in the West. High mass unemployment created the conditions for this, as well as East German lack of experience with the capitalist system and East-West competition. This was shown by the completion of arrangements in the public services, the replacement of unlimited working conditions with limited and flexible ones during company transformations and clauses opening up wage scales at company level.

At present, in Germany as a whole, intense debate is raging within the unions, as well as controversial discussion between the political parties and the unions about agreeing to reductions in working hours together with wage concessions and part-time work, as well as about the new jobs which companies have guaranteed to create by way of compensation. In this area too, there are various different viewpoints in East and West Germany ('Wunder gibt es immer wieder' [Miracles still happen], *Express - Zeitung für sozialistische Betriebs- und Gewerkschaftsarbeit*, No. 3, March 1997).

The cancellation of collective agreements by unilateral notice on the part of the employers was just avoided by the first ever East German strike action and threatened appeals to the Constitution. In the East German metal industry, this success in defending the existing system of industrial relations has had a significant mobilisation effect. However, the fact that the structure of this industry is predominantly small and medium-sized prevents the emergence of strong centres of power from which counter-attacking positions can be created and qualified bargaining with an overall effect can be pursued.

Thus, for example, in IG Metall in the Zwickau region, only 45 of the 217 companies in the metal sector are in the employers' association, i.e. some 20 per cent. By comparison, the figure in West Germany is around 80-90 per cent. As a result, the process of decline in the employers' associations, which abide exclusively by traditional wage policies, is proceeding even faster than in the unions (*Freie Presse*, 16 January 1997, 4). Thus, in the view of IG Metall, the employers are waging war on two fronts. Wages are either raised or undercut as a result of leaving the employers' association. IG Metall has lost some 50 per cent of all its members in Zwickau since the changeover. Of the remaining 30,000 members, only 16,000 are working in companies, the rest have taken early retirement or are pensioners. In total, this leaves 10,000 fewer members than expected.

The issue of productivity versus East-West wage harmonisation is often used to justify wage differences and yet the pressure to conform on the remaining small businesses in the East, whether as subsidiaries or as suppliers at the beck and call of large Western companies, is very real. In 1996, according to figures from the association of the Saxon metal and electrical industry, two-thirds of East German metal and electrical companies recorded losses. In the building sector in Saxony, some 15,000 jobs are expected to be lost in 1997 alone. Lack of company capital after privatisation or new business creation, mismanagement and the lack of will on the part of the banks to tide over financial crises simply add to the problems (*Freie Presse*, 27 December 1996).

The obvious de-industrialisation and dependence on the West of East German subsidiaries is hardly something to increase the present level of bargaining power. They make the harmonisation of Eastern and Western conditions difficult and can contribute to the acceptance of unsafe and precarious labour relations in the East in the long term.

Thus, Eastern Germany with its de-industrialised structure remains a laboratory for changing industrial relations and the adaptation of trade union organisation to new challenges. It also remains the preferred location for the adaptation of labour relations between Eastern and Western Europe and between northern and southern Europe. The shift in the main emphasis of industrial relations to company level is obvious here. To what extent unions co-operate with works councils, how the overall system of German industrial relations can be reformed and how it can face the manifold corporate, national and European challenges - these are issues which to some extent will be decided here.

References

Altmann, N. (1992), 'Rationalization Strategies and Representation of Workers Interests', in N.Altmann et al (eds), *Technology and Work in German Industry*, Routledge, London/ New York.

Andreff, W. (1993), 'Französische Privatisierungstechniken und -erfahrungen', in L. Fritze, V. Kreißig and E. Schreiber, *Privatisierung und Partizipation: ein Ost-West-Vergleich*, Working Papers of the SAMF, 1993/4, Gelsenkirchen.

Clarke, T. (1993), 'Privatisierung und Umstrukturierung von Unternehmen in Großbritannien: Lehren für Osteuropa?', in L. Fritze, V. Kreißig and E. Schreiber (eds), *Privatisierung und Partizipation: ein Ost-West-Vergleich*, Working Papers of the SAMF, 1993/4, Gelsenkirchen.

Dümcke, W. and Vilmar, F. (1996), *Kolonialisierung der DDR: kritische Analysen und Alternativen des Einigungsprozesses*, Agenda Verlag, Münster.

Grabher, G. (1996), 'The Elegance of Incoherence. Institutional Legacies, Privatization and Regional Development in Eastern Germany and Hungary', *WZB-Mitteilungen*, No. 66 (December).

Hennersdorf, B. (1996), 'Erfahrungen in einem reprivatisierten Textilbetrieb des Freistaates Sachsen', in V. Kreißig and J. Gerlach (eds), *Ökonomische Transformation und Arbeitsbeziehungen in der Textil- und Bekleidungsindustrie. Die Rolle des sozialen Dialogs in den neuen Bundesländern Deutschlands*, Protokollband Euro-Seminar, Chemnitz vom 06.09. 1996 (Unpublished), p. 6.-4.

Kreißig, V. (1992), 'The German Unification Process and the Organisation of Trade-Union and Co-Determination Structures in East Germany', Shigeycshi Tokunaga et al (eds), *New Impacts on Industrial Relations. Internationalisation and Changing Production Strategies*, Monographien aus dem Deutschen Institut für Japanstudien der Philipp-Franz-von-Siebold-Stiftung 3, Iudicum Verlag, München, p. 341-64.

Kreißig, V. (1996a), *Kombinate - Privatisierung - Konzerne – Netzwerke. Ostdeutsche Automobil- und Zulieferindustrie und industrielle Beziehungen im Transformationsprozeß*, Rainer Hampp Verlag, Munich/Mering.

Kreißig, V. (1996b), 'Transformation of Industry: the East German Experience in the Textile and Automobile Industries', Paper given at the *Friedrich Ebert Foundation Conference, 'The Partnership Agreement between Egypt and the EU'*, Alexandria, 16-19 May 1996.

Lubk, R. (1995), 'Erfahrungen mit dem sozialen Dialog im Freistaat Sachsen', in V. Kreißig and I. Ermischer (eds), *Ökonomische Transformation und Arbeitsbeziehungen: die Rolle des sozialen Dialogs in den neuen Bundesländern*, Seminar proceedings of 15 December 1995, p. 46-56.

Martens, H. (1989), *Unternehmensmitbestimmung und gewerkschaftliche Reformstrategien. Entwicklungschancen eines unfertigen Modells*, Campus-Verlag, Frankfurt-am-Main/New York.

Vilmar, F. and Dümcke, W. (1996), 'Kritische Zwischenbilanz der Vereinigungspolitik: eine unerledigte Aufgabe der Politikwissenschaft', in *Das Parlament*, 27 September 1996, Supplement B40/96.

Wenzel H.-M. (1996), 'Wege zur erhöhten Wettbewerbsfhigkeit', Lecture presented at the conference *Ökonomische Transformation und Arbeitsbeziehungen in der Textil- und Bekleidungsindustrie - die Rolle des sozialen Dialogs in den neuen Bundesländern Deutschlands*, Chemnitz, 6 September 1996.

PART II
TRADE UNIONS AND THE CHALLENGE OF IMMIGRANT WORKER CULTURES

PART II

6 Trade Union Policies towards Immigrants: The Case of Belgium (1944-97)

ALBERT MARTENS

Introduction

Whenever I hear the words 'cultural diversity, class identity and integration in the labour movement', I am always reminded of the front page of the Communist Party Manifesto (London, 1848) by K. Marx and F. Engels. Indeed, on the cover and below the main title of this leaflet, we find the words, 'Proletarier aller Länder vereinigt euch' (workers of all countries unite). The foreword concludes with the following phrase.

> It is high time that Communists should openly, in the face of the whole world, publish their views, their aims, their tendencies, and meet this nursery tale of the Spectre of Communism with a Manifesto of the party itself.
> To this end, Communists of various nationalities have assembled in London, and sketched the following Manifesto, to be published in the English, French, German, Italian, Flemish [sic] and Danish languages (Marx and Engels, 1948/1976, vol. 6, p. 481).

Even when the (First) International was founded, the cultural and national diversity of the workers could not be overlooked. A strong (international) labour movement could only exist in so far as this diversity was accepted - and transcended - by the movement: 'Workers of all countries, unite!'

The meaning of the term 'unite' at that time (1848) probably differs considerably from what we (in this contribution) understand by the title 'cultural diversity' (within the same national labour organisation). Then, it was concerned with the international organisation of 'national' workers' delegations and associations within one institution. The merger of all these (national) organisations was to show the workers that they could overcome their national diversities and together proclaim, 'Workers have no fatherland'.

This historical reminder is not without significance because, later, under different circumstances and in a very different institutional context, the phrase 'workers have no fatherland' and proletarian internationalism were to be invoked to wipe out the cultural diversity of workers *within* one and the same country. The Marxist and socialist-inspired social movements and parties will primarily be the ones to pursue this basic doctrinal premise (Martens, 1996, 200-17). This also applies to Belgium and is the reason for this digression.

The Basic Premises for Understanding Trade Union Policy towards Immigrants in Belgium

Foreign employees have been present in Belgium for over half a century. Nonetheless, it is not easy to reproduce the various features of trade union reaction in a few sentences.

Before the Second World War, in the 1920s, Belgian employers recruited foreigners to work underground in mines. During the 1930s, the government - under pressure from the trade unions - sketched the outlines of an employment policy towards immigrants. Its central features were controlling and protecting the national labour market. The trade union organisations wanted to prevent or, in any event, restrict the recruitment of foreigners. With effect from 1936, an employer could no longer employ a foreigner if he had not received prior authorisation from the Minister of Employment. Foreigners coming to Belgium to work had to be in possession of a work permit before they crossed the border (Martens, 1973).

However, it was principally after the Second World War that hundreds of thousands of foreigners were recruited, firstly to extract coal (the recruitments by Fédéchar, the coal employers' national organisation; graph 6.1), then for heavy and/or less qualified work in industry, building and the services (see appendix 6.1). At present (1996) these foreign workers represent some 15 per cent of the total number of employees and, together with their families, make up approximately 10 per cent of the total population. In other words, we are talking about a population group of more or less than one million people.

In order to chart the trade union policies - which were developed after the Second World War - three basic starting points must be used:
a) a theory of the social movement;
b) the division into phases of the waves of worker immigration;
c) the pillarisation (theory) applied to the Belgian labour movement.

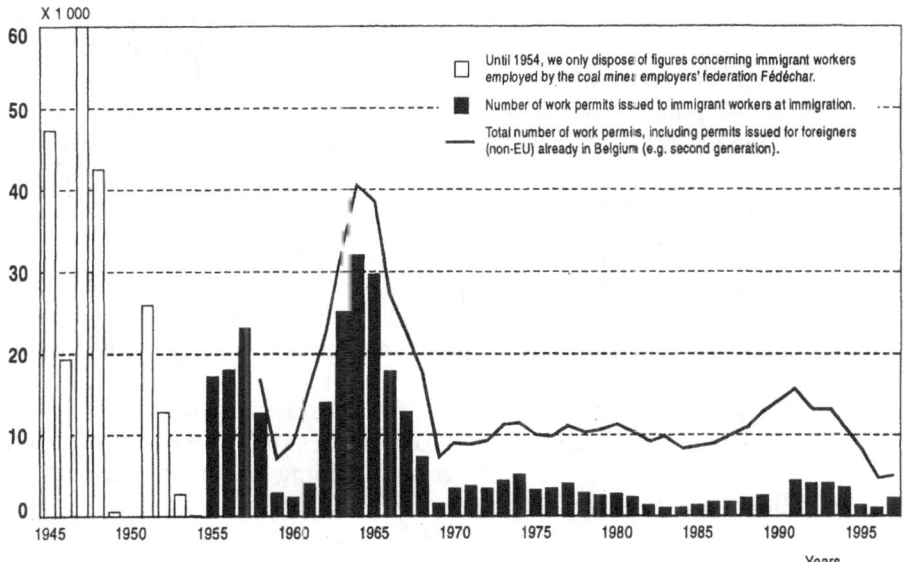

Graph 6.1 Number of work permits issued annually to foreigners in Belgium, 1945-97

These points are presented briefly below.

a) What is a social movement?

Any social movement can only be conceived and 'operate' if three elements are present and interact with each other:
- a logos: a word, language, doctrine, point of view which tells the members, the (potential) adherents, the activists, the grassroots and the opposition who you are, who the opponents are, what the ultimate aim of the movement is and what the short-term and long-term objectives are;
- a practice: a series of actions which are used to motivate and mobilise the members (mobilisation, demonstrations, campaigns, strikes, negotiations, etc.) to achieve the stated aims;
- an organisation as an institutional and structural foundation of the movement; an apparatus with rules, statutes, buildings, offices, secretariats, funds, etc.

In other words, to put it in terms of personalities, every social movement presupposes the combination of three emblematic figures: the ideologist, the activist and the apparatchik. The fact that these three actors

are simultaneously 'indispensable' and do not all have the upper hand at the same time produces many surprises. This is why the study of social movements is important.
Trade union policy towards immigrants will be examined in the light of these three elements or perspectives. Both the language and doctrine as well as the actions (not) undertaken and the place within the apparatus will be examined in turn.

b) The successive waves of immigration since 1945:
   After the Second World War, as worker immigration increased in scope, the points of view, actions and method of organisation of the trade unions changed with respect to immigrants. Four periods can be identified (appendix 6.1A):
   - 1945-62: immediately after the Second World War, significant immigration of Italians (70,000) and, to a lesser extent, Spaniards (7,800) and Greeks (3,400) for underground mining in the minefields of Wallonia and Limburg (Martens, 1973, 210);
   - 1962-74: the arrival of North African and Turkish immigrants for heavy, unskilled, dangerous or unpleasant work in most branches of industry, building and services (personal care, cleaning, etc.). Immigration is no longer restricted to the coal basins, but also spreads to the major industrial cities (Brussels, Ghent, Antwerp, Liège, Charleroi);
   - 1974-91: the emergence of the 'second generation' in a period of economic restructuring, company closures and high unemployment. Access to the labour market is now a serious problem for the immigrants who have either come to Belgium to be reunited with their family or have been born in Belgium;
   - 1991-97: pressure from extreme right-wing movements and parties is forcing democratic movements and trade union organisations to redefine their points of view and actions with respect to immigrants. This does not alter the fact that foreign workers are still actually not gaining access to the jobs' market.

   I believe that these four immigration periods or situations have significantly influenced trade union policy towards immigrants. An analysis of this policy will therefore be presented in this classification.

c) **Pillarisation:**
   Belgium has three recognised trade union federations. The largest (in terms of members) is the christian trade union (the ACV, with 1,300,000 members), followed by the socialist trade union (the ABVV, with 1,100,000 members) and the independent, liberal trade union (the ACLVB, with 50,000 members).

Trade union pluralism has incontrovertibly left its mark on trade union policy, including with respect to immigration and immigrants (Martens, 1993a, 39-50). Just after the Second World War, the doctrinal positions of the various federations differed significantly. The socialist trade union (ABVV), the oldest, proclaimed a radical social-democratic doctrine and granted a high degree of autonomy to its national unions. The christian trade union experienced a breakthrough after the Second World War, it is doctrinally less distinct but more highly centralised (one central strike fund for the entire trade union) and provides more efficient services for its members. In recent years, we have observed greater harmonisation between the trade union organisations - under external (and internal) pressure - in terms of positions, actions and forms of organisation.

To conclude this theoretical introduction, we will just reiterate how the analysis of trade union policy towards immigrants is presented below: by immigration period and according to the (doctrinal) positions, actions and institutional organisation of the two largest trade union federations.

The Period 1945-62: Integration within Miners' Trade Unions

The trade union organisations were not indifferent to the arrival of 70,000 workers from Italy in 1945-46. Severely hard-hit by the war, the trade unions attempted to restructure themselves, both in terms of organisation and doctrine.

Neither trade union organisation openly opposed the mass recruitment of foreigners. The trade union federations accepted the macro-economic attitudes of the coalition governments (socialist/christian/communist):

a) national reconstruction and the essential export of industrial production require large quantities of cheap energy;
b) coal is the only available source of energy;
c) in order to achieve (a), the coal has to be extracted as cheaply as possible;
d) for this reason, miners' wages cannot rise above a certain rate;
e) if the domestic supply of labour is insufficient, foreign miners can (again) be recruited to do the job.

The acceptance of these principles by the trade unions does not mean that the arrival of these Italian workers was applauded by the unionised Belgian miners.

The doctrinal line taken by the trade union organisations with respect to the foreign workers in this period could be presented as follows:
- stopping these non-unionised, vulnerable, inept workers becoming the victim of additional extortion;
- avoiding these foreign miners remaining aloof from the collective struggle, adopting an anti-trade union position and breaking strikes, as well as vice versa;
- stopping them joining extreme left-wing and revolutionary (communist) movements (Martiniello, 1992, 261-91).[1]

In order to prevent this, the trade union organisations (immediately) had to open their ranks. The mobilisation and organisation of these workers was nonetheless tackled by the two major federations in very different ways.

In the socialist trade union ABVV, the so-called internationalist principles of solidarity and equality (no distinctions between gender, nationality, etc.) were assumed and any specific (nationalist/culturalist) approach to the problem was rejected. Immigrants had the same rights as the native, national workers, or at least they should have. A special approach would only have perpetuated the problem and further divided the working class. 'Workers have no fatherland' was the message.

The christian trade union ACV took a different view. In its opinion, it was precisely through special and specific recognition of this cultural individuality that these non-unionised foreign workers would find their way to the trade union organisations and become convinced of the joint struggle.

Trade union actions for and with these (Italian) workers reflected the dichotomy of these basic premises.

Very early on (1946) the christian trade union organisations, in the various coal basins, developed an entire network for providing support and assistance in Italian with the help of, for example, Italian priests. For this purpose, the ACV contacted the Christian Association of Italian Workers (Assoziazione cristiani dei lavoratori italiani, ACLI) (Morelli, 1988; Martiniello, 1992; Blaise and Martens, 1992; Dresse, 1997). In 1947, a department for foreign workers was even set up at federation level (ACV). This department assumed responsibility for support and co-ordination for the local divisions and represented the interests of these workers (in councils and committees) at national level.

---

[1] I am not referring back to the attitudes which are (at first sight) difficult to reconcile, which the trade union organisations must uphold with respect to 'external' workers: (a) the objection in principle to the recruitment of employees from abroad but, if they have nonetheless arrived in the country, (b) the unconditional acceptance of these employees within the labour organisations and radical action against discrimination and unequal treatment (Martens, 1996, 202-5).

The socialist trade union did not wish to organise special action, services or networks. The immigrants should have been able to assimilate themselves and to be active in the trade union without distinction in terms of nationality, language or culture. If necessary, they could still express their particular interests through the local sections or their respective political parties (the communist PCI and the socialist PSI).

The Period 1962-74: the Organisation of the Various Immigrant Communities within the Trade Union Organisations; the Support for Political Representation at Local Level

Following the arrival, in 1962-65, of substantial numbers of foreigners from various countries (Italy, Spain, Greece, Morocco, Turkey, Yugoslavia) with different languages, cultures and religions, the trade union organisations again faced problems of mobilisation and organisation.

At doctrinal level, a significant change took place compared to the previous period. For the first time since the 1930s, the trade union organisations accepted the renunciation of prior admission (for employers who want to recruit employees resident abroad). This made so-called 'tourist immigration' possible. Over 200,000 foreigners thus had the opportunity to work in Belgium. The former prior admission was not made compulsory again until 1967-68. 'Regular' immigration then applied again.

Actions towards further integration within the trade union organisations then assumed the following forms.

a) Within the respective trade unions:
within the christian trade union (ACV) the various national operations and provisions were further and better developed (training programmes, meeting days, newspapers in native languages, including in Polish, Italian, Spanish, Portuguese, Greek, Turkish, Arabic and Serbian).
The socialist trade union organisation (ABVV) now also followed this path and organised - although less high profile - specific activities and services for the employees of various nationalities.

b) Two important developments were observed between the trade union organisations:
- discrimination and restrictions imposed on foreign employees to participate in social elections in companies (voting rights and eligibility for the works council and the workplace safety, health and improvement committee) were reduced. As of 1971, full equality of rights between national and foreign workers became a reality;

- support for political expression by foreign workers at local level, firstly through the organisation of municipal advisory councils and later by working towards the granting of municipal voting rights to aliens. This latter demand has still not been granted. The first has been achieved fairly erratically. Here and there, municipal advisory councils have been introduced (Martiniello, 1992; Panceira, 1982). However, on the trade union side, no pressure is currently being exerted to continue the experiment with advisory councils systematically in all municipalities with a considerable number of immigrants. The trade union organisations have spoken out clearly for the voting rights and eligibility of aliens in municipal elections. However, this demand has not been supported by the general mobilisation of all trade union members. It is as if the specific interests of a particular group are at issue, which have to be defended more by political parties than by the trade union organisations.

The Period 1974-91: the Demand for Equal Treatment is Pushed to the Forefront

The advent of a period of regular and regulated immigration (1967-74) did not prevent employers employing (new) foreigners illegally. Under pressure from hunger strikes by clandestine workers, in 1974 the government decided that some illegally employed aliens were to be regulated (between 6,000 and 8,000 depending on origins) and that no further work permits would be granted for unskilled labour (a ban on immigration for unskilled workers).

However, the trade union organisations now faced new questions, specifically the lack of employment for the younger aliens resident in Belgium, the so-called second generation (including the children of foreigners who had previously arrived). This new question became very acute in regions and sectors where industrial restructuring was taking place (the coal industry in Wallonia and Limburg, the textile industry in Ghent) and in the larger urban centres (Antwerp, Ghent, Brussels, Liège, Charleroi).

During this period, the struggle for equal treatment was put forward as a (doctrinal) theme by the trade union organisations, but was however seldom, if ever, forced through, let alone converted into trade union actions.

Moreover, the presence of immigrants within the trade union organisational policy structures was disproportionately low. In the successive (company) elections - and in so far as figures show - immigrants were very rarely elected.[2] The employment crisis affected the immigrants more than the native employees (Rosvelds and Martens, 1993). The trade union organisations were unable or unwilling to do much about this phenomenon.

The Period 1991-97 and Beyond: the Emergence of the Extreme Right and the (Renewed) Struggle against Racism, Discrimination and Unequal Treatment, Including at Company Level

After the breakthrough and the electoral success of extreme right-wing parties, first in the municipal elections of 1988 and then in the 1991 and 1995 general elections,[3] the trade union organisations adopted a series of measures to combat racism and to protect the rights of immigrants (Persoone, 1995).

a) The battle against racism was fought using:
    - a joint campaign by the trade unions (ABVV, ACV and ACLVB) in the social elections of 1991 and 1995. The three trade union organisations openly proclaimed that any raising of the racist stakes during the elections would not be tolerated;
    - the proclamation by the trade union organisations (ABVV and ACV) of the incompatibility between activism for racist parties and trade union membership. On 28 October 1994, the ABVV, ACV and ACLVB signed an 'Agreement among trade union organisations regarding the 1995 social elections', to exclude extreme right-wing activists from becoming candidates in the social elections. Moreover, the ACV envisaged an exclusion procedure for trade union officials who may be or become members of extreme right-wing groupings;
    - the inclusion of an anti-discrimination clause and codes of conduct in the working rules of companies, departments or business sectors (Paritair Comité voor Uitzendarbeid, 1996). Initiatives were taken to

---

[2] The trade union membership of foreign workers in Belgium is not known. Pasture and Mampuys (1990, 231), give the following figures of the foreign membership of the ACV: 1947: 1.0 per cent; 1959: 2.0 per cent; 1969: 5.0 per cent; 1974: 5.6 per cent; 1981: 7.5 per cent; 1986: 6.3 per cent. Other sources indicate much higher percentages (e.g. Aerts and Martens, 1978 67 gives for 1968 8.4 per cent). Pittomvils (s.d., 12) estimates the foreign membership of the ABVV in 1968 was 5 per cent and 6.3 per cent in 1973. In the social elections of 1975, only 5 per cent of candidates for works council elections were foreigners (although they represent over 10 per cent of the total number of employees). Of the 6,501 elected from the ACV, 278 (4 per cent) were foreigners; of the 5,680 elected from the ABVV, 384 (6.7 per cent) were foreigners (Dresse, 1997, 184).

[3] In the 1991 elections, the Vlaams Blok received 10.3 per cent of votes in Flanders, compared to 12.3 per cent in 1995.

promote the 'Business without racism' campaign (Krzeslo, 1997, 24-5; Martens and Sette, 1997).

b) The promotion of 'equal treatment' and the 'equal opportunities policy' within companies: within the national unions, actions have been launched to encourage militants at company level:
   - to investigate where and under what circumstances immigrants are (or are not) employed; using a checklist, to check who works where and for what wages (ABVV, 1992a and 1992b; ACV, 1993). If this reveals an 'unequal' presence of women, immigrants, etc., the trade union representatives must report this in the information and advisory bodies of the companies and present it for discussion. To do this, they can appeal to the collective labour agreement (CAO) 9bis. Concrete steps and training courses are proposed in anti-discrimination programmes;
   - in order to promote the recruitment and promotion of immigrants, language teaching on the shopfloor is organised ('Dutch on the shopfloor' programmes).

Conclusion

We can state that trade union policy towards immigrants has been shifted in the following ways since the Second World War (1945-97) (see table 6.1):

a) at doctrinal level (logos):
   - a certain rapprochement of positions has been observed between the christian and the socialist trade unions, associated with the recognition of the cultural identity and individuality of the immigrant communities. The radical position on republican ideals (universality and equality without (cultural) difference of meaning, which is also translated into the pronouncement, 'the workers have no fatherland') which was found in the socialist trade union, has been tempered by a certain recognition of the cultural identity (language, culture, religion) of the immigrants. The concern for cultural and religious individuality remains a high priority in the christian trade union, but is now developing more outside rather than within the trade union structures;
   - a redirection of trade union work, where more attention has been devoted to defending the rights and positions of 'immigrants' within companies. The immigrant question, which previously had to be dealt with primarily by interprofessional, local and federation trade union work, is now gradually being pushed towards the national unions.

The position is now less 'integration' but more 'struggle against racism, for equal rights, opportunities and treatment';

b) as far as trade union practice is concerned:
   - in implementing the above, the three federations have been attempting, by presenting a joint trade union front, to put forward propaganda and to take action against the infiltration of extreme right-wing groups and/or ideas;
   - attempts are being made to make the presence (or absence) of immigrants within companies a subject for discussion. The trade union company representatives (union delegation, those elected to the works council and the prevention committee, etc.) are encouraged and trained to investigate and defend the equal rights of 'minorities' (women, immigrants, young people, etc.). This does not take place without underlying or open resistance from the unionised employees. Within the public services, for example, the trade unions are still resistant to the recruitment of employees who are not of Belgian nationality;

c) as far as the institutional structures are concerned:
   - the federation-level immigrant department(s) and institutions are being dismantled in the christian trade union in favour of the 'existing' (education) departments and the take-over of immigrants' demands by the national unions;
   - the broader cultural demands of immigrants (language, religion, art, etc.) are now supported by the development of independent 'self-organisations', but ones which are recognised by the immigrant communities.

Over the past half century, the trade union organisations in Belgium have undergone a complete revolution. While in other countries (UK, the Netherlands, France), the trade union organisations had to incorporate workers' compatriots from the (former) colonies (Africa, Asia, Central America) who shared the nationality of the mother country, this was not the case for Belgium, also a (former) colonial power. These were foreigners, alien workers. Since they were barely familiar with how to deal with immigrants (other languages, cultures, religious perceptions, etc.), the trade union organisations could not rely on earlier examples. Improvisation often took place 'on-the-job', rather than thinking things through first.

I hope that this attempt at classification offers a better overview of what happened. Perhaps this will give new impetus to reflection on the subject.

References

ABVV-Vlaams Intergewestelijk Komitee (1992a), *Controlelijst over de werksituatie op jouw bedrijf*, Vlaams ABVV.
ABVV-Vlaams Intergewestelijk Komitee (1992b), *Voorsprong nemen. Werkdocument voor een gelijkekansenbeleid*, Antwerp/Brussels, 14 February 1992.
ACV (1993), *Integratie van migranten. Een syndicaal werkboek voor de onderneming*, Brussels.
Aerts, M. and Martens, A. (1978), *Gastarbeider, lotgenoot en landgenoot*, Kritak, Leuven.
Bastenier, A. and Targosz, P. (1991), *Les organisations syndicales et l'immigration en Europe*, Sybidi Papers No. 11, Academia-Erasme, Grem, Louvain-la-Neuve.
Beauchesne, M.-N., Nayer, A., Nys, M. and Zinbi, T. (1991), *La discrimination dans l'accès à l'emploi et l'intégration professionnelle en Région Bruxelloise*, CeRP, Institut de Sociologie, Université Libre de Bruxelles.
Blaise, P. and Martens, A. (1992), 'Des immigrés à intégrer. Choix politiques et modalités institutionnelles', *Courrier hebdomadaire*, No. 1358-1359, CRISP, Brussels.
Denolf, L. and Grieten, C. (1991), 'Positieve acties voor vrouwen, ook voor etnische minderheden?', *Tijdschrift voor Sociologie*, Vol. 11, No. 5-6, p. 495-535.
Dresse, R. (1997), 'L'action des syndicats', in P. Blaise, M.-T. Coenen and R. Dresse et al, *La Belgique et ses immigrés. Les politiques manquées*, Pol-His, De Boeck Université, Brussels, p. 166-97.
El Mouden, A. (1990), *De toegang tot de betrekkingen in overheidsdienst en de nationaliteitsvoorwaarde*, Sociologisch Onderzoeksinstituut, Leuven.
Fonteneau, G. (1993), *Les instruments juridiques concernant le droit des travailleurs migrants et leurs familles*, Confédération Européenne des Syndicats, Brussels.
Krzeslo, E. (ed) (1997), *Les syndicats contre le racisme, la xénophobie et la discrimination sur le lieu de travail*, Confédération Européenne des Syndicats, Brussels.
Martens, A. (1973), *25 jaar wegwerparbeiders. Het Belgisch immigratiebeleid na 1945*, Katholieke Universiteit Leuven, Sociologisch Onderzoeksinstituut.
Martens, A. (1993a), 'De integratieproblematiek binnen een multiculturele samenleving: het verzuilingsmodel als hypothese', in F. Demeyere (eds), *Over pluralisme en democratie. Verzuiling en integratie in een multiculturele samenleving*, VUB Press, Brussels, p. 39-50.
Martens, A. (1993b), 'Gelijkheid in de werkgelegenheid: "Fair Play or Fair Scores?"', *De Gids op Maatschappelijk Gebied*, Vol. 84, No. 8-9, p. 659-73.
Martens, A. (1996), 'Trade Unions and Migrant Workers in Europe: A Changing Ideology as a Reflection of Variable Principles', in P. Pasture, J. Verberckmoes and H. De Witte (eds), *The Lost Perspective? Trade Unions between Ideology and Social Action in the New Europe*, Volume 2: Significance of Ideology in European Trade Unionism, Avebury, Aldershot, p. 200-17.
Martens, A. and Sette, K. (1997), *Belgische gevallen voor het opmaken van een compendium van betekenisvolle voorbeelden van bestrijding van racisme op de werkplaats*, European Foundation for the Improvement of Living and Working Conditions, Dublin.
Martens, R. (1996), *Inspraak en participatie van allochtonen in de vakbonden*, Antwerps Centrum voor Migrantenstudies en Stedelijke Migrantenraad Antwerpen, Workshop, 20 November 1996.
Martiniello, M. (1992), *Leadership et pouvoir dans les communautés d'origine immigrée. L'exemple d'une communauté ethnique en Belgique*, L'harmattan/CIEMI, Paris.
Marx, K. and Engels, F. (1976), *Collected works*, Vol. VI, Lawrence & Wishart, London.

Morelli, A. (1988), 'L'appel de la main-d'oeuvre italienne pour les charbonnages et sa prise en charge à son arrivée en Belgique dans l'immédiat après-guerre', *Revue belge d'histoire contemporaine*, Vol. 19, No. 1-2, p. 83-130.
Panceira, S. (1982), 'Les conseils consultatifs communaux des immigrés', *Courrier hebdomadaire*, No. 923, CRISP, Brussels.
Paritair Comité voor Uitzendarbeid (1996), Collective Labour Agreement of 7 May 1996. Code of Conduct to Prevent Racial Discrimination (agreement registered on 21 May 1996 under number 41822/CO/322), *Belgian Official Gazette*, 6 November 1996, p. 28328-30.
Pasture, P. and Mampuys, J. (1990), *In de ban van het getal. Ledenanalyse van het ACV*, HIVA-reeks 13, HIVA, Leuven.
Persoone, M. (1995), *'ACV weert extreem-rechts': een ideologische verkenning en instrument voor vakbondsvorming*, Degree dissertation, Faculté Ouverte Politique, Economique et Sociale, Université Catholique de Louvain, Louvain-la-Neuve.
Pittomvils, K. (s.d.), *Het ABVV, internationale arbeidsmigratie, en 'gastarbeiders' in de periode 1960-74: internationalisme versus nationale verdediging*, Interuniversitaire attractiepool 37, Centrum voor de Interdisciplinaire Studie van Brussel, VUB (politiek-historisch luik).
Rosvelds, S. and Martens, A. (1992), 'Vrouwen van etnische minderheden op de Belgische arbeidsmarkt', in B. Gademann, J.J. van Hoof and F. Loth (eds), *Dubbel gediscrimineerd? Allochtone vrouwen op de Europese arbeidsmarkt*, Kluwer, Open Universiteit (Arbeid en Organisatie), Deventer.
Rosvelds, S. and Martens, A. (1993), *Zelfde zweet ander brood. Onderzoek naar de arbeidsmarktpositie van Belgen en migranten op twee lokale arbeidsmarkten: Antwerpen en Gent*, DPWB, Programma Maatschappelijk Onderzoek, Migrantenstudies, Brussels.
Secretariat of the female labour commission (1992), *Non-discriminatory job offers*, Ministry of Employment and Labour, Brussels.

Appendix 6.1: Schematic Representation of Trade Union Logos, Praxis and Organisation Regarding Immigrants

A. 1945-62: Integration within the Trade Unions

Logos	Praxis	Institution
▪ Cultural diversity accepted and recognised (ACV) ▪ Proletarian universalism and internationalism (ABVV)	Inclusion and integration. Invitation to combine: ▪ with specific mobilisation (ACV) ▪ without specific attention for the cultural differences (ABVV)	At confederal level: ▪ specific services (ACV) ▪ none (ABVV) In the national unions: no specific recognition, but de facto marginalised

B. 1962-74: the Organisation of the Immigrant Communities

Logos	Praxis	Institution
■ Cultural diversity accepted, recognised and supported by the christian TU ■ Acceptance and some support of the cultural diversity; sympathy for left-wing members or political refugees (ABVV)	■ Inclusion and Integration; implementation of the logic of representation: - with strong acceptance of the cultural diversity - with precarious attention for the cultural differences (ABVV) ■ Supporting political expression	At confederal level: specific services (ACV and ABVV) No more legal discrimination in union elections (individual companies)

C. 1974-91: the Demand for Equal Treatment and Political Representation

Logos	Praxis	Institution
■ Acceptance of the immigration restrictions (also family reunification) ■ Equal treatment	■ Campaigns against racism and discrimination ■ Supporting immigrants activists within the confederal structures ■ Action for political representation at the local level (unsuccessful)	Idem as before

D. 1991-97: the Renewed Struggle Against Racism and Far Right

Logos	Praxis	Institution
■ The proclamation of the irreconciability of militancy in racist parties and union responsibilities ■ Necessity of combating racism on the work place ■ Promotion of equal opportunities and chances	■ Campaigns against racism and discrimination ■ Mobilisation for equal right actions at the plant level and within the individual companies ■ Promotion of the independent self-organisations of migrants	At confederal level: reduction of the immigrant services At the level of the national unions: integration in the TU actions

Appendix 6.2: Summary of Trade Union Policy towards Immigration and Immigrants, 1945-97

Period	Core idea	Logos	Practice	Institutional development
1945-62	How to convince foreign employees to unionise	- ACV: with acceptance and recognition of cultural diversity - ABVV: worker universalism and internationalism	Recruitment, integration and organisation actions. Invitation to join: - with specific mobilisation channels (ACV) - without particular attention to cultural differences (ABVV)	*At federation level:* - own organisation and operation (ACV) - none (ABVV) *Within the national unions*, no particular recognition and often marginalisation in practice
1962-74	The organisation of immigrants (communities) within and by the trade union organisations	- ACV: an effective opportunity must be offered for the recognition and support of cultural diversity. The best way to make true trade unionists of foreign employees - ABVV: acceptance and limited support for cultural diversity. Openness and sympathy towards political refugees from left-wing parties	Inclusion and integration practices. Attempts to appeal to and train valid representatives through: - open acceptance of cultural individuality (ACV) - implicit and cautious recognition (ABVV) - Actions to support political involvement at local level (municipal advisory councils)	- Own alien departments at federation level (ABVV and ACV) - Social elections: abolition of distinction between Belgian and foreign employees regarding voting and eligibility rights

Period	Core idea	Doctrine Logos	Practice	Institutional development
1974-91	Demand for equal treatment and for political representation	▪ Acceptance of the various immigration restrictions imposed by the government (especially in connection with reuniting families) ▪ Promotion of equal treatment	▪ Campaigns and actions against racism and discrimination ▪ Support for immigrants, militants and representatives within the federation-level structures ▪ Support for political involvement and representation by immigrants at local level (without success)	Same as during the previous period
1991-97	Renewed struggle against racism and extreme right (including at company level)	▪ Proclamation of incompatibility of trade union office with membership of an extreme right wing organisation or party ▪ Need to combat racism in the workplace ▪ Promotion of an equal opportunities policy	▪ Launch of campaigns against racism and discrimination ▪ Mobilisation within companies, development of equal opportunities policy ▪ Promotion of self-organisation by immigrants	At federation level, reduction and/or abolition of immigrant services At the level of national unions, integration into trade union operations

7 Trade Union Policies Regarding Immigration and Immigrant Workers in the Netherlands (1960-95)

JUDITH ROOSBLAD

Introduction

After a decade of reconstruction following the Second World War, labour markets in Western European economies were confronted with labour shortages. Depending on factors such as the speed of the economic reconstruction, the demographic situation and labour market participation (e.g. of women), the need to import additional labour to guarantee optimum production manifested itself sooner or later in various countries and in various sectors of economic activity. By the middle of the 1950s most Western European countries had in fact become importers of workers, who mostly filled in the gap left by the (increasingly educated) national labour forces. Systems for recruitment and employment of these imported workers were developed. It was not only the employers and the governments that had to formulate policies with regard to the recruitment and employment of foreign workers, but the trade unions, as important intermediaries, also had to play their role.

Since the European trade unions were one of the (potentially) powerful and influential institutions within western economies, and since in many cases they co-operated with the government and employers' associations in the socio-economic decision making process,[1] they had to take a stand on immigration policy. They also had to formulate their policies relating to the migrant workers who actually arrived and became part of the working force

---

[1] E.g. the Social Economic Council (*Sociaal Economische Raad*, SER) in the Netherlands, in which representatives of employers and employees together with so called 'crown members' (independent experts appointed by the government) determine to a considerable extent the socio-economic policies of the government.

the unions were meant to represent. This made trade unions very important organisations for the socio-economic position of foreign workers in the receiving countries. Through their membership in a trade union, the foreign workers had the possibility of influencing the political decision making process indirectly. This helped them to improve their socio-economic and political position in society.

The main goal of the trade unions was to protect the individual and collective interests of the workers against the employers and other authorities that were in a position to affect the workers' socio-economic situation. It was in the interest of the trade unions to represent as many workers as possible. Therefore, the trade unions seemed to be the obvious organisations to protect the interests of the foreign workers. However, for various reasons this turned out not to be an easy task. The trade unions found themselves confronted with several dilemmas. The first was whether to resist the immigration policies of the employers and the state, or else to co-operate and try to avoid the possible negative consequences. The second dilemma arose when the migrants had arrived: 'should they be included as members of the trade unions or not?' And if the answer was yes, then another dilemma manifested itself: 'should special services, facilities and policies be established for these migrant workers within the unions, or not?' (Penninx and Roosblad, 1993; see also Martens, 1994). We will discuss these dilemmas briefly in what follows.

When international labour migration started to increase, the trade unions feared, on the one hand, that the arrival of immigrant labour would directly clash with the interests of 'their own' indigenous members, since labour migration would tend to keep wages low. Obviously, trade unions considered it their chief task to protect their members against this tendency. On the other hand, the trade unions did realise that immigrant labour was necessary to keep production going, at least in times of economic expansion. Moreover, the trade unions had always had a tradition of international solidarity, so that too open a resistance against immigrant workers (should that be the policy) would definitely not be in keeping with this ideology (Castles and Kosack, 1974; De Jongh et al, 1984; Vranken, 1990).

With respect to those immigrants who were already settled, the trade unions had to redefine or even change particular points of view. Choices had to be made with several considerations being taken into account. On the one hand, the trade unions were only too well aware of the fact that once it had become clear that a large number of immigrants intended to stay permanently and the immigrant workers themselves were attempting to improve their labour position by means of various actions, then it was of the utmost importance that immigrant workers should join the trade unions.

Moreover, the exclusion of immigrants would lead to a rift in the labour movement which would result in a weaker position of the unions during negotiations. On the other hand, the inclusion of immigrant workers might clash with the interests of native members, or certain factions within the labour movement might come to hold this view (Castles and Kosack, 1974; De Jongh et al, 1984; Vranken, 1990; Edye, 1987; Wubben, 1986).

To complicate matters even more, the two options with regard to immigration and immigrant policy were inextricably linked. Castles and Kosack (1973, 128) have expressed this as follows:

> The trade unions find themselves in a dilemma. It may seem logical to oppose immigration, but once there are immigrant workers in the country, it is essential to organise them - not only in their own interests, but also in the interests of the workers. If the unions oppose immigration initially and even continue to do so, they may find that the immigrants do not trust them and are unwilling to join. Where this happens, the unions have the worst of both worlds. Not strong enough to prevent immigration, their attempts to do so only serve to alienate the new workers from them. The result is a weakening of the unions and the deepening of the split in the working class. Thus there is a potential contradiction between trade union policies towards immigration, on the one hand, and policies towards the immigrant workers once they are in the country, on the other.

Hence Castles and Kosack argue that trade union policies towards immigration and trade union policies towards immigrant workers should be studied in relation to each other.

Even if trade unions are in favour of the inclusion of immigrant workers based on the view that native and immigrant workers belong to the same class, fundamentally having the same rights, they are still confronted on a daily basis with existing or alleged differences between the two categories (De Jongh et al, 1984). These differences are partly due to the specific needs of foreign labourers, and this leads to a third dilemma. Should a trade union exclusively attend to the common interests of indigenous and immigrant workers, or should a union also stand up for the specific interests of their immigrant members? In the first case, the trade union will be running the risk of being unjust when they do not make a distinction in their treatment of cases which are not equal. Migrant workers are at a disadvantage, and if given the same treatment as indigenous workers this disadvantage will remain. However, if a trade union pays special attention to its migrant members, then there is a chance that indigenous workers will feel slighted and might even oppose the giving of special treatment to migrant workers. In summary, the trade unions are faced with a choice between two alternatives, each of which carries negative consequences.

This dilemma is called the 'equal versus special-treatment dilemma' by De Jongh et al (1984, 219).

The trade unions are not only faced with these dilemmas within their own organisation, but also within society at large. Do they support the inclusion or exclusion of migrants and ethnic minorities in society at large? And if they are in favour of the inclusion of these groups in society, do they support special measures and special policies for stimulating their integration into society, or do they only stand up for the common interests of these two groups and of the indigenous population?

The question is how trade unions in the Netherlands dealt with these dilemmas and if there are differences in approach between the different trade unions. The aim of this paper is to describe and analyse the development of trade union policies in the Netherlands with regard to immigration and immigrant workers. The paper will look not only at official trade union policies, but will also give attention to their factual behaviour and the arguments trade unions put forward to justify (the gap between) these official policies and their factual behaviour.

Trade Union Positions in the Netherlands Regarding the Recruitment of Foreign Labour

The official recruitment of foreign workers under the supervision of the Dutch government began in 1960 after a recruitment agreement between the Dutch and the Italian governments (Schumacher, 1987). Soon after that, recruitment agreements with other Mediterranean countries followed, such as Spain, Portugal and Turkey (1964), Greece (1966), Morocco (1969) and Yugoslavia and Tunisia (1970). The immigrants recruited form these countries mainly came as temporary contract workers to the Netherlands. the so-called 'guest workers'. The official recruitment took place on the base of tripartite consultation between the Department of Social Affairs and Employment and representatives of the employer and employee organisations which started in 1960. The employee organisations were represented by the three major trade union confederations in Dutch society: the social democratic Dutch Trade Union Confederation (NVV), the Dutch Catholic Trade Union Confederation (NKV) and the Confederation of Christian Trade Unions in the Netherlands (CNV). The NVV and the NKV merged in the FNV (Confederation of Dutch Trade Unions) in 1976. Agreements were reached within a consultative body concerning the principal of recruiting and the actual implementation of the recruitment and employment of foreign workers (Janssen, 1967, 39). The recruitment of foreign labour was seen as a temporary measure: when the Dutch economy would no longer need foreigners, then the foreign workers would return home. The main concern of the government - but also of employers and trade unions - was to set up good structures for recruiting and employing foreign workers (as long as they were needed for the Dutch economy).

The attitude of the Dutch trade union confederations toward the recruitment and employment of foreign workers was rather positive in the first half of the sixties. Just like the government and employers, they also took the view that the recruitment of foreign workers was necessary in order to provide for the shortage of manpower, especially in the industrial sector.

However, they were also concerned with the direct material interests of the Dutch workers. For example, the officially recruited foreign workers enjoyed certain specific conditions of employment, in addition to what was due them on the grounds of the general collective labour agreements. It was the employer's duty to take care of housing and food (the worker had to contribute to cover the costs), and the workers got extra holidays. All this was understandable, but was considered by (part of) the Dutch colleagues as 'discrimination' against them. The trade unions had a hard time explaining why the foreign workers would need such special facilities. Furthermore, they feared that employers would be happier with foreign workers, because these workers were more eager to earn as much money as possible and therefore more willing to work overtime.

In order to minimise the 'unfair competition' between Dutch and foreign workers, and in order to improve the squalid conditions under which foreigners had to live, the trade unions advocated the equal treatment of foreigners and Dutchmen. However, at the same time they used this equality policy as a tool for limiting recruitment. For example: if employers could not take care of good housing in times of housing shortage, then they would not be permitted to recruit foreigners (Marshall-Goldschwartz, 1973, 63-70).

In the mid-sixties the initially positive attitude of the trade unions towards recruitment changed. This was due to the great flow of foreigners and because of the brief economic recession that occurred in 1966-67 and the mass discharges that followed that recession. The trade unions opposed further recruitment of foreign workers. They urged the government to come up with well-balanced and well-controlled policies regarding the recruitment and admission of foreign workers and the co-ordination of policies regarding their housing and integration into society. The trade unions themselves, however, did very little to protect the interests of foreign workers, and no attempts were (yet) made to formulate integration policies. Because the trade union activities were not tailored to foreigners, the foreigners were not much inclined to join the unions. Social assistance and

Differences in Attitudes between the Trade Unions Regarding Foreign Workers

At the level of the federations not much difference can be observed in the policy towards foreign workers. The policies of the three trade union federations NKV, NVV and CNV are to a significant extent attuned to one another. At the level of the affiliated unions, however, differences can indeed be noted in the manner in which these unions approach foreign workers.

When, for example, we focus on the transport sector, then we note that foreign workers barely played a role in the period 1960-69. There were probably few foreign workers employed in the sector in this period. This impression is reinforced when we consult the annual reports and the trade union journals of the transport unions NKV, NVV and CNV on this point. In the period 1960-69, neither the annual reports nor the union journals devoted hardly any attention to the recruitment and employment of foreign workers. The scarce articles that were published in the union journals of the three transport unions about foreign workers were informative in nature and intended to cultivate understanding among the indigenous rank and file for the difficult situation of the foreign workers. It is revealing, for example, that the first article about foreign workers that appears in the union journal of the transport union CNV was placed in the Christmas issue and was entitled 'My Neighbour is a Turk'.[2] In this article there is a strong appeal to the indigenous rank and file for feelings of compassion and tolerance.

Although Dutch Rail (Nederlandse Spoorwegen) had started the recruitment and employment of foreign workers in 1961, it was only after 1967 that the number of foreign employees increased substantially. At the end of 1967 the number of foreigners employed was 552, at the end of 1969 this number nearly doubled (992).[3] From the beginning the transport unions were involved in the recruitment and employment of foreign workers. Firstly, they had a say in the countries foreign workers would be recruited from. For example, initially in 1961 the recruitment was limited to Belgian workers, because the trade unions thought that Mediterranean workers

---

[2] *Het seinlicht*, Vol. 55, 1964.
[3] As appears from the annual reports of the *Personeelsraad* (Personnel Council), 1961-1969. Dutch Rail, Utrecht. The Personnel Council is a co-operative body of the transport unions NKV, NVV and CNV.

would have language problems and problems to integrate with Dutch society. Later, in 1964, when the trade unions and Dutch Rail had agreed to recruit Mediterranean workers, the base on which that happened differed from that of the Belgian workers. The Mediterranean workers were employed on temporary contracts, while the Belgium workers had been employed on permanent contracts, because Dutch Rail and the trade unions assumed that Belgium workers would have no problems to adapt to Dutch society.[4] The trade unions also had a say in the terms of employment. Apart from the duration of the employment contracts, they ensured that foreign workers were employed under the same terms as indigenous workers. In addition, a number of secondary terms of employment were agreed upon for the benefit of foreign workers, such as extra leave days for vacation in the country of origin. Despite the involvement of trade unions in the recruitment and employment of foreign workers it was not until the end of the 1960s when the transport unions really started paying attention to foreign workers on the workplace.

There are great differences between the transport unions regarding policies for the benefit of foreign workers. One indicator is the attention that is given to foreign workers in the journals of the three different transport unions. Here it is a question of the extent to which and the manner in which the journals of these unions write about foreign workers. It may be that this says nothing about the actual behaviour of the unions toward foreign workers, but it does reveal how the unions depict the foreign workers to the rank and file and what 'attitude' the unions want to propagate among their members.

Beginning in the 1970s, both the CNV transport union and the NVV and NKV transport unions started to report more on foreign employees. There are differences, however, regarding the nature of the articles, the style in which they were written and the number of articles that were devoted to the topic.

During the period 1970-76[5] in the journal of the CNV transport union, *Het seinlicht*, there were considerably more articles about foreign workers than in the journals of the NVV and the NKV (34, 27 and 10, respectively). The articles were mainly positive and argued that attention should be given to the situation of foreign workers. The CNV did its best to promote the rights of the foreign workers ('Foreigners must have equal rights' in 1974), and sometimes opposed government policy on this point ('Bill discrimi-

---

4   Idem.
5   In 1976 the NVV and NKV transport unions merged to form the FNV transport union. The journals of the NVV and NKV transport unions joined forces in the FNV transport journal *Onderweg*.

nates against foreign workers' in 1975.[6] They also reported (more than in the journals of the other two transport unions) on foreign workers who wanted to improve the position of their companions in adversity.

In this period, the reporting in *Steeds voorwaarts*, the journal of the NVV transport union, was mainly positive and informative in nature. Nevertheless, there was a single article in the period 1970-76 that spoke negatively of foreign labour, namely in 1973 ('No more workers from abroad').[7] *Richting*, the journal of the NKV transport union, reported the least on foreign workers (only ten articles between 1970 and 1976). In addition, we note that two of these articles were clearly detrimental to the foreign workers and probably could have had a polarising effect. In 1972 for example we find an article with the headline 'Director of French company *Entrepose:* Northerners prefer unemployment. Unions furious about threat to replace Dutch workers with immigrant workers' reporting on a French company that wanted to import foreign workers because the Dutch workers were not prepared to work more hours than was agreed upon in the construction industry collective labour agreement.[8] Another article in 1971 contained a proposal by the NKV that suggested to revise the collective agreements between the Netherlands and the Holland overseas territories (the so-called *koninkrijkinstituut*) so that workers from Surinam and the Netherlands Antilles would no longer automatically have the right to settle in the Netherlands. This would discourage the 'turbulent flood of immigrants' from the region. On the other hand, the NKV also stood up for the foreign workers. For example, one article criticised the repatriation grant for foreigners ('Head of department against repatriation grant for foreigners').[9]

In the second half of the 1970s, after the NVV and NKV transport unions had merged to form the FNV transport union, the tone in which the articles were written changed. If up to then it was mainly a matter of informing the readers of the NKV and NVV journals, in this period there was a clearer stand being taken for the interests of the foreign workers. Headlines such as 'Turks as merchandise. Koops BV has work only for underpaid foreigners';[10] 'Punish discrimination in the labour market';[11]

---

[6] *Het seinlicht*, Vol. 66, No. 23, 1975.
[7] *Steeds voorwaarts*, Vol. 18, No. 17, 1973.
[8] *Richting*, Vol. 21, No. 7, 1972.
[9] *Richting*, Vol. 23, No. 7, 1974.
[10] *Onderweg*, Vol. 3, No. 10, 1978.
[11] *Onderweg*, Vol. 4, No. 13, 1979.

'Illegal workers must bleed for their own exploitation';[12] 'A slave in the inland shipping trade'[13] are regular features.

Also in this period much more attention was given to foreign workers in the journal of the CNV transport union. In the period 1977-80 the journal of the CNV transport union devoted 33 articles to foreign workers, as opposed to fourteen in the journal of the FNV transport union. As to the nature of the articles, they were chiefly a defence of the foreign workers, though in a somewhat more moderate tone. What is striking is that in the CNV there was more information for foreign workers and there were also reports including criticism by foreign workers of the union ('Foreign employees are dissatisfied with trade unions').[14]

Another indicator of the difference in approach between the three trade unions is the facilities that were provided for foreign workers within the different unions. In the early 1970s facilities were created within the CNV transport union specifically for foreign workers. An administrator was appointed to concentrate on the problems of the foreign workers. In 1971 the Foreign Workers Section was established. In this section, problems specific to foreign workers such as housing, religion, etc. were raised and passed on to the Executive Committee. Thus a number of issues were dealt with by the section. The chairman of this section - just as the chairmen of all the other sections - sat in the Industrial Confederation Committee. The chairman of the Foreign Workers Committee also became a member of the Works Council in 1973. Facilities for the benefit of foreign workers were created in the NVV and the NKV as well. Training courses and the like were organised. In 1976 the NVV/NKV, a working group for foreign workers, was established. This working group had difficulty in getting off the ground, however.

A clear difference could be observed between the CNV, on the one hand, and the NVV and the NKV, on the other in the approach taken to foreign workers. In CNV circles, this difference was explained in terms of religious belief. The Biblical motivation to demonstrate concern for foreign workers (defending the weak) was strongly emphasised by the CNV. Their religious character was seen to be an important reason for religious foreigners to join the CNV unions. According to the CNV, the fact that the NKV was also a trade union based on religious principles was of lesser importance in this period. It believed the NKV had abandoned its religious ideology with its (then imminent) fusion with the NVV, and for this reason less importance came to be attached to religious belief in the NVV. My

---

[12] *Onderweg*, Vol. 5, No. 10, 1980.
[13] *Onderweg*, Vol. 6, No. 14, 198_.
[14] *Het seinlicht*, Vol. 69, No. 8, 1978.

assumption, however, is that the merger between the NVV and the NKV did not only have an effect on the religious ideology of the (ex)NKV, but also had a significant effect on the ideology of the CNV. Because of the merger (plans), the CNV came to present itself more in terms of its religious character. The CNV wanted to become a union that organises all believers.

Here the attention is focused on foreign workers who, for the most part, are Moslim or catholic. In this way, however, the door was also opened to autochtone catholic workers, who had no desire to join a socialist-dominated FNV. Through emphasising its basis in christian principles, the CNV wanted to create a distinct profile for itself as opposed to the much larger FNV. At the same time, this was a means of recruiting a new group of members, namely those workers who on religious grounds did not feel at home in the FNV.

Trade Union Policies Regarding Foreign Workers in the 1970s

The policy on foreign workers pursued in the 1970s by the three trade union federations, the NVV, the NKV and the CNV, was formulated in the 1971-75 action programme of the Co-operation Committee of the NKV, NVV and CNV.

Three important starting points for general policies were stated in this action programme. First, a restrictive admissions policy was considered an absolute necessity. From the mid-1960s to the end of the 1970s the government, which was also in favour of restrictive policies, gradually introduced a number of measures that made it more difficult for foreign workers to enter the country. The trade unions supported these restrictive immigration policies of the government.

Second, as foreign labour was viewed as a temporary phenomenon, the foreign workers should be encouraged to return to their country (after the expiration of their contracts). The idea was to bring the jobs to the people instead of taking the people to the jobs. When government promoted the idea of a so-called return bonus for those foreign workers who wanted to return to their home country, the federations stressed the importance of 'return projects' as part of development aid. In collaboration with the Ministry of Development Co-operation and the government of the country of origin, returning migrants received help in setting up small businesses.

This policy met with criticism, however. Since the economic recession of 1967, a debate had developed concerning the significance and function of foreign workers in the Dutch economy. On the one hand, it was clear that foreign workers functioned as a buffer against economic fluctuations.

In periods of economic boom it was fairly easy to attract them in large numbers via official recruitment or via the personal relations of the foreign workers already present in the country. In periods of recession, this recruiting was halted and a number of foreign workers flowed back to their countries of origin because they found no more work here and they were either denied the rights of an unemployed worker or else these rights were granted only for a very short period of time.

On the other hand, the crisis made it clear that the greatest part of the foreign workers in the Netherlands were also indispensable in times of recession. They occupied positions in the Dutch economy that the Dutch workers no longer considered desirable. Even though both government and business - and even the trade unions - had said that it was a temporary mobilisation of foreign workers who, on a temporary basis, would make up for the manpower shortage, already in 1967 it had become clear that foreign labour in the Netherlands was to be granted a longer life than originally expected (Penninx and Van Velzen, 1977).

There was also criticism of the policy in trade union circles. The union secretary for labour policy of the NKV declared himself to be against repatriation grants because he was of the opinion that workers should not be treated like merchandise to be disposed of when they are no longer needed.[15]

Thirdly, foreign workers already present in the Netherlands needed to have the same rights and obligations as Dutch workers. Based on such arguments of equality, they opposed bills proposed by the government that violated the rights of foreign workers. One example of such a proposal was the Foreign Workers Employment Bill (*Wet Arbeid Buitenlandse Werknemers - WABW*) of November 1975. The Foreign Workers Employment Bill stated that employers had to have a work permit for a foreign worker before they could employ that particular foreign worker. Furthermore, the bill set a limit on the number of foreign workers employers were allowed to employ. This meant that foreign workers could only be employed by companies which had not yet reached their limit. The limits set by the government constituted a new instrument the government could use in controlling and reducing the number of foreign workers. The bill was severely criticised because its provisions were considered discriminatory against foreign workers. In a joint statement, the FNV and the CNV, pointed out the 'unacceptable consequences' of the proposed regulations, because they held that foreign workers, once they had been admitted to the Netherlands, should have the same employment opportunities as Dutch

---

15 'Commandeur tegen vertrekpremie voor buitenlanders' [Head of section against repatriation grants for foreigners], *Richting*, Vol. 23, No. 7, 1974.

workers (Penninx and Van Velzen, 1977, 38-40). Despite the severe criticism of the bill, it was passed in 1979, and the trade union federations resigned themselves to the fact.

As far as the protection of the interests of foreign workers in the labour market was concerned - a task which was supposed to fall to the trade unions - much less effort was made. The immediate promotion of the interests of foreigners was still mainly done by welfare organisations for foreigners. Even though union leaders were on the boards of some of these organisations, there were often controversies between the two institutions. The numerous action groups of and for foreigners that came into being at the beginning of the seventies grew in importance (WRR, 1979, 121; Köbben, 1983, 12-3). They drew the attention of the unions to their responsibilities towards foreigners. The federations gradually established special measures for foreign workers. These special measures included, for example, separate consulting hours, the provision of courses for foreigners, the publication of important documents (e.g. forms, folders on legislation, calls for strikes) in different languages, and the creation of special advisory committees. To co-ordinate these activities on behalf of foreign members, the CNV established a Foreign Workers Committee in 1971, and in 1979 it instituted a Secretariat for Foreign Workers. In 1972 the NVV followed with the institution of the Secretariat for Foreign Workers and the Contact Committee for Foreign Workers.

These measures were essentially unable to improve the position of foreign workers (Slob, 1982, 80-1). Notwithstanding these measures, the level of organisation of foreign employees remained low. Less than 15 per cent of foreign employees were union members, as compared with roughly 40 per cent of indigenous workers. According to the unions, this was due to language problems, the temporary nature of their stay, bad experiences with trade unions in the country of origin, difficulties in collecting union dues from people who often changed their address (*Handboek Buitenlandse Werknemers*, 1973). According to (some of the) foreign workers, these secretariats and activities of the trade union federation served as an excuse for some of the member unions to make no real efforts to protect foreigners' interests, but rather to leave this to the secretariats.

In labour conflicts, as well, the interests of foreign workers came to take low priority. The relatively scarce evidence - for example a study by Van de Velde and Van Velzen in 1978 - relating to the participation of foreign workers in a nationwide strike in 1977, shows that the unions made little effort to inform foreigners and involve them in their actions. According to this study, the organisers of the actions, the industrial unions of the NVV and NKV (later merged into the FNV industrial union), made almost no efforts to involve foreigners in the decision making process, even though in some plants foreigners made up 20 per cent of the work force.

The First Attempt to Formulate Minorities Policies

At the end of the seventies the economic crisis got an ever greater grip on social life. In 1979 in the Memorandum on Aliens Policies (*Notitie Vreemdelingenbeleid*), the government expressed the need for even more restrictive policies. High population density was presented as a major argument for restrictions. In addition, however, it was argued that 'the Dutch tradition of hospitality should no longer be expressed in terms of admitting larger numbers of foreigners', but rather 'by setting up immigrant policies stressing the quality of life of those who are already in the country' (*Notitie Vreemdelingenbeleid*, 1979, 8). In other words, the curtailing of immigration was considered a prerequisite for the development of sound immigrant policies.

The long-standing official denial that the Netherlands was in fact a country of immigration had prevented the development of clear immigrant policies. This holds not only for government policy. Up to that point, the labour unions, as well, had never formulated a minorities policy. They had never been able to do this, moreover, because they had always assumed the temporary status of the immigrant labour, and it was also under this condition that they had agreed to the recruitment and employment of foreign workers. This explains why it was only a good twenty years after the recruitment and employment of foreign workers that the trade unions for the first time began formulating a structural integration policy.

The need for coherent policies was publicly recognised in 1979 in the Scientific Council for Government Policies (*Wetenschappelijke Raad voor het Regeringsbeleid*), a high-level advisory body to the government, which advised the government to proceed on the assumption that foreign workers were going to be a permanent part of society. After this report the government hesitatingly came to realise that foreigners had settled permanently and that policies should be directed at overcoming their deprived position.

In The Memorandum on Minorities (*Minderhedennota*) of 1983 the government finally recognised the fact that the Netherlands was an immigration country and that special immigrant policies were needed, irrespective of the nationality of the immigrants and their reasons for immigration (Entzinger, 1985). Government policies focused predominantly on removing disadvantages suffered by ethnic minorities,[16] as well as on creating a multi-cultural society. Employment, education, housing and welfare were stressed in practice.

After the report of the Scientific Council for Government Policies, the trade unions also accepted the fact that the Netherlands was indeed an immigration country and immigrants were going to be a permanent element of the labour market. The change in the official stance of the FNV (the former NVV and NKV) on return migration was typical of this change of course. The initiation of remigration projects, as previously advocated, was abandoned because it had proved to be unproductive.

One important result of the minorities policies of the government and the acceptation of the fact that the Netherlands was indeed an immigration country, was that trade unions as well, following the government, began focusing on all minorities instead of solely focusing on the category of foreign workers which did not include the colonial and other categories of minorities. This was expressed within the FNV by changing the name of the secretariat. Previously it had been called the Foreign Workers Secretariat, but from 1985 onward it was referred to as the Workers' Interests Ethnic Minorities Secretariat.

Following the national policies of the government, the CNV and the FNV gradually started to formulate minorities policies. Within the FNV the basis for such policies was laid in the 1982 memorandum 'Together rather than separate'; the CNV came out in 1980 with the brochure 'The alien within the gate'. The latter CNV brochure was meant to inform the Dutch rank and file about their foreign colleagues, but also to convince foreign workers that this union was serious about promoting their interests and that they should join the CNV. The CNV also recognised the importance of foreigners having their own organisations and the federation was prepared to co-operate with such organisations. The aim of the FNV's memorandum 'Together, rather than separate' was to create a discussion among the member unions in order to formulate more detailed minorities

---

[16] In the former situation immigrant groups in the Netherlands after World War II could be divided in two main categories. Firstly, colonial immigrants from the Dutch Indies, Moluceas, Surinam and the Dutch Antilles. The protection of their interests, social guidance and integration into Dutch society was mainly a matter of the government and (private) welfare organisations (for more details see Lucassen and Penninx, 1994). The trade unions did not perceive this as of special concern to them. Secondly, the so-called 'guest workers'. In the new minorities policies of the government this division into categories was abolished. Those immigrant groups who were socially and economically deprived and were considered as 'culturally different' were brought together into a single group and labelled 'ethnic minorities'. In the late 1980s this term became less popular because of the negative connotation it had according to some people, and the term 'allochthones' came into use.

policies. Only in second instance was it intended to create a basis for these policies among the rank and file. The memorandum concentrated on problems such as housing, education and the integration of foreign workers. Remarkably enough, it did not say very much about ways to improve the labour market position of minorities. Furthermore, the memorandum was rather brief on what the member unions themselves could do to improve the position of foreign workers. Despite the moderate tone of the FNV memorandum, it received much criticism from member unions and the Dutch rank and file. They felt that the memorandum was too much in favour of the foreign workers and did not sufficiently take into account the interests of Dutch workers. The indigenous members of the FNV wanted to show solidarity with foreigners only as long as these foreigners had the same rights and duties as Dutch workers and as long as there was no 'affirmative action'. Moreover, Dutch FNV members seemed to have the idea that by virtue of having longer vacations and other advantages, the foreign workers were in a preferential position. According to the rank and file, in exchange for solidarity, the foreigners had to adapt to Dutch society (De Jongh et al, 1984).

Trade Unions' Attitude towards Minorities in Practice

In society at large the trade union confederations seemed to become even more aware of the importance of their task of protecting the social interests of minorities. They stood up for the social rights of minorities in political debates. For instance, in the SER in 1983, the trade union federations opposed the 'country of residence' principle. According to this principle foreigners would get lower child allowances for children who were still in the country of origin. The action against this plan, taken in co-operation with other organisations, was successful. The government withdrew its proposal to introduce this principle. The price for this solidarity was a general, though minor, lowering of child benefits (De Jongh et al, 1984; Ritsema, 1993).

They also presented themselves as a social movement in the struggle against racism. When in the general elections of 1982 the extreme right Centrum Democratic Party won a seat in parliament, the trade unions publicly raised their voice against racism and right-wing extremism. The FNV, together with the CNV and organisations of and for foreigners, initiated the 'Anti-Discrimination Consultative Body'. As a consequence of these consultations, the federal council of the FNV decided that people who were members of or openly sympathised with racist organisations should be deprived of their union membership. The CNV, as well, stated that within their organisation there was no place for members of an extreme-right party. During the general elections of 1994 the trade unions also spoke out strongly against such parties. Especially when research had shown that quite a number of FNV members (56,000, or 2.8 per cent of the membership) were voting for the Centrum Democratic Party, (which implied that one fifth of Centrum Democratic supporters were also members of the FNV). In the elections of 1994 the FNV brought out a negative voting recommendation, calling on its members not to vote for an extreme-right party. The unions proceeded to put into effect the decision to expel those who were members of or openly sympathised with such parties. The FNV produced a practice-based manual on how to fight day-to-day racism in order to counter racism within its own ranks. Furthermore, a manual was produced especially for staff members charged with education and training. These manuals were distributed among the unions.

Still, as far as the position of minorities in the labour market was concerned, not much had changed. The minorities policies of the government did not succeed in improving the social position of minorities. In addition, the minorities policies of the trade unions did not seem to have much effect. Especially in the labour market, minorities found themselves in a deprived position. Studies had shown that the disproportionate unemployment rate of ethnic minorities could to a significant extent be explained in terms both of direct and indirect discrimination against minorities in recruitment and selection by employers, and in terms of the over-representation of immigrants in the case of (mass) redundancies. The governments' Advisory Committee on Research Relating to Minorities (ACOM) therefore recommended affirmative action in 1986, as had been implemented in the United States and Great Britain (Bovenkerk, 1986). These recommendations of the ACOM were not well received, however. Although the SER in its recommendation of 1987 proposed a number of measures in the area of training immigrants and of joint action by employers and trade unions to improve the position of minorities, it categorically rejected any form of obligatory affirmative action.

An Attempt to Improve the Labour Market Position of Minorities

The government, as an employer, decided in 1986 to implement affirmative action within its own ranks, because in government service the proportion of minorities was also very low. However, the government did not intervene in the private sector. Here the government left it to the social partners to come up with a solution. When it became clear to the government that its reserved attitude towards the private sector was unproductive, it urged the social partners to reach solid agreements. If not, the government threatened to take legislative measures. The threat of possible legislation in the private sector resulted in an agreement between employers and trade unions in the Labour Foundation (*Stichting van de Arbeid*)[17] in 1990, on how to reduce unemployment among minorities. The aim was to reduce unemployment among minorities to the level of that among the indigenous population within five years (the so-called STAR Agreement). In order to attain this objective, 60,000 additional jobs for minorities would have to be created in co-operation with employment agencies. But within two years it became evident that this agreement was not going to work. The STAR Agreement was not considered binding by employers. Furthermore, in collective bargaining the agreements on ethnic minorities were of secondary importance. Priority was given to claims on wages and other primary conditions of employment.

The disappointing results of the STAR Agreement made the government (and also the opposition) prepare for legislation. In 1994 the Promotion of Proportionate Employment Participation by Allochthonous Workers Act (an initiative of the opposition) was accepted. The act obliged firms with over 35 employees to report on the ethnic composition of their workforce, to develop a recruitment policy for minorities, to register migrant employees and to draw up an annual public report on the efforts they had made to employ ethnic minorities and the results of these efforts. They were also required to set up a plan of action, indicating how they intended to implement employee recruitment from minority groups. However, the act did not carry any penalties for firms which did not comply with the act.

As could be expected, the act was severely criticised, both by advocates and opponents of legislative measures. Advocates of legislation stated that the act was not forceful enough, because no penalties were imposed on employers who did not make enough effort to increase the number of allochthonous employees. Opponents of legislation - particularly employers - stated that legislative measures were unnecessary, because of the STAR Agreement. They threatened they would no longer co-operate under the STAR Agreement if there would be additional legislative measures. This threat was not very realistic, because this act was a reaction to the fact that in practice the agreement had hardly produced any results. A remarkable fact is that the trade union federations did not lobby to get the legislation passed. They kept a low profile. They had committed to the STAR Agreement they had made with the employers, and were obviously not in

---

[17] The Labour Foundation (*Stichting van de Arbeid*) consists of representatives of the social partners. It advises the government in social and economic matters.

favour of additional legislation. This led to a somewhat irritated reaction from one of the members of Parliament who had submitted the bill, Green Left member of Parliament Rosenmöller: 'The unions do a lot of talking about what the politicians should do. But when we do something that is not in accordance with their agreements with the employers, then they do not approve' (*De Volkskrant*, 2 February 1994).

The Position of Minorities within the Trade Unions

The STAR Agreement made clear to the trade unions that within their own organisations the percentage of minority employees and also the percentage of minority members in staff position was very low.[18] But minorities inside and outside the trade unions also confronted the trade unions with the fact that within the trade unions far too little was being done on behalf of minorities. In addition to the secretariats, both the CNV and the FNV had installed advisory bodies for minorities affairs. These bodies did not work very well, however. They performed merely an advisory function. The real decisions were taken at the board level, and the advisory bodies had a hard time trying to get their issues on the boards' agendas.

Within the FNV the Workers' Interests Ethnic Minorities Secretariat recognised the fact that the minorities policies of the FNV were (so far) mainly paper policies. It stated that in practice not much had happened to improve the position of minorities within the labour market, and in fact not much had happened even to improve their position within the trade unions. In order to do something about this, the FNV and its member unions formulated a 'non discrimination code' in 1993. The code was intended to be a step in the direction of overcoming the deprived position of migrant workers, both in the labour market and within the trade unions. The main measures proposed were affirmative action to prevent the disproportionate representation of minorities in employment, to improve the selection procedures, and to screen these procedures for direct and indirect discrimination. But once again the practical implementation of the policies proposed remained rather vague. Given the severe criticism that some of the member

---

[18] It is not quite clear to what extent the minorities are organised. The problem with estimating the degree of organisation among ethnic minorities is the way in which the unions register their (migrant) members: if they register on the basis of 'ethnic background' at all, this is done according to the criterion of 'nationality', not 'country of origin'. This means that immigrants with Dutch nationality remain invisible. Various unions are now developing a registration system which also registers 'ethnicity'. This, however, is done on a voluntary basis: those who do not want to be labelled as 'ethnic minority' are not registered as such, and this results in an incomplete picture.

unions (especially the mighty industrial union FNV) raised against the proposed measures, and in particular against affirmative action, it remains to be seen what will come of this code.

Conclusion

In the early phase the trade unions had been rather positive as far as the recruitment and employment of foreign labourers was concerned. But when the number of foreigners increased and when in 1967 an economic recession occurred, the resistance of the trade unions and the rank and file towards recruitment grew. The trade unions employed a number of strategies to reduce the number of foreign workers in the country. Because of their firm position in the national socio-economic decision making process, the trade unions were able to co-regulate the recruitment. The first strategy was to demand equal treatment and equal pay for foreign and Dutch workers alike and to demand that employers must take care of housing for their foreign employees. They did this not only (or not in the first place) out of concern for foreign workers, but rather to make foreign labour more expensive and consequently less attractive for employers. The second strategy was to press the government into making more restrictive immigration policies in order to reduce recruitment. The third strategy was to put emphasis on return migration, not by force but rather by creating and supporting good opportunities for foreign workers to return to their home countries. These strategies did not have very much effect because, in the first place, it turned out that the employers were willing to pay the high cost for foreign labour, and few migrants were actually interested in these return projects. And secondly, due to family reunification, the government's more restrictive immigration policies did not lead to less immigration.

Although on the one hand the trade unions were very much in favour of reducing recruitment, on the other hand they emphasised the integration of foreign workers into Dutch society. However, they did not do very much to protect the interests of foreign workers. Beginning in the seventies, they created a number of activities for promoting the interests of foreigners and they even installed secretariats to co-ordinate these activities, though it was still mainly the welfare organisations that looked after the interests of foreign workers.

At the end of the seventies and the beginning of the eighties, the trade union federations finally came out with minorities policies. They did not start to formulate minorities policies until twenty years after the official start of the recruitment and employment of foreign workers because it was not until that time that the government and the trade unions finally recognised that the foreign workers were not going to return home but would be staying and would become a permanent element in Dutch society. Only then did it become really important for the government to integrate them into Dutch society. Only then did it became clear to the trade unions that minorities would be a permanent part of their membership and that therefore something had to be done to include them not only in society but also within the trade union organisations.

The inclusive attitude of the trade unions in their minorities policies involves three domains. Firstly, the trade unions strove for improvement of the social position of minorities in Dutch society at large. In this domain the trade unions took firm stands: for example their opposition to several laws that worsened the social rights of foreign workers, such as the Foreign Workers Employment Act and the 'country of residence'-principle, their stand against racism, discrimination and right-wing extremism, and their emphasis on good housing and education for minorities. In this domain they presented themselves as a social movement.

With regard to the domain of the labour market, however, the trade union federations were rather vague. Unemployment among the minority populations was very high. In the 1982 minorities policies of the FNV, not many proposals were made to improve this situation. In the 1993 'anti-discrimination code', certain proposals were made in the area of affirmative action. These proposals ran up against much resistance from some of the member unions: especially the powerful industrial union FNV and (part of) the Dutch rank and file.

Finally, with regard to the inclusion of foreign workers within the trade unions, we can note that although the trade unions created special facilities on behalf of foreign workers in order to include them in the trade unions and they even installed special secretariats to deal with and co-ordinate the interests of foreign workers, nevertheless the attention given to issues involving foreign workers still remained very low. Even in 1995 there was still an under-representation of minorities in the rank and file and as employees of the trade unions.

It is clear from the foregoing discussion that the minorities policies of the trade unions revealed an inclusive attitude mainly with respect to integrating the immigrant workers into society. Within their own organisations and within the labour market, however, the trade unions had a much harder time substantiating their inclusivist claims.

References

Bovenkerk, F. (1986), *Een eerlijke kans. Over de toepasbaarheid van buitenlandse ervaringen met positieve actie voor etnische minderheden op de arbeidsmarkt in Nederland*, Ministry of Foreign Affairs, Den Haag.
Castles, S. and Kosack, G. (1973) *Immigrant Workers and Class Structure in Western Europe*, Oxford University Press, London.
Castles, S. and Kosack, G. (1974), 'How the Trade Unions Try to Control and Integrate Immigrant Workers in the German Federal Republic', *Race*, Vo. 15, No. 4, p. 497-514.
CNV (1987), *De vreemdeling binnen de poort*, Third revised edition, CNV, Utrecht.
De Jongh, R., van der Laan, M. and Rath, J. (1984), *FNV'ers aan het woord over buitenlandse werknemers*, 16th edition. Rijksuniversiteit te Leiden, Centrum voor Onderzoek van Maatschappelijke Tegenstellingen, Leiden.
Edye, D. (1987), *Immigrant Labour and Government Policy*, Gower Publishing Company Limited, Hants.
Entzinger, H. (1985), 'The Netherlands', in T. Hammar (ed), *European Immigration Policy. A Comparative Study*, Cambridge University Press, Cambridge, p. 50-88.
FNV (1982), *Samen, beter dan apart. De FNV en de buitenlandse werknemers*, FNV, Amsterdam.
FNV (1985), *FNV-informatiebulletin*, FNV, Amsterdam.
FNV (1992), *Onder ons - gezegd, maar niet meer gezwegen. Naar een implementatie van anti-discriminatiebeleid bij FNV en bonden*, FNV, Amsterdam.
FNV (1993), *Non-discriminatiecode voor FNV en bonden. Richtlijnen voor de vereniging en werkorganisatie*, FNV, Amsterdam.
Janssen, J.W. (1967), 'Opvattingen en beleid van de werkgevers- en werknemersorganisaties', in R. Wentholt et al, *Buitenlandse arbeiders in Nederland*, Spruyt, Van Mantgern en De Does nv, Leiden, p. 33-56.
Köbben, A.J.F. (1983), *De zaakwaarnemer*, Erasmus Universiteit Rotterdam/Van Loghum Slaterus, Deventer.
Kok, H. (1978), 'Beleid belicht', *Tijdschrift voor maatschappijvraagstukken en welzijnswerk*, Vol. 32, No. 6, p. 178-83.
Lucassen, J. and Penninx, R. (1994), *Nieuwkomers, nakomelingen, Nederlanders. Immigranten in Nederland 1550-1993*, Het Spinhuis, Amsterdam.
Marshall-Goldschwartz, A.J. (1973), *The Import of Labour. The Case of the Netherlands*, Rotterdam University Press, Rotterdam.
Martens, A. (1994), 'Migratiebewegingen. Huidige toestand en vooruitzichten. Proeve van theorie voor vakbondspraktijk', *De gids op maatschappelijk gebied*, Vol. 85, No. 6-7.
Ministerie van Binnenlandse Zaken (1983), *Minderhedennota*, Staatsuitgeverij, 's-Gravenhage.
Niessen, J. (1987), *Emancipatie in internationaal perspectief. Het organiseren van Marokkaanse arbeiders in Nederland*, VU Uitgeverij, Amsterdam.
NKV (1975), *Visieprogram*, NKV, Utrecht.
NVV (1974), *Jaarverslag 1974*.
Overlegorgaan NVV-NKV-CNV (s.d.), *Actieprogramma 1971-75*.
Penninx, R. (1979), *Naar een algemeen etnisch minderhedenbeleid? Schets van de sociale positie van Molukkers, Surinaamse en Antilliaanse Nederlanders en mediterrane werknemers en een inventarisatie van het Nederlandse overheidsbeleid*, Voorstudie bij het WRR-rapport 'Etnische minderheden', Den Haag.

Penninx, R. and Roosblad, J. (1993), 'Trade Unions, Immigration and Immigrant and Ethnic Minority Workers in Western Europe 1960-93. A Proposal for an International Comparative Study', Unpublished manuscript.

Penninx, R and Van Velzen, L. (1977), *Internationale arbeidsmigratie. Uitstoting uit 'thuislanden' en maatschappelijke integratie in 'gastlanden' van buitenlandse arbeiders*, SUN, Nijmegen.

Ritsema, G. (1993), *De participatie van Turkse werknemers in de FNV*, Wetenschapswinkel Universiteit van Amsterdam, Amsterdam.

Schumacher, P. (1987), *De minderheden. 700 000 migranten minder gelijk*, Van Gennep, Amsterdam.

Slob, A. (1982), *De buitenlandse werknemers en de Nederlandse vakbeweging*, Vakgroep Sociologie, Faculteit der Economische Wetenschappen, Erasmus Universiteit Rotterdam.

Stichting van de Arbeid (1990), *Méér werk voor minderheden*, Publication no. 6/90, Stichting van de Arbeid, 's-Gravenhage.

Van de Velde, B. and Van Velzen, J. (1978), 'De Nederlandse vakbonden, internationale solidariteit en buitenlandse werknemers: ideologie en werkgelegenheid', in F. Bovenkerk, *Omdat zij anders zijn: patronen van rasdiscriminatie in Nederland*, Boom, Amsterdam/Meppel, p. 166-88.

Van Twist, K. (1977), *Gastarbeid ongewenst. De gevestigde organisaties en buitenlandse arbeiders in Nederland*, In den Toren, Baarn.

Vermeulen, H. and Penninx, R. (1994), *Het democratisch ongeduld. De emancipatie en integratie van zes doelgroepen van het minderhedenbeleid*, Het Spinhuis, Amsterdam.

Vervoersbond CNV (1976), *Leven en werken in Nederland. Een sociologisch onderzoek onder de Turkse werknemers in dienst bij de NS*, Vervoersbond CNV, Utrecht.

Vranken, J. (1990), 'Industrial Rights', in Zig Layton-Henry (ed), *The Political Rights of Migrant Workers in Western Europe*, Sage Modern Politics Series, Volume 25, 4773, Sage, London.

Windmuller, J.P. and de Galan, C. (1979), *Arbeidsverhoudingen in Nederland*, Third revised version, Het Spectrum, Utrecht.

WRR (1979), *Etnische minderheden*, Rapporten aan de regering 17, Staatsuitgeverij, 's-Gravenhage.

Wubben, H.J.J. (1986), *Chinezen en ander Aziatisch ongedierte. Lotgevallen van Chinese immigranten in Nederland, 1911-40*, De Walburg Pers, Zutphen.

X (1973), *Handboek buitenlandse werknemers*, Samsom Uitgeverij, Alphen aan den Rijn.

Zwinkels, A. (1972), 'Buitenlandse arbeiders en vakbonden', *Informatiebulletin werkgroepen buitenlandse arbeiders*, No. 3, p. 71-9.

8 Immigrants as a Special Target: Ambiguity of Solidaristic Action

MAURIZIO AMBROSINI

Immigrant Workers in Italy

Italy, traditionally an emigration country, has faced remarkable immigration phenomena only during the last decade. Just as in other southern European countries, the arrival of people searching for a job seemed mainly to be caused by push factors and to be a consequence of the closing of the national borders by other European countries. In the beginning, these were mostly undocumented immigrants, mainly concentrated in the central and southern regions, where it was easier to establish a precarious existence. They did not appear to be destined to achieve any valuable function in the labour market, except that of feeding the conspicuous sector of the underground economy.

Nevertheless, a new set of dynamics came into play with the 1986 and, above all, with the 1990 immigration laws. Immigrants have had easier access to regular jobs, and they have been moving to areas in the production system where there is a demand for labour which can no longer be filled by the internal migrations of recent decades. According to the most recent INPS (National Institute of Insurance) data - although these do not include agricultural and independent workers - at the end of 1994, 95,686 foreigner workers were regularly employed by firms in Italy, and about 43,000 foreigners were employed as housekeepers by families. Moreover, the tendency which seems apparent from the working insertion numbers for 1995, which state that 111,248 foreign workers either found or changed a job in Italy in that year (in 1993 the number was 85,000, and in 1994 less than 100,000), indicates that this process is continuing to grow.

The majority of employees in factories work in manufacturing industries (49 per cent), followed by services (37.2 per cent), and then by the building industry (13.8 per cent). As for agriculture, we can state that it has accounted for 18.5 per cent of the 1995 work insertions.

The territorial distribution is rather interesting. Of the housework, 42 per cent is concentrated in the Rome and Milan areas, while the rest is scattered all over the country, mostly in the central-southern regions.

By contrast, 70 per cent of the work in factories is concentrated between Lombardia and the northeast (Triveneto and Emilia-Romagna) (table 8.1). This is no coincidence, since at the present time this is the most dynamic region in the Italian production system. In fact, these regions are distinguished by a still strong industrial sector, mostly composed of small and medium-sized firms, belonging partly to the traditional manufacturing sectors, though export oriented, and compelled to emphasise traditional flexibility features: timely adjustment to order requests, high work intensity, shifting and overtime work, and atypical schedules. At the same time, unemployment in these regions is remarkably lower than the national average (5-7 per cent) and is concentrated in certain sectors of the population which are considered to be unavailable or unfit for the roles and conditions that the production system requires. It is within this context that immigrant labour finds its place, with heavy tasks, not infrequently dangerous, harmful and unhealthy, often temporary and, at any rate, precarious; the incidence of shift work is higher than the average, with night and holidays shifts. These are not necessarily underpaid jobs, but they generally correspond to low social status. They are, at least for the most part, '3-D' jobs: dirty, dangerous and demanding (Abella et al, 1995).

At the same time, from a socio-economic point of view, we can assert that the position of immigrants in the production system is indicative of the great territorial differences with respect to the economy and the labour market, as various studies have reported (Zanfrini, 1991; Sciarrone, 1996). If we just focus on the industrial sector, it is no coincidence that Vicenza is the number one province in terms of foreign immigrant employment figures; Brescia is second; Milan comes in only third place; Turin is far behind. Thus, foreign immigrant employment appears to be concentrated for the most part in recently developed areas, and it could be perceived as a sign of dynamism and prosperity in the local economies. In these areas, the demographic decrease of the younger population, together with growth both in terms of education and level of wealth, have led to a decrease in the manual and the unskilled labour supply (Ambrosini, 1995; 1996). On the other hand, internal migration from southern regions has virtually come to an end, at least as far as blue-collar workers are concerned; factors such as lower wages, higher housing costs, loss of the advantages deriving from being part of a larger family group and from the possibility of entering into seasonal activities or some interstice of the underground economy, have made the old emigrant's way of life unattractive to unemployed youth in the south.

Table 8.1 Extra EEC dependent workers in firms, sectors and regional distribution, 1994

Regions	Industry	Building industry	Services	Total
Abruzzo	386	256	517	1,159
Basilicata	25	11	17	53
Calabria	64	18	86	168
Campania	221	50	267	538
Emilia-Romagna	8,045	2,441	4,668	15,154
Friuli-Venez. Giulia	1,847	815	1,815	4,477
Lazio	945	673	4,243	5,861
Liguria	226	396	749	1,371
Lombardia	14,483	2,658	9,758	26,899
Marche	1,887	422	839	3,148
Molise	13	4	14	31
Piemonte	3,530	1,317	2,440	7,387
Puglia	323	66	296	685
Sardegna	31	345	259	117
Sicilia	265	95	714	1,074
Toscana	2,385	784	2,269	5,438
Trentino-Alto Adige	1,253	649	2,895	4,797
Umbria	386	422	461	1,269
Val d'Aosta	41	95	167	303
Veneto	10,412	1,703	3,642	15,757
Total	46,868	13,220	35,598	95,686

Source: ISMU's elaboration of INPS data.

A separate discourse appears necessary to explain immigrants' (and, more precisely, women's) insertion in domestic work. The weakness of the Italian welfare system, the increasing number of women employed in extra-household occupations, the rapid growth of the elderly population - with no appropriate level of social assistance - traditions of care of the household and food, has led to a shift in the demand for domestic help beyond privileged upper middle class, primarily in large urban areas where family and neighbourhood synergies are more difficult to achieve, and where the distances from home to work reduce the time available for care activities. This peculiar segment of the labour market is also fostered by the large abundance of worker supply, fed by migration chains based on family and friendship links. Moreover, the household environment makes it easy to hide undocumented immigrants, as the findings of the last sanatoria (expired on March 31st 1996) largely confirmed.

Migration chains, ethnic organisational ability and the labour supply all concur to explain different occupational outcomes amongst the various national groups and their insertion into the different niches in the job market. Some groups with female supremacy, mostly the Asians and Latin Americans (e.g. Filipinos and Peruvians), have become a standard fixture in many households, though they are striving to expand their range of employment. Industry reveals different components, depending on the local markets. In Veneto we may find mostly Eastern Europeans; in Emilia, North Africans; in Eastern Lombardia, Senegalese and Ghanese. Indians have distinguished themselves in the field of livestock. In Milan, the Egyptians are well settled into the lower services and they have started up a good number of independent activities: 1,500 people, born in Egypt, are registered with the Chamber of Commerce as enterprise managers (Baptiste and Zuchetti, 1994; Ambrosini and Schellenbaum, 1994). The efficiency of ethnic networks, together with their earlier entry into the country and their ability to meet specific needs of the local labour market, explain these results far better than presumed cultural characteristics. In fact, in Milan, the Senegalese are mostly illegal street vendors of poor quality items and thus almost beggars, while a few miles away, in Bergamo and Brescia, they are the best integrated immigration components in industry. Moroccans and Tunisians, generally regarded as unstable and unreliable workers in Lombardia, are, to the contrary, well established in the industries of Emily, and so on.

The third type of factor that contributes to explaining immigrant insertion into the labour market is the activities of groups, associations, and local institutions. All these organisations, in compensating, as far as possible, for the feebleness of state action and the absence of the entrepreneurs, have sometimes created certain minimal external conditions that have allowed the immigrants to settle and the labour supply to meet the labour demand. This has been accomplished, for example, by organising public dormitories, by helping with bureaucracy, employers, health services, and so on. Among these agencies, which I have defined as 'supporting institutions', we find the trade unions, which to varying degrees are involved, with more or less incisiveness and connections, with many local institutions and social forces.

The following figure shows how supply is meeting demand, highlighting the above-mentioned role of the supporting institutions.

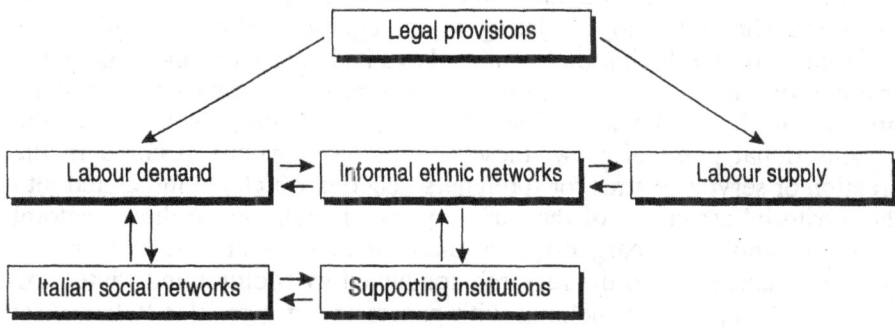

Figure 8.1 **Labour supply and demand, and the role of the supporting institutions**

Trade Union Policy toward Immigrants: Solidarity Centred on Social Needs

The attitude of the Italian trade unions toward immigration has developed within a context which is completely different from that of other countries. Martens has pointed out that the immigration of workers into industrialised societies has been stimulated by employers, and that the trade unions have responded in two different ways: first by trying to contain foreign labour, and then by campaigning for equal conditions with native workers (Martens, 1996; see also Bastenier and Targosz, 1991).

In Italy, however, immigration has been regarded neither as a threat to native workers nor as a remarkable phenomenon from the economic point of view. Especially in the beginning, the actions undertaken in behalf of this population were considered to be rather the result of a political attitude which has never limited itself to the mere protection of the workers, but has also been interested in a variety of broader political issues (peace and disarmament, southern regions development, protest against oppressive regimes, the fight against terrorism, etc.) and has endeavoured to extend the radius of trade union action to include the socially disadvantaged (the unemployed, temporary workers, persons evicted from their homes and, above all in recent years, the retired, who make up a considerable portion of the membership of trade union organisations). Indeed, in the seventies the trade unions were the first to welcome the Chilean and Argentine political refugees, some of whom found work within the trade unions or other related activities.

Theirs was ultimately a solidaristic action that had little to do with the traditional activities of the trade unions and that had even less to do with European Union ideology relating to immigration. Thus, the initiatives undertaken by the Italian trade unions have had charitable and solidaristic features that have often served to compensate for the faults and procrastination of the public authorities (Mottura and Pinto, 1996). From the organisational point of view, these actions have usually resulted in the creation of service centres for foreigners - centres which are integrated into the territorial structures of the trade unions (though, not in those sectoral structures entitled to bargain). The functions these centres have been carrying out, according to the research conducted by Mottura and Pinto, are, in order of importance: helping with papers to get a regular Italian visa; searching for housing accommodations; and solving all the problems related to the first housing situation. It is only in the fourth and fifth places that we find all the work-related activities, and these for the most part concern individual protection and employment problems, while negotiating, organising conflicts, and the managing and promoting of mass protests are even less frequent activities.

The usual interlocutors in these kinds of actions would logically be public institutions and not the employers. The target public can be characterised as being composed of foreigners, regardless of their working condition or legal status. Furthermore, all the services supported by the trade unions have played an important role in the process of legalising undocumented immigrants. During this process, trade unions have often operated in co-operation with associations and volunteers' groups, promoting both actions and demonstrations. This has happened in the struggle against racism, as well in the campaign of the trade unions for new laws to facilitate the legalisation of immigrants who have already entered Italy, or, again, when the trade unions committed themselves to direct supportive actions, such as gathering money to buy or restore houses for immigrants. Just as voluntary services associations have done, the trade unions have also supported interethnic organisations, as well as groups of immigrants coming from the same country and anti-racism groups; CISL, for example, has supported an association for immigrants (ANOLF) that is now a stable presence in many local contexts. It is in charge of aggregation ('socialisation') and activities of cultural promotion activities, preparing the path to initial enrolment ('pre-unionisation'). Continuity, communication and the overlapping of trade unions and social organisations are emphasised by the fact that many trade union operators are also individually engaged in social activities.

A number of foreigners have been employed as operators, either full or part-time, in the trade unions, especially in service centres for immigrants (132, according to Mottura and Pinto, but this data is underestimated), even when their nationality only partly coincides with that of the most prevalent groups. These are mostly educated and politically engaged individuals who have often arrived in Italy as students or refugees. Hence, among them we may find Chileans, Palestinians, Eritreans, Lebanese and Iranians, who belong to national groups that are scarcely represented in the highly variegated and heterogeneous immigrant scene in Italy. Whereas, at least according to the available data, far more numerous groups, such as the Filipinos, Tunisians and Chinese, do not yet have any union representatives from among their ranks. The activities of these foreign operators, rather limited in their extent, take on a much greater significance when we note their territorial concentration: trade unions operating in the northern and central regions, with higher concentrations of foreigner workers, are those that more often are staffed with foreign operators. These operators play a significant representative and intermediary role with respect to the immigrants, the trade unions and local societal needs. Immigrants are variously inserted into trade union organisations, and are also unified in informal regional and national boards ('co-ordinations'). These boards mainly serve a 'lobbying' function, or else they provide a 'public voice' which speaks up for the interests of the various immigrant communities. Their ability to have an effect on trade union bargaining and organisation policies, though, does not seem to be particularly great.

At any rate, we can affirm that these trade union policies have had a number of positive aspects, namely:
- making the trade unions become protagonists in the most relevant social issues of contemporary Italy, and reaffirming their role as 'political actors' capable of conceiving and creating enlarged circles of solidarity;
- the protection of immigrants, without discrimination, whether they be employed or unemployed, whether legal or illegal;
- putting the trade unions into contact with the world of social associationism and voluntary services. This a very dynamic sector of Italian society, but on the whole the trade unions lag far behind in attaining the strategically desirable frequency of contact with these movements and organisations;

- drawing trade unions closer to the immigrant population, which has quickly learned to regard them as allies and a source of support in the difficult process of integrating themselves into Italian society;
- promoting at least a small minority of immigrants to qualified positions as union operators or cultural mediators.

However, the increasing numbers of immigrants entering the labour market in the strongest regions of the Italian economic system is highlighting the limits of this policy, which is unavoidably tied to the phase when immigration was perceived as a social problem, as a consequence of external causes (push factors), and not as connected with the Italian labour market. In Piemonte, for example, CGIL, CISL and UIL have proposed a document on immigration policy, which is to be discussed with the regional government. In this text the basic demands were referred to broad social questions: in the migration process are described as follows: entrance, stay, return, co-operation to development of the countries of origin, and citizenship rights. Work was included under the first question (entrance), and was discussed essentially in terms of legalising those immigrants who have already entered the country and been informally inserted into the economic system. A second document proposed by trade unions (*Piemonte: proposals on social protection*) began presenting data on immigrants' regular hiring reduction (occurred in 1993), and then put forward proposals regarding: the presence of immigrant representatives in local consultations on migration; requesting constant updating by public personnel operating in different services sectors; the insertion of foreigner operators as cultural mediators in public offices; initiatives on housing problems. Recently (late 1996), a new platform was formulated by the regional co-ordination office for immigrants of CGIL, CISL and UIL. Once again, the platform starts with data on work and then puts forward several requests to the Region on housing solutions; participation and representativeness; the role of associations; school and education; initiatives and cultural activities. I think this example allows us to glimpse beyond the positive aspects and see the limits and the still prevailing position of trade unions toward migration phenomenon:
- trade unions tend to mix with other agencies of social solidarity, with the volunteers world, and even with the immigrant offices of local institutions. Hence, as a foreigner union operator told us: 'Immigrants cannot tell a trade unionist from a social worker';
- immigrant policies often risk having volunteering and specialised features which are often dependant, among other things, on the operators' individual motivation, with no adequate links to bargaining strategies and the general policies of trade union organisations;

- the operators' competence tends to be oriented more towards social and legal problems, and thus more towards relationships with public actors, than towards working for the protection of immigrants on the job. They generally know everything about legalisation procedures, but very little about the 'black' and 'grey' work done by immigrants;
- the employers are not adequately involved and aware: as a matter of fact, they get the greatest benefit from immigrant labour but, apart from individual cases of personal availability or commitment, they are completely absent, as social actors, from any discussion dealing with migration and the improvement of the integration of immigrants;
- and then there is a growing risk of remaining stuck in the logic of charity - 'doing something *for* the immigrants' - when the distinctive task of the trade unions should be to 'do something *with* the workers' and, moreover, to organise individually weak actors, thus enabling them to become collective actors, capable of bargaining for their own working conditions.

Immigrant Attitudes toward Trade Unions: Looking for Social Protection and Support

The merits and faults of the distinctive approach taken by the trade unions to dealing with the immigrants are reflected in the attitude of the population that is the target of the previously described policies.

We could say that attitudes of acknowledgement and consent towards trade unions are unexpectedly widespread among immigrants who have not lived in Italy for more than ten years and who have hardly had any chance to participate to major protests in the factories. Mottura and Pinto estimate that nearly 100,000 foreigners were enrolled in Italian trade unions at the end of 1994. This is a rough and underestimated figure: at the moment, as one national leader of CISL recently declared to me in an interview, CISL alone has about 80,000 foreign immigrant members. On the other hand, the survey we conducted in Milan and Brescia in 1991 (IRER, 1991) identified in that period a trade unionisation rate higher than 20 per cent in a population whose legal workers were a minority who often had not yet been living in Italy for more than one year. Many members are still not receiving any salary. They have asked the trade unions to satisfy needs that are different from labour protection. They have had the chance to adhere to territorial structures, instead of to industrial structures, paying the low enrolment fees that Italian union confederations apply in these cases.

It is even more interesting to note that foreigners who have regular jobs, assiduously submit requests to the trade unions to have them check the legality of their working conditions, to provide precise explanations, and to compare different situations. They appear to be anything but subdued and inexperienced, and they frequently ask the trade unions to open individual disputes to defend their own rights. As an employer from Lombardia told me during an interview: 'They had just arrived, and yet they knew how to read their payroll'. It is mostly within the local contexts where trade unions are traditionally deep-rooted and strong that immigrant worker participation in the trade unions is rather high.

There are new cases of foreign immigrant representatives in trade unions, elected by their fellow workers, in spite of language problems, occupational instability and difficulties in areas outside of the workplace, primarily in the area of housing.

But immigrant attitudes on the whole express essentially the fear of being exploited and the desire to be fairly treated. They ask trade unions for protection and support, and they seldom become activists or assume militant attitudes.

A study of immigrant labour in the area of Bergamo - a province in eastern Lombardia with a consistent production system which, though export oriented, remains traditional - has made it possible, among other things, to analyse the relations between immigrants and trade unions (Zanfrini, 1996). I will discuss the major findings that emerged from this study.

It has generally been confirmed that trade unions are perceived to be structures which function to meet individual and specific needs, but which are not perceived as a collective good and don't give rise to feelings of belonging or of co-responsibility.

Secondly, immigrants' opinions about their relationship with trade unions are largely influenced by the level of availability and empathy perceived in the operators' behaviour, so that personal and relational factors affect the choice of initial enrolment, stable membership, as well as disaffiliation or change of organisation. Ideology, on the other hand, seems to play a minor role in the making of these decisions.

Operators in trade union services, then, by solving many personal and family problems, and by responding to requests that go beyond the sphere of work, end up playing a referential role. Trade unions are often confused with other institutions and service agencies, such as local and voluntary service organisations. There are some organisations that, from the immigrants' point of view, are interchangeable since, in any case, they are always looking for people ready to listen to them and help them in a disinterested and concrete way. The fact that in Bergamo, as anywhere else, the same people work in different institutions, contributes to this perception: in fact, numerous operators are also involved in voluntary services, and they are often members of multiethnic associations.

It is very common for people to request help from trade unions for personal disputes with employers, and these requests are usually motivated by claims related either to pay or to job loss.

In some sectors, such as commerce and housework, individual disputes are particularly numerous. As one trade unionist told us: 'They use the 'tam-tam' system among themselves. If the dispute is successful, the next day or in a week's time, all the people they know are knocking on our door. They come in crowds. They have their disputes. They are very demanding. And afterwards they have their own meetings. An Italian housekeeper, on the other hand, who has already had one dispute, will think twice before starting a second one. But these immigrants come back again and again. And, God knows, they do suffer from unfair conditions'.

Disputes are often a reaction to unfair working conditions, but they can also be used to achieve other less noble ends, which themselves, however, are the result of a multitude of difficult and atypical working conditions: immigrants often accept a salary inferior to the contractual minimum in exchange for living accommodations. When the working relation comes to an end, they initiate a dispute to recover the money that was not paid, including interest. This is a perfectly justifiable behaviour, and it is also understandable from the immigrant's point of view, but it is awkward for the trade union operators, who feel used and who thereby develop difficult relationships with the employers.

Back to the Future? Toward New Union Policies for Immigrant Workers

The future of relations between trade unions and immigrants seems to depend on the ability of the organisations to develop policies which I would characterise as 'strictly trade unionist': in other words, policies which are more integrated into the strategy of those industry structures that determine collective agreements and which are more in accordance with the typical bargaining action of trade unions. This should happen without losing the broad-minded values, the attention to the social and political dimensions of the immigrants' conditions, as well as the links with the world of voluntary groups and associations. These are elements that have all contributed to determining the immigrants' conditions in the course of the previous phase. In other words, there is the need to maintain the sense of the specificity of the immigrants' condition, while developing a more appropriate concern for their condition as a working population, all the while inserting this specificity into the whole of the bargaining actions.

This is not an easy task for those organisations that, in Italy as in other countries, have always essentially insisted on the common interests of the workers, fearing the risk of a fragmented working class. There has been a struggle for the acknowledgement and protection of specific groups, such as women and youth. The risk, in this case, is to redirect them to specialised commissions or workshops, with no other consequence on the general bargaining strategies of the unions. As far as immigrants are concerned, the risk is that the same specialised services of which they are the target, will continue to work as specialised units and will be destined to follow a certain type of issues, with little influence on or links with bargaining and workers' organisational strategies.

Some local experiences go in the direction that we propose and, above all, the awareness of the importance of this transition for the improvement of immigrant workers' rights is spreading among the unions. First of all, they tend to increase the enrolments in industrial sector federations, rather than the enrolments in territorial service agencies. Secondly, some programmatic papers have been elaborated by immigrant and national commissions, which have underlined some of the priorities and bargaining solutions. This is the case, for instance, in the areas of: accident prevention; specific training; bargaining for holidays that will be long enough to allow immigrants to return to native countries (possibly by means of biennial accumulation); modifying schedule and shifts to facilitate religious practices; diversifying cafeteria menus in the firms; verifying professional skills possessed by already working immigrants (Regional Commission for Immigrants, Emilia Romagna, 1993).

However, we shouldn't forget the difficulties, both political and cultural, of this inversion:
- first of all, it is not easy for trade unions to talk about immigrants' rights in a country with more than 2.7 million unemployed, concentrated for the greatest part in regions considered among the poorest in Europe;
- even in the northern regions, solidarity with the immigrants is not a very popular message: we shouldn't forget that regions like Lombardia and Veneto, where a conspicuous number of immigrants are concentrated, are the same regions where 'Alga Nod' finds the bulk of its electoral following - and Alga Nod is probably also the most popular party among working-class and blue-collar groups;
- great social problems still need to be solved - such as housing, which hinders integration processes in local communities. These processes are difficult in any case, since even if we recognise the role immigrants play in the production system, we still tend to affirm that work is the least problematic sector of the immigrants' condition;

- the transition from solidarity with the immigrants, as poor and needy individuals, to a statement of equal rights and an acknowledgement of their professional skills, requires a further cultural step, and can also lead to conflict with the interests of the native workers. At the current time and in the current workplaces, interethnic conflicts are almost non-existent, because immigrants are accepting jobs for which there is no supply of Italian workers, and they do not really compete for promotion or for more qualified duties and supervising roles;
- there is an organisational viscosity, in consequence of which specialised services and offices, created following a certain logic, have acquired experience in doing only some things but not others, and they tend to reproduce the same model that they have been trained for.

Nevertheless, I believe that the crucial transition to a new phase of trade union policies on immigrant employment is actually the evolution from a kind of solidarity that is quite close to social assistance (as well deserved and necessary as this may be) to an approach in which solidarity will be expressed in terms of those bargaining instruments which are most characteristic of trade union action.

Table 8.2 has been drawn up to outline the differences between the 'protective' and the 'bargaining' model.

It might seem fallacious or vaguely *passé* to think about trade union policies for immigrants in apparently narrow-minded bargaining terms rather than in the broad context of a praxis that is very open to social problems extending beyond the narrow sphere of work. Nevertheless, this goal readjustment seems necessary to free trade union policies from an excessive mingling with the functions of other service agencies and other social counselling offices, and to fit the problem of immigrant workers into the mainstream of bargaining strategies, as well as into the totality of trade union policies, thus resolving the ambiguity of a supply of specialised services which have little to do with the genuine issues determining the future of the trade union movement.

Table 8.2 Differences between the 'protective' and the 'bargaining' model

Approaches	Charitable protection	Bargaining
Organisation centre	Trade union horizontal structures	Trade union vertical industrial structures
Target	Foreign immigrants in general	Working immigrants
Focus	Response to social needs	Promotion in the workplace
Counterparts	Public institutions	Employers
Linked actors	Voluntary services organisations, anti-racism groups	Other trade union structures
Operators' professional profile	Nearly social operator	Typically trade unionist
Type of action	Legal and bureaucratic advice, network co-operation with public and no-profit institutions, pressure on public institutions, direct help	Bargaining, initiating individual and collective disputes, representatives training on the spot
Matters of evidence	Legal status, housing, family reunions, creation of associations, employment	Rights in the workplace, recognition of competence and professional promotion, recognition of diversity in the workplace

References

Abella, M.I., Park, Y. and Bohning, W.R. (1995), *Adjustment to Labour Shortages and Foreign Workers in the Republic of Korea*, International Migration Papers, ILO, Geneva.

Ambrosini, M. (1995), 'Il lavoro', in ISMU, *Primo rapporto sulle migrazioni 1995*, Angeli, Milano.

Ambrosini, M. (1996), 'Il lavoro', in ISMU, *Secondo rapporto sulle migrazioni 1996*, Angeli, Milano.
Ambrosini, M. and Schellenbaum, P. (1994), *La comunità sommersa. Un'indagine sull'immigrazione egiziana a Milano*, Quaderni ISMU 3.
Baptiste, F. and Zuchetti, E. (1994), *L'imprenditorialità degli immigrati nell'area milanese: una ricerca pilota*, Quaderni ISMU 4.
Bastenier, A. and Targosz, P. (1991), *Les organisations syndicales et l'immigration en Europe*, SYBIDI papers no. 111.
Colasanto, M. and Ambrosini, M. (eds) (1993), *L'integrazione invisibile. L'immigrazione in Italia tra cittadinanza ecoonomica e marginalità sociale*, Vita e Pensiero, Milano.
IRER (1991), *L'immigrazione extracomunitaria in Lombardia: il ruolo delle politiche regionali*, Milano.
ISMU (1995), *Primo rapporto sulle migrazioni 1995*, Angeli, Milano.
ISMU (1996), *Secondo rapporto sulle migrazioni 1996*, Angeli, Milano.
Martens, A. (1996), 'Trade Unions and Migrant Workers in Europe: a Changing Ideology as a Reflection of Variable Principles', in P. Pasture, J. Verberckmoes and H. De Witte (eds), *The Lost Perspective? Trade Unions between Ideology and Social Action in the New Europe*, Vol. 2, Avebury, Aldershot, p. 200-17.
Mottura, G. and Pinto, P. (1996), *Immigrazione e cambiamento sociale. Strategie sindicali e lavoro straniero in Italia*, Ediesse, Roma.
Regional Commission for Immigrants, Emilia Romagna (1993), mimeo, Bologna.
Sciarrone, R. (1996), 'Il lavoro degli altri e gli altri lavori', *Quaderni di sociologia*, Vol. XL, No. 11, p. 9-49.
Zanfrini, L. (1991), 'L'immigrazione straniera nei mercati del lavoro', in IRER, *L'immigrazione extracomunitaria in Lombardia: il ruolo delle politiche regionali*, Milano.
Zanfrini, L. (ed) (1996), *Il lavoro degli 'altri'. Gli immigrati nel sistema produttivo bergamasco*, Quaderni ISMU 1.

9 Organised Labour and the Black Worker in England: A Critical Analysis of Postwar Trends

SATNAM VIRDEE

This chapter provides a critical analysis of the historical and contemporary relationship between black[1] labour and the British trade union movement. It begins with an investigation of how, during the era of postwar capitalist expansion and initial black labour migration, many trade unions and white labour colluded with employers to ensure that the traditional strategy of operationalising restrictive practices to maximise the terms and conditions of existing members took on an added dimension when the ideology of racism was utilised to exclude migrant labour from key sectors of employment, especially skilled work. This chapter goes onto describe the industrial action taken by black workers from the mid-1960s against such racist exclusionary practices and the continued failure of the organised labour movement to support such action. However, important wider developments affecting the trade union movement served to create the conditions for a shift in policy and practice to take place in relation to black workers by the mid-1970s. In addition to discussing the nature of these developments, particular attention is paid to a dispute that demonstrated working class unification could be achieved between black and white labour. The chapter then moves on to discuss the contemporary relationship between white and black labour during an era which has witnessed a weakening of trade unionism. Particular attention is paid to the rise of 'bureaucratic' self-

---

[1] I use the term 'black' to reflect the social construction developed by Asian and Caribbean trade unionists during the period under discussion. However, when necessary, I also distinguish between different 'ethnic' groups by using the terms 'Asian' and 'Caribbean'. That all of these terms are social constructions and not 'objective' categories is captured by the controversy in the USA and Britain over self-categorisation (see Davis, 1991; Modood, 1988).

organisation within one public sector trade union, NALGO, and its relative effectiveness in tackling the problems faced by black workers and its implications for working class unification. The chapter concludes with an analysis of recent measures undertaken by the TUC to build solidarity between black and white labour.

Racist Exclusionary Practices as a Feature of Workplace Relations

Large-scale migration from the Caribbean and the Indian subcontinent began in the late 1940s and early 1950s and was facilitated through a combination of both 'push' and 'pull' factors of which the most important were the relative underdevelopment of the migrant worker's country of origin and the demands of an expanding postwar British economy (Castles and Kosack, 1985). According to Fryer (1984, 373), 'In some industries the demand for labour was so great that... black workers were actively recruited in their home countries'. Employers such as the British Transport Commission, the London Transport Executive, the British Hotels and Restaurants Association and the Regional Hospitals Board all established arrangements with Caribbean governments to ensure a regular supply of labour (Ramdin, 1987, 197). By 1958 and a decade of black labour migration, there were 125,000 Caribbean and 55,000 Indian and Pakistani workers in Britain (Fryer, 1984, 373).

As was mentioned briefly above, the immediate postwar British economy underwent a period of great capitalist expansion characterised by full employment and rising real wages. Under such economic conditions, labour supply was scarce, and many trade unions found themselves in a favourable position when it came to negotiating with employers for improved terms and conditions for their members. Through the employment of the traditional strategy of restrictive practices, they were further able to restrict the supply of labour and thereby ensure that the price of labour already in an industry remained high. If such restrictive practices did not succeed, then trade unions and shop stewards could resort to short, unofficial strikes, commonly known as 'wildcat' strikes which were normally sufficient to ensure success in negotiations with employers in this period (Hyman, 1972; Beynon, 1984).

Precisely because such trade union strategies were normally sufficient to ensure improved living standards, this period was characterised by a growth in working class reformism amongst much of the white trade union movement, with little sense of a common class consciousness that transcended individual workplaces. This was reflected in that nearly all the leaders of the major unions were right-wing and advocated a policy of caution (Callinicos, 1982) whilst the increasingly important shop stewards responsible for bargaining at the plant or workgroup level also articulated 'restrictive, sectionalist attitudes and the defence of local rather than general [working class] interests' (Verberckmoes, 1996, 223).

While such a strategy no doubt served to secure improved living standards for many groups of white workers, the evidence from this period suggests that many trade unions and white workers actively colluded with employers to ensure that such restrictive practices took on an added racist dimension by excluding migrant labour from key forms of employment, especially skilled work (Sivanandan, 1982; Fryer, 1984; Wrench, 1986; Ramdin, 1987). Elements of the organised labour movement drew on the prevailing ideology of racism in society and used it to institutionalise a major division within the trade union movement between black and white labour. According to Fryer (1984, 376), 'in many industries, white trade unionist's resisted the employment of black workers, or insisted on a 'quota' system limiting them to... about 5 per cent.' As a result, and despite the heterogeneous class structure of the migrating populations, they came to overwhelmingly occupy a position at the bottom of the British class structure, undertaking work of an unskilled or semiskilled nature (Daniel, 1968; Smith, 1977). The Caribbeans worked in the service industries such as transport, health and hotels while the Indians and Pakistanis found themselves in factories, foundries and textile mills (Sivanandan, 1982, 5).

When such racist practices came under threat of being breached, white workers would take industrial action to defend them. In February 1955, in the West Midlands, white workers at the West Bromwich Corporation Transport system began a series of Saturday strikes in protest against the employment of an Indian trainee conductor (Ramdin, 1987, 200). Similarly, and also in 1955, white transport workers in Wolverhampton decided to ban all overtime from the 1st September in protest against the increasing employment of black recruits. The local union contended that the 5 per cent quota which had been informally agreed with management had been breached because 68 of the 900 total workforce were black workers (Ramdin, 1987, 200). There were also other racist exclusionary practices agreed between white trade unionists and employers which served to impact adversely on black workers: the principle of 'last in first out' was not applied at a time of redundancy if it meant that white workers would lose their jobs before black workers (Wrench, 1986, 6).

One might have expected that an important source of opposition to such disunity in the organised labour movement may have been the Trade Union Congress (TUC) - the federation of British trade unions. However, according to Miles and Phizacklea (1977, 3) the TUC and its executive body:

> The General Council failed to acknowledge that there existed considerable hostility towards black workers amongst white trade unionists and increasingly came to adopt the position that the problems arose from the immigrant's refusal to 'integrate'.

Apart from isolated cases such as the campaign mounted by black community organisations and some individual whites against the operation of a 'colour bar' introduced by white bus workers in Bristol in 1955 (Dresser, 1986), there is little evidence of organised resistance to such racist practices from Caribbean, Indian and Pakistani workers during this period. According to Sivanandan (1982, 5) 'resistance to racial abuse and discrimination on the shopfloor was more spontaneous than organised'.

Overall then, this initial period of migration and settlement between 1948 and 1964 was characterised by the organised labour movement being severely divided by racism with white workers and trade unions utilising the ideology of racism and actively colluding with employers to restrict the job opportunities open to black workers.

Black Self-organisation as a Strategy of Resistance to Racism: 1965-73

Whilst the period between 1965-73 continued to be characterised by continuing divisions between black and white workers, it also provided the first evidence of organised resistance to racist exclusionary practices by black workers themselves. An important catalyst in the development of such organised black resistance was the arrival in Britain in 1965 of the two leaders of the American anti-racist movement: Malcolm X and Martin Luther King met with representatives of the black British community and encouraged them to establish organisations to combat racism. Two national anti-racist organisations were established: the Racial Action Adjustment Society (RAAS) influenced by the ideas of Malcolm X and the philosophy of radical black nationalism and the Campaign Against Racial Discrimination (CARD) influenced by the teachings of Martin Luther King (Sivanandan, 1982).

The first evidence of organised resistance to racism and exclusionary practices in the workplace emerged shortly afterwards. In May 1965, Asian and Caribbean workers went on strike at Courtauld's Red Scar Mill in Preston, Lancashire. This was a large rayon mill which produced industrial textiles. About one-third of the total workforce of 2,400 were of Caribbean or Asian origin. However, they were overwhelmingly located in the tyre cord spinning department where they formed two thirds of the total workforce; the rest being Italian and East European migrants.

Towards the end of 1964, TGWU officials entered into negotiations with management about a new productivity agreement for workers in the tyre cord spinning department. On 15th April 1965, management, the TGWU official and the four local stewards representing the tyre cord spinning department came to an agreement which amounted to the workers having to work more machines for proportionately less pay. In effect, the agreement amounted to a 50 per cent increase in work for a 3 per cent increase in pay. The workers were furious and refused to accept the agreement. Eventually, the Caribbean and Asian workers walked out in protest leaving only the European workers to carry on working. However, not only did the TGWU fail to support the black workers by refusing to make the strike official, they actively colluded with management to state that the strikers did not have a legitimate grievance. The vice-chair of the factory-wide shop stewards organisation used racist imagery by telling a reporter that the dispute was 'tribal' in nature while another steward claimed that '"several hotheads" are stirring up trouble for their own selfish interests' (cited in Foot, 1965, 6). Although there was no support forthcoming from white trade unionists, the black workers were able to continue the strike for three weeks through the active support of RAAS and individual white radicals.

Another strike by black workers quickly followed which again illustrated both trade union inaction and racism. In 1967, at a Coneygre Foundry in the West Midlands, management precipitated the strike by Asian workers through the use of racially discriminatory redundancy procedures: management refused to operate the generally accepted trade union principle of 'last in first out' and selected 21 Indians - and no whites - to go. However, the Asian workers' trade union, the TGWU, refused to make the strike official and rejected the idea that racial discrimination was involved. Moreover, white workers in another trade union, the Associated Union of Foundry Workers (AUFW), refused to support the strike and continued to cross the Asian workers' picket line, encouraged by the local AUFW official, who explained that his members were not involved in the redundancies. Despite the obvious lack of solidarity shown by white trade unionists, the strike was sustained by the support provided by other Asian workers and the Indian Workers Association (IWA). It was this support from the community that eventually forced management to take back all of the 21 Asian workers made redundant who wished to return (Wrench, 1986, 7; Duffield, 1988, 86-9).

Whilst Asian and Caribbean workers were beginning to collectively resist the racist exclusionary practices that had served to exclude them from skilled work, elements of the white working class were being mobilised to consolidate further such divisions within the trade union movement. When Enoch Powell, a former health minister who had been responsible for the recruitment of Caribbean nurses to Britain in the 1950s (Fryer, 1984) made an inflammatory speech in Wolverhampton in April 1968, warning against the dangers of 'race mixing', 'London dockers struck work and marched on parliament to demand an end to immigration. Three days later they marched again, this time with the Smithfield meat porters' (Sivanandan, 1982, 24).

A substantial number of strikes by black workers continued throughout the late 1960s and early 1970s and according to Sivanandan (1982, 22) 'nearly all of them showed up trade union racism'. Due to the constraints of space, only two of the more prominent disputes are discussed in this chapter.

The high-point of black self-organisation as a strategy to combat racism and exclusionary practices was the Mansfield Hosiery Mills dispute which took place in the East Midlands in October 1972. Mansfield Hosiery was a company that made pullovers. The process involved three groups of workers: the 'knitters' who earned the most and who were all white and the 'runners-on' and the 'bar-loaders' who earned the least and were overwhelmingly of Asian origin. The 500 strong Asian workforce had effectively been denied access to the best-paid jobs on the knitting machines over a long period of time. In October 1972, a strike was called over this and other anomalies in the payment system. Management responded by agreeing to train two Asian knitters and so the strike was called off. However, almost immediately the white workers on the knitting machines, fearing that their jobs were under threat, came out on strike. According to Moore (1975, 75) 'This strike had been promised by the local union leadership if the whites were, in his words, "flushed out" of the knitting jobs'. Under pressure from the local union, the National Union of Hosiery and Knitwear Workers (NUKW), management backtracked on its promise to train Asian knitters and instead offered them a small increase in pay. This resulted in the escalation of the dispute with 400 Asian workers including Asian workers from another company factory coming out on strike in sympathy. The company immediately dismissed these workers and began to recruit white trainees for the knitting jobs. It was at this point, that the union was forced to request that management stop recruiting 'scab' labour. However, it was not until the strikers occupied the union offices that the union finally made the strike official although it still refused to call out its white membership. Again the Asian strikers had to rely on the support they received from the Asian community rather than the trade union movement to sustain the strike. Eventually, they succeeded in winning all their demands and 28 Asian workers were selected for training as knitters (Moore, 1975, 75-7; Sivanandan, 1982; Wrench, 1986, 7).

This strike had important repercussions within the trade union movement. After almost a decade of organised resistance to racism by black workers, the first indications of a change in attitude within parts of the labour movement appeared. The Mansfield Strike Committee, which was born out of the dispute but which also comprised representatives of black political organisations, Asian workers from different areas as well as the strikers themselves, was central to the organisation of a major conference of trade unionists held in June 1973. Three hundred and fifty delegates from all the major unions as well as representatives from the black community organisations came together in Birmingham and from this merged the 'National Committee for Trade Unions Against Racialism' (NCTUAR) (Sivanandan, 1982).

However, this initial recognition of the need to challenge racism in the trade union movement was not solely attributable to the industrial struggles being waged by black workers; rather it also reflected the growing politicisation of important elements of the white organised labour movement which helped to create the political conditions for the ideas of anti-racism to gain at least a toehold in the trade union movement.

Government Attempts to Curb Trade Union Activity

The late 1960s and 1970s represented an era of continual government attempts to curb trade union activity (Marsh, 1992, 33). Political debate had come to focus on the trade unions and the development of industrial relations at the workplace level, in particular the increasing ability of shop stewards - unpaid trade union officials - to carry out bargaining in an informal manner at plant or workgroup level. The government contended that such a development encouraged disorder, and especially 'wildcat' strikes. As a result, the 'shop steward became a symbol of trade union irresponsibility, and workplace conflict came to be seen as *the* major problem underlying poor productivity performance and Britain's economic problems' (Eldridge et al, 1991, 25).

Although the Donovan Commission reported in 1968 that shop stewards were not the problem but poor management, the Labour government continued to seek a legal resolution to the problem of 'wildcat' strikes. In 1969, the government published a white paper called 'In Place of Strife' which outlined its proposals for curbing such activity. However, the bill was defeated due to the pressure brought to bear on the government by the trade union movement. Nevertheless, the Conservative government which took office in 1970 was able to successfully introduce an Industrial Relations Act in 1971 which replaced the collectivist laissez faire industrial relations with a comprehensive legal framework intended to restrict conflict (Verberckmoes, 1996).

The response of the trade union movement could not have been expected. According to Callinicos (1982, 18) 'attempts by the government and employers to... control the shop stewards led... to the biggest class confrontations for half a century'. The number of strike days lost increased dramatically: from an average of less than 4 million days a year during the 1950s and 1960s to 24 million days lost in 1972 alone (Grint, 1991, 172, table 7). Moreover, a significant proportion of these strikes were qualitatively different from those of the 1950s and 1960s: in the context of an economy that was heading rapidly into recession, the strikes were essentially defensive in so far as they sought to defend existing terms and conditions of employment rather than improve them as in the 1950s and 1960s. Relatedly, there was an uneven shift in consciousness taking place amongst key elements of the working class: in particular there was a growing move beyond the sectionalist class consciousness of the 1950s and 1960s to a form of class consciousness which recognised the importance of working class unity and collective action, if resistance to attempts to regulate the power of trade unions were to be successful. Critical to the organisation of this resistance were socialist trade unionists who had a political outlook that was internationalist in character. Verberckmoes (1996, 227) argues that, 'The relative strength of left wing tendencies in the trade union movement definitely played a mobilising role in the explosion of strike activity between 1968 and 1974'. By the mid-1970s, it was estimated that 10 per cent of all trade union officials were Communists (Verberckmoes, 1996, 227).

Although it was this growing politicisation of key elements of the white working class based around the ideology of working class solidarity coupled with ten years of independent struggle by black workers against racist practices that created the political conditions necessary for the ideas of anti-racism to seep into the trade union movement, it was the fear of growing far-right influence in the trade unions that finally resulted in a qualitative shift in the policy and the practice of the TUC and the affiliated trade unions from the 'problem of integration' to the 'problem of racism'.

The dispute that caused widespread concern about farright influence in trade unions took place in a firm called Imperial Typewriters in Leicester. Eleven hundred of the 1,650 work force were Asians, a large proportion from East Africa. Against a background of long-standing grievances over low pay, bad conditions and racial discrimination, a strike began involving 40 Asian workers. Management however, refused to recognise their grievances. Accompanying the general dissatisfaction with working conditions was the strikers' concern that there was only one Asian member of the shop stewards committee. Therefore, they also demanded the right to elect their own steward. However, the striker's union, the TGWU, publicly declared its opposition to the dispute and refused to make the strike official arguing that the Asian workers had not followed the correct negotiating procedures. The TGWU convenor in the factory refused to speak to the strike leaders on the grounds that union members were only eligible for election as shop stewards after two years membership. This lack of support from the union merely served to solidify Asian worker unity and over 400 workers were now out on strike. A critical factor in the dispute was the involvement of the farright, National Front, whose members regularly came to the factory gates to intimidate the picketing strikers and support the white workers who continued to work. Despite such intimidation and the refusal of the trade union to support the striking workers, the Asian workers were sustained throughout their action by support from the Asian and Caribbean communities. After three months on strike, management conceded to their demands (Miles and Phizacklea, 1978; Wrench, 1986).

Tackling Racism through Collective Working Class Action: 1974-79

Change followed quickly after the dispute. At the 1974 TUC Annual Conference, the General Council announced that it had submitted oral evidence and a memorandum to the Select Committee on Race Relations and Immigration where it acknowledged for the first time that black workers were subject to racism and discriminatory practices. Moreover, this evidence went on to state that 'trade unions should actively oppose racialism within their own ranks', both from the organised far-right and rank and file white trade unionists (Miles and Phizacklea, 1978, 199).

At the 1975 TUC Annual Conference delegates from several affiliated unions made speeches denouncing the racism and activities of the National Front and called upon trade unionists to warn their members of the dangers of racism to working class solidarity. Although a minority current of opposition to racism in the trade union movement had existed since the late 1950s (Miles and Phizacklea, 1978, 202), this opposition grew in the mid-1970s with local committees and trades councils becoming increasingly concerned about the need to tackle racism in the labour movement.

To further this aim, the General Council announced just after the 1975 TUC Annual Conference the establishment of a new sub-committee of the General Council, the Equal Rights Committee, whose main responsibility would be to develop policies to promote equal opportunity. Additionally, in 1975, the TUC General Council established the Race Relations Advisory Committee to work with the Equal Rights Committee on issues relating to 'race relations' (Miles and Phizacklea, 1978, 198). In July 1976, the General Council issued a press release which called for the trade union movement to actively tackle racial discrimination:

> Much needs to be done to eliminate the discrimination and disadvantage facing ethnic minorities and for their part the General Council are advising affiliated unions about steps they should take to strengthen the organisation among immigrant and black workers and unity between work people (Miles and Phizacklea, 1978, 199).

Hence, by the mid-1970s, there was growing recognition amongst increasing elements of the white trade union movement that working class solidarity could only be built by actively opposing the racism and disadvantage faced by black workers. This was demonstrated in practice in the Grunwick dispute (see Phizacklea and Miles, 1978; Sivanandan, 1982; Ramdin, 1987 for a more detailed discussion of this dispute). Grunwick Film Processing Laboratories Ltd was a firm that developed and printed colour films. There were two factories in Willesden, northwest London which employed about 440 people. The dispute lasted from August 1976 to July 1978 and was led by Asian women who worked long hours in appalling conditions for low wages.

An argument with a manager led to the dismissal of one worker which in turn led three others to walk out in protest. From this, the strike rapidly escalated with nearly a third of the 440 workers out on strike. The strikers decided to establish a union, and after advice from the local Trades Council, they joined the Association of Professional, Executive and Computer Staff (APEX). Once they had become members, APEX immediately made the strike official by announcing that strike pay would be given to the strikers. Grunwick's management responded by dismissing all the strikers. However, the strikers refused to concede and responded by stating 'If you refuse to talk to us, we will turn off all the taps, one by one, until you have to' (Phizacklea and Miles, 1978, 270). To do this, they required support from other workers and according to Ramdin (1987, 289), 'Support for the strike from sections from the British labour movement was quick and widespread'.

At the 1976 TUC Annual Conference, Roy Grantham, General Secretary of APEX called upon the entire trade union movement to give its support. He explicitly raised the issue of racism, arguing it was central to the exploitation that Asian workers suffered. Similarly, Tom Jackson of the Union of Post Office Workers (UPW) pledged support and agreed to stop the delivery of mail coming in or out of Grunwick which would effectively prevent the business from operating. It was not only senior white trade unionists that offered support to the strikers but also large numbers of rank and file white workers. Ramdin (1987, 292) describes how the local people of Brent responded with 'donations from Milliner Park Ward, Rolls Royce Works Committee, Express Dairies, Associated Automation (GEC), TGWU, the UPW Cricklewood Office Branch'. Importantly, on 1st November 1976, the post office workers in the UPW stopped delivering Grunwick's mail.

Despite such solidarity, Grunwick's management refused to concede to the strikers' demands. As a result, the strike committee responded by calling for the trade union movement to support a mass picket of the firm for one week in June 1976, which they hoped would cause maximum disruption during Grunwick's busiest trading period. The call for support did not go unheeded with up to 20,000 pickets (overwhelmingly white) supporting the Asian women strikers. Additionally, local post office workers continued to stop the delivery of mail coming in or out of Grunwick despite having their strike pay withdrawn by their union, the UPW. Contracted TGWU drivers, working for the police on picket duty at Grunwick refused to drive them into the firm's premises. Delegations of London dockers and Yorkshire miners came to the picket lines and supported the strikers. Mick McGahey, the then Scottish NUM leader called for workers to close down Grunwick and told the strikers 'You will win as night follows day... the whole of the Scottish miners will come here if necessary' (cited in Ramdin, 1987, 300). The dispute continued for two years until July 1978 and demonstrated clearly that, under conditions of high class struggle, it was possible for white workers to undertake collective action in support of black workers.

Throughout the late 1970s, there was a growing recognition amongst key parts of the organised labour movement that racism served only to weaken the trade union movement and that it had to be actively addressed. Several major unions including the GMBATU, BIFU, NUT, NATHFE, NALGO, and the CPSA issued positive statements against racism and set up bodies to monitor equal opportunity policies. Similarly, a resolution passed at the 1977 TUC Annual Conference called upon the General Council to conduct a campaign against racists in trade unions. This led to the production of a General Council statement on racism in 1978 and in 1979, the TUC sent a circular to all unions that had not adopted policies on tackling racists in their unions to do so (Labour Research, 1983, 182-3).

However, events were to take a turn for the worse for the British trade union movement in May 1979 when the Conservative Party came to power 'at least in part, because of the unpopularity of the unions as a result of the [1978/79] Winter of Discontent' (Marsh, 1992, 53). I shall now turn to explore how the trade union movement responded to black workers against a background of a severe weakening in their strength.

The Rise of 'Bureaucratic' Self-organisation in Trade Unions: 1980-95

Once in power, a two-pronged attack was mounted by the Conservative government to reduce the power of trade unionism. First, there was an increased 'willingness to confront union power through macho-management holding out against strikes' (Eldridge et al, 1991, 86), especially in the public sector (Batstone, 1988). Hence, the early 1980s were characterised by key sections of the organised labour movement being defeated in long, drawn out disputes including those in the steel industry, the civil service, the health service, the mining industry and British Leyland and GCHQ. Second, there was the extensive legal assault on collective and individual rights and the imposition of restrictions on various forms of unionised political activity (Eldridge et al, 1991; Ackers et al, 1996). Between 1979 and the end of 1993 nine pieces of legislation, including five Employment Acts had removed all barriers to the 'free and flexible' labour market lauded in new-right Conservative ideology (Wrench and Virdee, 1996, 240). The significance of Conservative employment legislation has been to deny workers access to resources of collective power (Smith and Morton, 1993, 99) and thereby 'increase employers discretion to determine the terms of the employment relationship' (Ackers et al, 1996, 17).

The resulting impact of these changes has been to severely weaken the strength of the British trade union movement and, in particular, the ideology of working class solidarity that had gained strength throughout the 1970s. Secondary industrial action, the single most potent means of success in pursuing a strike has been outlawed while the number of days lost to strike action has suffered a dramatic decline from 29,474 millions days in 1979 to just over 4 million days a year throughout the 1980s (except for 1984 and the yearlong miners dispute) (Eldridge et al, 1991, 124, table 5.3).

Against such a backdrop of severe setbacks for the organised labour movement, one might have expected trade union work on tackling racism to have declined in importance. However, this has not proved to be the case: as a result of the lessons learnt by the British workers movement in the 1970s, coupled with the continuing pressure brought to bear on the trade union movement by many anti-racist black and white trade unionists, combating racism continues to be an important feature of many British trade unions' work (Virdee, 1992; Virdee and Grint, 1994; Wrench and Virdee, 1996).

The most important development of the last 15 years in tackling racism in the workplace and trade unions has been the establishment of specific organisational structures in most large trade unions to encourage the development of a layer of black worker activists (Virdee and Grint, 1994). The underlying assumption leading to the creation of such 'bureaucratic' forms of self-organisation is that only those experiencing a particular form of oppression, in this case, racism, can most effectively lead resistance to it. As one delegate to the first NALGO Black Members' Conference put it:

> It is not self-organisation for the sake of being separate. It is to ensure exactly the opposite - that black issues and rights are addressed by the trade unions [to] which we belong in a way acceptable to black members. As black trade unionists we believe in the principles of solidarity and support but these can never happen if they work only for some (cited in Virdee and Grint, 1994, 209-10).

In order to investigate this claim, I carried out depth interviews with black and white stewards in three London branches of NALGO - the local government worker's trade union. This union was chosen because debates about the relative effectiveness of 'bureaucratic' self-organisation in tackling racism have advanced furthest within this union (Virdee and Grint, 1994). Thirty black stewards and fifteen white stewards were interviewed and asked to prioritise objectives related to both conventional trade union and anti-racist polices. Table 9.1 below ranks the top three priorities of each of these stewards.

Table 9.1 Stewards' priorities ranking in top three (in per cent)

	Black stewards (n=30)	White stewards (n=15)
Tackling racial harassment	78	53
Implementing equal opportunity policies	74	33
Helping the low paid	74	47
Protecting jobs	30	73
Improving working conditions	26	60
Negotiating higher pay	11	27
Increasing union membership	11	7

Given the relatively small number of black and white stewards, I make no claim that the differences between black and white stewards are valid across unions. Nonetheless, the data does suggest that the differences were systematic and it is particularly noticeable that black stewards were more consistently concerned with what may be typically regarded as 'black issues' than were the white stewards. For white stewards it was the more conventional 'bread and butter' issues of trade unionism, such as protecting jobs and conditions of employment, that appeared to be most significant. Clearly, given the occupational position of many black workers, such bread and butter issues are also important to them, but the implication is that black stewards do perceive of their role differently from white stewards. As one leading black activist with many years of trade union experience reflected:

> White stewards have singularly failed to adequately represent black workers. That is why black self-organisation in the trade union movement has absolutely mushroomed over the last few years. Black workers have places and have seen how things have changed because of self-organisation. The black shop steward is better able to represent black members who have suffered racial harassment than any white steward - no matter how well-meaning that white steward is. That's because the black steward also shares the experience of racism.

Nevertheless, it is equally important to emphasise that a significant layer of white stewards also recognised the importance of tackling racism: half the white stewards considered tackling racial harassment to be one of their three most important objectives. The interviews revealed that most of these anti-racist white stewards held radical political views and saw anti-racism as an essential element of trade union solidarity. Furthermore, these white stewards also attached importance to the actions and influence of black stewards and black organisations in helping to develop solidarity between black and white workers. As one white steward commented:

> I didn't always support autonomous black members' groups because I thought it was possible to challenge racism by united activity through the normal trade union channels... But now I see them as essential in the fight against racism.

What is particularly important here is to note the significance attached to the learning process. Self-organised groups are not self-evidently advantageous to trade unions but their actions may demonstrate such utility. In the words of a second white steward:

> I've seen a lot of activists who were in the black NALGO group who are now active in the mainstream of the union. That's very important to me... I feel I should support them in their battles.

Another advantage of 'bureaucratic' self-organisation has been its ability to encourage trade union activity amongst a layer black workers who previously would not have considered taking part. Attendances at most union meetings are notoriously low: between 5 and 15 per cent with an average of 7 per cent being a representative figure for all unions (Salamon, 1987, 135). In one of the NALGO branches studied, prior to the existence of the Black Workers' Group, a mere 5-10 black workers were regular attenders at the branch meeting. By 1988, despite staff cuts of 25 per cent due to local government cutbacks, black attendance was regularly 100 - amounting to 30 per cent of the entire branch membership. Relatedly, the number of black work representatives and shop stewards rose from 1 in 1982 to 30 by late 1989. The local branch secretary estimates that two thirds of the current black representatives had come through the ranks of the Black Workers' Group, while one third had risen through the more conventional trade union channels.

A very similar experience was detected in a second NALGO branch. In 1986, before the Black Workers' Group existed, only two of the branch's shop stewards were black, three years later there were seventeen. As one black member noted:

> I joined NALGO because a Black Worker's Group existed... they act as a support structure to black workers in a union that still hasn't properly addressed the issues of racism within its ranks... I believe the Black Workers' Group enables black members to come into the union mainstream more easily.

Hence, the impact of 'bureaucratic' self-organisation at a local grassroots level has been advantageous in several ways. First, it appears that black stewards who have come through the ranks of local black workers' groups appear to attach a higher priority to tackling racism and other issues which impact directly on black workers. Second, in addition to directly facilitating the increase in the number of black workers in positions of representation, self-organisation also appears to have encouraged greater attendance at union meetings amongst rank and file black workers. Importantly, self-organisation has also played a key role in constructing a unity between black and white activists, with a layer of white stewards recognising the importance of self-organisation to black members and to the development of a united trade union.

Continuing Change in the TUC

Anti-racist trade unionists have not only pressed individual trade unions to adopt more positive policies towards the tackling of racism, but also the TUC. Briefly, the TUC has taken action in four key areas. First, they have established specific organisational structures to facilitate the participation and representation of black members. Hence, since 1991, an annual TUC

Black Workers Conference has been held. Trade unions affiliated to the TUC send delegates in proportion to the size of their union. The largest section of the TUC Race Relations Advisory Committee (RRAC), established in the mid-1970s to facilitate and promote the interests of black trade unionists in the TUC, is elected at this conference. Additionally, in 1993, the General Council of the TUC agreed to include three additional positions for black trade unionists of which one must be filled by a women. According to the 'race' equality policy officer at the TUC 'These structural changes allow ethnic minority workers to have access to and participate in the governing body of the organisation' (personal communication with author: 20th January 1997).

Second, the TUC has attempted to create a layer of black and white lay and full-time officials who are capable of tackling racism and promoting equality of opportunity in the workplace. Regular training courses for shop stewards and full-time officials are held at the TUC National Education Centre in north London. Several documents have been produced for use on such courses (TUC, 1989; 1990a; 1990b; 1996a). In 1995, the TUC initiated a programme of regional 'race' discrimination seminars designed to help union full-time officials and lay officials to develop an understanding of the law, identify cases of 'race' discrimination and learn to take practical steps needed to support such cases at industrial tribunals.

Third, the TUC has given increasing attention to tackling racial discrimination within its own organisation. They have undertaken several measures, such as adopting an equal opportunities policy; conducting an ethnic monitoring exercise of TUC employees; ensuring that all job vacancies are advertised in the ethnic minority press; and ensuring that staff responsible for recruitment are trained in equal opportunity recruitment and selection. A particularly important development has been the creation of the post of the aforementioned 'race' equality policy officer who specialises in 'race' equality issues and who works in the TUC Equal Rights Committee.

Fourth and finally, although Britain, unlike many parts of Europe, does not have a farright party of national electoral significance, the farright British National Party (BNP) has managed to secure significant electoral support in a number of socially-deprived inner-city wards, particularly in east London. The election of the BNP candidate, Derek Beackon, in a Millwall ward of the London borough of Tower Hamlets in September 1993, meant the farright gained their first seat on a local council since the National Front won two seats in May 1976 in Blackburn (Virdee, 1995). As a direct response to this development, the TUC launched a 'Unite Against Racism' campaign. In one of its documents, the TUC declared that racism was 'unacceptable in a civilised society' and recognised the important role trade unions could play to prevent it: 'unions have access to millions of people and are ideally placed to spread the word against racism, and to popularise anti-racism' (TUC, 1996b). The first public event in this campaign took place in March 1994 and was a demonstration organised in the London borough of Tower Hamlets - the area of highest racist activity. A second demonstration was organised in October 1995 in Manchester where over 10,000 people from all over the country protested against racism. In July 1996, over 80,000 people attended a festival in Finsbury Park in North London where the message was 'value and respect the contribution made by all communities that make up Britain'.

Conclusion

For many writers in Britain, the trade union movement and the white working class have been written off as an agency of progressive social change. It has been contended that they derive both an economic and an ideological benefit from the racism that black workers have been subjected to (Rex and Tomlinson, 1979, 276; Gilroy, 1987, 246). From the historical and contemporary evidence provided in this chapter, it is clear that such a conclusion is rather premature and only partially correct. There is little doubt that the traditional trade union strategy of utilising restrictive practices to maximise the terms and conditions of employment of workers already in a particular industry took on an added dimension when the ideology of racism was used to exclude black migrant labour from key areas of work, especially skilled employment. In this sense, parts of the white working class were an active social agent in the manufacture of this division in the British trade union movement. Moreover, this division was amplified by the industrial action taken by black workers against such racist exclusionary practices from the mid-1960s and the failure of the trade union movement to support them.

However, as I have shown in this chapter, the attempts to curb trade union activity in the late 1960s and early 1970s served to generate a politicisation of key elements of the white working class. In particular, there began to take place a significant shift beyond the narrow, sectionalist consciousness of the 1950s and 1960s to a more politicised form of class consciousness which recognised the importance of class solidarity and collective action. This major development coupled with almost a decade of industrial struggles against racism by black workers and growing fear of farright influence in trade unions created the 'pre-conditions' for the ideas of anti-racism and solidarity between black and white labour to gain a wider audience in the trade union movement. By the mid-1970s, the TUC and some affiliated trade unions explicitly recognised that working class unification could only be achieved through combating racism, and, as a result, policies and practices were introduced to tackle racists in trade unions. However, the most visible manifestation of solidarity between black and white labour came during the course of the Grunwick dispute when thousands of white workers including miners, dockers, transport workers and post office workers actively supported Asian women on strike. This dispute demonstrated that amidst the growing politicisation of parts of the organised labour movement, many white workers were able to overcome the ideology of racism and act in solidarity with black workers.

Despite the weakening of trade union power in the 1980s and 1990s, the organised labour movement has continued to recognise the importance of tackling racism. Through the creation of 'bureaucratic' forms of black self-organisation within affiliated trade unions as well as in the TUC; campaigns against racism in the wider community and the organisation of training courses for trade union activists on tackling racism, the organised labour movement has ensured that there are a significant number of black and white anti-racists activists in British trade unions today.

References

Ackers, P., Smith, C. and Smith, P. (1996), 'Against All Odds? British Trade Unions in the New Workplace', in P. Ackers et al (eds), *The New Workplace and Trade Unionism: Critical Perspectives on Work and Organisation*, Routledge, London.
Batstone, E. (1988), *The Reform of Workplace Industrial Relations. Theory, Myth and Evidence*, Clarendon Press, Oxford.
Beynon, H. (1984), *Working for Ford*, Penguin, London.
Callinicos, A. (1982), 'The Rank-and-File Movement Today', *International Socialism*, Vol. 17, Autumn, p. 1-38.
Castles, S. and Kosack, G. (1985) *Immigrant Workers and Class Structure in Western Europe*, Oxford University Press, London.
Daniel, W.W. (1968), *Racial Discrimination in England*, Penguin, London.
Davis, F.J. (1991), *Who is Black? One Nation's Definition*, Pennsylvania State University Press, Pennsylvania.
Dresser, M. (1986), *Black and White on the Buses: the 1963 Colour Bar Dispute in Bristol*, Bristol Broadsides, Bristol.
Duffield, M. (1988), *Black Radicalism and the Politics of De-Industrialisation. The Hidden History of Indian Foundry Workers*, Avebury, Aldershot.
Eldridge, J., Cressey, P. and MacInnes, J. (1991), *Industrial Sociology and Economic Crisis*, Harvester Wheatsheaf, Hemel Hempstead.
Foot, P. (1965), 'The Strike at Courtaulds, Preston: 24 May to 12 June 1965', *IRR Newsletter*, Supplement July.
Fryer, P. (1984), *Staying Power. The History of Black People in Britain*, Pluto Press, London.
Gilroy, P. (1987), *There Ain't no Black in the Union Jack*, Hutchinson, London.
Grint, K. (1991), *The Sociology of Work*, Polity Press, London.

Hyman, R. (1972), *Marxism and the Sociology of Trade Unionism*, Pluto Press, London.
Labour Research (1983), 'Race at work', *Labour Research*, July, p. 182-3.
Marsh, D. (1992), *The New Politics of British Trade Unionism. Union Power and the Thatcher Legacy*, The Macmillan Press Ltd, London.
Miles, R. and Phizacklea, A. (1977), *The TUC, Black Workers and New Commonwealth Immigration: 1954-73*, Working Papers on Ethnic Relations no. 6, Research Unit on Ethnic Relations, University of Bristol, Bristol.
Miles, R. and Phizacklea, A. (1978), 'The TUC and Black Workers: 1974-76', *British Journal of Industrial Relations*, Vol. 16, No. 2, p. 195-207.
Modood, T. (1988), 'Black, Racial Equality and Asian Identity', *New Community*, Vol. 14, No. 3.
Moore, R. (1975), *Racism and Black Resistance in Britain*, Pluto Press, London.
NALGO (1986), *Proceedings of the First National Black Members' Conference*, NALGO, London.
Phizacklea, A. and Miles, R. (1978), 'The Strike at Grunwick', *New Community*, Vol. 6, No. 3, p. 268-78.
Ramdin, R. (1987), *The Making of the Black Working Class in Britain*, Gower Publishing Company Ltd, Aldershot.
Rex, J. and Tomlinson, S. (1979) *Colonial Immigrants in a British City*, Routledge and Kegan Paul, London.
Salamon, M. (1987), *Industrial Relations. Theory and Practice*, Prentice Hall International, London.
Sivanandan, A. (1982), *A Different Hunger. Writings on Black Resistance*, Pluto Press, London.
Smith, D.J. (1977), *Racial Disadvantage in Britain*, Penguin, London.
Smith, P. and Morton, G. (1993), 'Union Exclusion and the Decollectivisation of Industrial Relations in Contemporary Britain', *British Journal of Industrial Relations*, Vol. 31, No. 1, March.
TUC (1989), *Tackling Racism. A TUC Workbook*, TUC, London.
TUC (1990a), *Racial Harassment at Work*, TUC, London.
TUC (1990b), *Race Discrimination at Work*, TUC, London.
TUC (1996a), *United Against Racism in Europe*, TUC, London.
TUC (1996b), *Unite Against Racism Campaign*, TUC, London.
Verberckmoes, J. (1996), 'The United Kingdom: Between Policy and Party', in P. Pasture, J. Verberckmoes and H. De Witte (eds), *The Lost Perspective? Trade Unions between Ideology and Social Action in the New Europe*, Vol. 1, Avebury, Aldershot.
Virdee, S. (1992), *Part of the Union? Trade Union Participation by Ethnic Minority Workers*, Commission for Racial Equality, London.
Virdee, S. (1995), *Racial Violence and Harassment*, Policy Studies Institute, London.
Virdee, S. (1997), 'Racial Harassment', in T. Modood et al, *Ethnic Minorities in Britain. Diversity and Disadvantage*, Policy Studies Institute, London.
Virdee, S. and Grint, K. (1994), 'Black Self-Organisation in Trade Unions', *Sociological Review*, Vol. 42, No. 2, May, p. 202-26.
Wrench, J. (1986), *Unequal Comrades. Trade Unions, Equal Opportunity and Racism*, Policy Papers in Ethnic Relations no. 5, CRER, University of Warwick, Coventry.
Wrench, J. and Virdee, S. (1996), 'Organising the Unorganised. "Race", Poor Work and Trade Unions', in P. Ackers et al (eds), *The New Workplace and Trade Unionism: Critical Perspectives on Work and Organisation*, Routledge, London.

10 The French Trade Union Movement and the Struggle Against Racism in the Workplace

PHILIPPE BATAILLE

A number of unionists from the French Democratic Workers' Confederation (Confédération Française Démocratique du Travail, or CFDT) recently became concerned by the phenomenon of increasingly intense expressions of racism in the companies where they worked, and informed their union organisation of their concern. However, both tradition and conviction prevented the union organisation from accepting these reports of ideological deviation, not in the least because they sometimes involved union members, and in certain cases even militants. In view of the French ideological context and the chronic weakening of the anti-racist movement in France (Galissot, 1986), it also seemed clear that a simple reminder of correct standards by the confederation leadership would not be enough. After all, in calling upon their confederation, the unionists were drawing the attention to the fact that racism was taking hold amongst workers, and that it was carving out a place for itself within work relations and work structures. The CFDT therefore decided to go ahead with a national enquiry to investigate the ideology at the bottom of the racist behaviour which was being seen amongst workers.[1]

---

[1] Scientific responsibility for this research was entrusted to Michel Wieviorka (Cadis, EHESS). Philippe Bataille has directed the enquiry, assisted by Anne Sauvayre and Claire Schiff. Michel Caron, national secretary of the CFDT, assisted by confederation secretaries Stéphane Larigon and Francois Scrozynski, have helped its progress. They have ensured a link between the researchers and the union sections involved in the research.
This research is financed by the European Union, in particular by the Social Action Fund (Fonds d'Action Sociale or FAS) and the Population and Migration Department (Direction population et migrations or DPM).

The confederation was not claiming to have uncovered this problem - it was already a long-standing one among workers - but was admitting that racist conduct was now more frequent within work relations and work structures, whilst the researchers were working on the theory that there had been a shift in the ideology at the bottom of such conduct. But for this working hypothesis, the traditional means of unionist intervention would have sufficed to respond to the calls from the grassroots, and it would not have been necessary to undertake an inquiry.[2]

The Militants' Call

The militants denounced racist attitudes affecting immigrant or illegal workers, obliging the unionist movement to repeat its message of fighting to defend the status and rights of these workers (Gallissot, 1988). However, these attitudes equally affected French people of foreign origin, notably those of Algerian or Moroccan background, or indeed people originating from the Antilles or from the island of La Réunion - in other words, coloured French people. Subsequently, other aspects of the research would confirm that the legal distinction employed in relevant statute between French and foreign workers in fact has become blurred in such a way as to set up a distinction introducing racial criteria, especially that of skin colour, into work structures and access to jobs.

With this realisation, the lack of knowledge of the logic behind racist ideas among workers became clear. But there is no doubt that the CFDT was likewise taken by surprise by the National Front's announcement that it was organising unionist structures to convey its party line within the unionist context (*Le Monde*, 24 and 25 March and 3 April 1996). This declaration of intent is a clear indication of the National Front's political desire to ally to its own ideology sentiments and attitudes which have become widespread among workers. Further, as far as advancing the cause of racism among workers is concerned, the present economic situation, which provides considerable cause for concern, would be placed under the banner of an ideological conflict revolving around crucial and long-standing issues to do with work relations and work structures.

In this context, the point of an investigation into racism among workers goes far beyond the simple recording of existing situations. For the CFDT it is in fact a question of tracing the broad outlines of possible unionist

---

[2] To give some idea about the scope of the inquiry, it gathered material from transcripts of two hundred individual conversations, to which were added some fifty group meetings which were likewise recorded and transcribed.

action against racism and xenophobia. Thus, without alarmism about recording the current situation, and without excessive indulgence in the course of contacts with the unionists, our approach rests on a double observation, placing the unionist in an analysis of his current practice after having recorded the logic which he sees unfolding and which he claims to wish to reverse. In other words, our analysis, made in close collaboration with unionists who received us in their workplaces, aims to be of help to them as they proceed to act in future. And we will of course observe what becomes of the actions they instigate.

Xenophobia and Racism

Racism as an ideology rests on the basic principle of the existence of different races. However, the essential point about the racist is that he attributes positive or negative value to racial criteria that are the product of ideology. The appeal to the notion of races - ranked in order, with a distinction between 'superior races' and 'inferior races' - is without scientific foundation. For instance, extreme right-wing groups in Northern Europe nowadays refer to a Celtic race, and a considerable specialised press describes with admiration its supposed biological features, such as pale skin, clear eyes and a virtuous character. Worse still, the workings of ideology lead to a confusion whereby the idea of race ends up being used to define national spaces. The expedient resorted to here is an appeal to the idea of culture. When people talk about 'French culture', they refer to the historical reality of the construction of a national space with certain characteristics. But they create the impression that this culture is the reflection of a distinct ethnic character. However, if one may talk of a 'French culture' at all, to attribute an ethnic character to it is highly misleading and a product of racist thinking. Confusing the concept of race with that of culture, present-day racist theories refer to ethnicity and use the concept to further their cause, while other people fighting against the selfsame cause at the same time proclaim their own right to an ethnic identity (Wieviorka, 1997). From this contradiction originate any number of confusions and polemics turning round the crucial question of how to define the identity of one group or another. However, these debates remain somewhat crudely defined features on the French intellectual and political scene (Wieviorka, 1993).

Taking advantage from the present-day uncertainties, racist ideology has set itself the task of racialising social relations. France today has not of course reached the end point of this tendency, and at most there exist certain political groups who keep it alive and meet with a certain degree of electoral success (1997 general election). Therefore, in analysing racism in social relations, it is better to start out by referring to xenophobia, and to draw the attention to the thinking of certain politicians who have attempted to connect this pervasive attitude with an ideology which is undeniably based on racism as far as they are concerned (*Le Monde*, 13 September 1996), and whose electoral success is increasing (*Le Monde*, 27 May 1997). For us, looking at racism in this light raises the question of the reality of a racist intention in most of the behaviour and the attitudes which supposedly typify it. Put more simply, we believe that racism in France has simply been created and sustained by the work of racist ideologists. Their ideological discourse has developed against a background of social crisis, and by encouraging certain xenophobic reflexes it has ended up gaining a real political influence on the *Front National*, which for many years struggled to survive on the political scene with insignificant electoral support (Perrineau and Mayer, 1989).

In addition, a gap is opening up today in France between efforts which are made to give a precise definition of racism on a purely theoretical basis, and explanations of racist behaviour. Ruling out for the moment the hypothesis that most of those who go in for racism do so out of conviction, we have to explain it by other means than the power of ideology. This is true (and here lies the difficulty) even when we are no longer ignorant of the fact that such behaviour contributes to the success of the racist ideologists.

The Invitation to Racism

The slowing down of the French economy, with the effect this has had on employment, seems the best explanation today if one is looking for reasons why the social crisis has given rise to xenophobic and racist attitudes. The desire to protect self and family from the ravages of the social crisis which is destroying community bonds such as those which used to exist in certain working class areas, creates fertile ground for cultural and political thinking based around nostalgia for a ravaged social class (Wieviorka, 1992). From the beginning this seized upon the issue of immigrants. Although they were no more numerous during the 1980s than they had been at any other period in the history of immigration in France, immigrants and their children had to endure people calling into question their presence in France. They were systematically branded as responsible for a large number of social, political and cultural problems. Their behaviour, which wavered according to circumstances between resignation and indignation, invariably diminished their chances of being seen and recognised for what they were, i.e. people with the potential to integrate into society - a possibility, however, that was denied to them on the grounds that they could not be assimilated. Claiming concern about social issues whose critical nature could not be denied, and drawing on the background of a general debate about immigration, one electoral party has increasingly tended towards a more cultural and ideological explanation of social ills. Their position is that the Other, the foreigners, vaguely characterised as Arabs or as North Africans by tendentious ideology, are the primary causes of current social problems, or, at the very least, that if they were repatriated it would reduce the harmful effects of the economic crisis. It is at the point where someone subscribes to this idea that it becomes correct to talk of them taking the first steps down a path leading towards racist conduct and actions. What happens in the world of work provides a perfect illustration of this.

The Working Environment

For those who have a job, work relations presuppose that they participate in a set of relational exchanges in an environment which consumes and produces references of identity. But running through the experience of work are also a profusion of other experiences not obviously bearing any connection with work. All of these participate in the building of various identities, and not only that of the worker himself.

At the same time, debates and discussions within the work relation draw on a considerable body of events and facts whose origin is outside the workplace. Nowadays, as in the past (Sainsaulieu, 1977), conversations at work revolve around life in the local community and relationships with the neighbours, about children at school, about people's state of health; there are discussions about France's foreign policy, or sports, or what was on TV the night before. The workplace provides a forum within which it is easy to air opinions which are formed without any link whatsoever with the realities of the work experience. Everything takes place in a context where the common experience of work does not have any connection with the appraisals and perceptions which are being expressed, and still less with interpretations.

Moreover, although they sometimes have similar jobs, workers are far from sharing the same interests. Cultural practices and references concerning all aspects of life in society are varied in their expression, and are thus often to be linked with ideological sensibilities which in turn show great diversity. Behaviour and attitudes in the workplace will thus always be guided by ideological references, but the latter do not necessarily originate in the workplace, and more particularly in the tradition of the workers' movement. This is why, at the point where the ideological references bound up with the workers' movement seem to be crumbling away, albeit without necessarily disappearing, it is better to speak of the splitting up of a pre-existing ideological space rather than of its collapse as such. It is probably enriching the sum of ideas in circulation in many ways, whilst at the same time offering opportunities for ideologies without a foothold to gain in importance. This would seem to be the case with racism.

To better illustrate this last remark, during the first contacts made with the unionist teams, the CFDT unionists often considered racism to be a 'taboo' subject, implying the significance of its presence in the reality of people's behaviour, especially when combined with the strength of silences which punctuate certain conversations. Thus racism is not really legitimate, as it has long been fought against by the tradition of the workers' movement, and can scarcely be said to be laid claim to from any quarter, since adherence to racist ideas would not for the moment have any representative framework at work. And yet it is nonetheless present in a fairly specific form. One may therefore speak of a certain climate in the workplace, or, more precisely, of a certain atmosphere which is often described by the victims of racism, such as the policemen from the Antilles who talk about the breaking off of conversations when they go over to their colleagues, or the pressure brought to bear on one of them not to formalise a complaint about harassment of a racist nature.

The overriding impression is of people avoiding any flare up, as though the situation which has long existed can continue, but no one would know how to handle any disturbance to the equilibrium which might arise. Our research was to fall victim to this feeling on several occasions. Unionists who alerted the confederation about what was happening in their workplace, and who called for the intervention of the researchers, ended up by backing down after having presented the initiative they had taken before the rest of their section. This was not because the problem they had brought up had been solved, nor even because it was denied by the others, but because the majority either simply did not believe that there was any possible solution, or feared a disturbance to the equilibrium that existed in these areas in their company. On the strength of this kind of argument, they preferred to block their comrades' initiative.

As a privileged observer of a climate whose deterioration he dreads, the unionist who wishes to modify its basic nature asks himself to what extent work relations have given way or resisted in the face of temptations to participate in racial hatred. He should also know in what circumstances it will be possible for him to mobilise his forces to contest work structures when these institutionalise discriminatory practices based on racial criteria. Moreover, according to our approach, if one talks of racism amongst workers, this presupposes that the way work is structured formalises racist aspirations implicit in working relationships, which would thus find expression in the systematic domination of others by virtue of some supposed racial or ethnic difference (unless it consists of systematically upholding this kind of distinction away from the work process). The responsibility of the unionist who desires to curb racist tendencies which he sees developing would therefore consist of uncovering the logic at the bottom of this way of encountering people in order to denounce it and fight against it. To achieve this, he must use his trade union experience in order to have an effect on work relations, and in certain circumstances he can contest the lines along which a company is organised.

Work Relations and Work Structures

We studied situations where pronounced forms of racism have already become commonplace. This is especially the case in an employment catchment area in the south of France. In this former mining region, the population of North African origin is deprived of access to hundreds of jobs. This situation has existed since the time when miners changed jobs to become workers at mechanical engineering companies some twenty years ago. Foreigners originating from North Africa, especially Moroccans and Algerians, who started out as miners, were deliberately denied access to the facilities for seeking re-employment offered by the mines which were closing. A rule of preferring native born Frenchmen was unofficially implemented by those responsible for economic policy at the time. This discrimination in status has since been transformed into a racial discrimination affecting Frenchmen with foreign parents, who have had exactly the same school careers as those who nowadays get the jobs. Also, amongst the hundreds of jobs provided by these companies, there are no more than one or two young people of North African origin, and this applies even to children of mixed marriages.

A study of the system of recruitment very quickly reveals that the situation can only be explained by analysing a combination of factors, amongst which is prominent a racism that is no longer disguised, without, however, being openly displayed by any of the parties involved, for example, those currently responsible for economic policy.

In this employment catchment area, the two companies which we studied adjoin one another, and provide more than a thousand jobs. A long-term job offer only comes after a trial period which candidates who are initially selected on the criteria of their competence qualify for. However, supervisors and workers alike admit that the application of a child of a member of staff, or brother, or brother-in-law, are generally favoured. All employees are aware of the power that string-pulling has, having themselves benefited from it. The notorious absence of young people of North African origin in a good number of local companies, although they are found in the schools and in the local neighbourhoods, would thus be explained by the traditional form the recruitment system now takes. None of their parents being 'on the inside', they have no hope of getting in themselves. Such at least is the systematic explanation which seems to satisfy everybody, and many of those who offer it consider that none of this provides any evidence of racism.

However, first of all, it sometimes happens that employees who have a mixed marriage put in a word for their North African spouse. These candidates, who have all the necessary skills, as well as the benefits of some string-pulling, are nonetheless systematically rejected, on the pretext that they would have difficulties adapting to their fellow workers. Secondly, there are trainees of North African origin or young people under temporary contract who work in these companies. Their racial origins would only create a real problem at the moment of a long-term job offer, because meanwhile, having been kept in menial underpaid jobs, they do not contradict the assumptions whose victims they are, because they do not really pose a threat to employment. Thus the historic hypothesis about the system of recruitment is not enough to explain the absence of young people of North African origin.

However (and this also applies to the situation which has just been described), it is difficult to talk of racism, not in the least because a racist intention is not evident in any readily identifiable party. And yet it is possible to follow step by step the unspoken process of transformation of a system of discrimination resting on the exploitation of foreign fathers, into a system of segregation which brings about the exclusion of their sons and the daughters. Nobody bears direct responsibility for these facts, even though all the world is perfectly aware of them, and more or less assumes their part of the responsibility. For the workers, it is a question of protecting jobs and of applying the principle of preference for native born Frenchmen which bears a strong resemblance to a preference based on ethnic and community criteria. For the supervisors and the management, it is rather a question of maintaining social and relational equilibrium, at the risk of formalising an implicit racism. Finally, in the two companies which we studied, the few unionists who took the initiative to denounce the situation were not to find any real support, except from their management, who gave particular support to the conducting of the enquiry.

Oral Expressions of Racism

In other companies, often very large ones, as for example in the car industry, racist overtones are more tangible, even if they do not necessarily translate into the way work is organised. This climate produces ideological divisions, and the young people under short term contract who are involved in the work process show themselves particularly sensitive to these divisions. Whether they are of foreign origin or not, they come up against expressions of racism of a kind that is new compared with what they have encountered in their neighbourhood or at school. These virtual outsider witnesses of the world of work say in particular that they do not immediately grasp the importance of things left unsaid or hidden meanings which they consider to be numerous, and which are contained in certain jokes or stories making fun of one or other category of worker. For them, the principles of solidarity to which they spontaneously refer, having developed them in the common experience of the 'penal servitude' as was defined by François Dubet, no longer have their place in the work experience. Their frames of reference are thus turned upside down and left to be taken for granted in situations where the prevailing ideological viewpoint tends to suppress their better nature in favour of views and attitudes tinged with racism. These young people often feel discouraged, and say that they avoid discussions which they think would undermine the perspective that was theirs when they were taken on. Thus, they tolerate rather than oppose. On the other hand, they repeat in their own families, and in the company of their friends, the opinions which they have heard, thereby feeding a cycle of hatred which spills out beyond the world of work, but from which one can no longer say that the world of work is protected, as it is its stage.

In other cases, especially in the civil service, one may speak of a kind of professional behaviour which brings implicit racism to the fore. Here, it is no longer only a question of work relations, but of the service given to the general public. It has to do with openly uttered discrimination or with insults at the counter in the presence of the person concerned. This kind of behaviour is often complained about, but the complaints are not necessarily brought to the knowledge of the legal system by their victims.

In the case of the civil service, these facts are all the more liable to create tensions amongst civil servants, given that they are rarely sanctioned by the hierarchy. This is particularly the case in *prefectural* or community services intended for the reception of foreigners. Unionist sections of the CFDT set up in the *prefectures* clearly state that the tightening up of laws concerning the status and fate of foreigners gives free rein to racist attitudes on the part of many of their colleagues, especially as far as escorting immigrants back to the frontier is concerned.

In work situations like this, unionists who denounce their colleagues' displays of excessive zeal in interpreting the law in practice are accused of calling into question the political and legislative bases of their authority. They indicate that because of the absence of anyone who will speak out in an ideological confrontation concerning the place of foreigners in French society, and because of the state of public opinion about these matters, this lack of discernment in the way the law is interpreted in practice receives encouragement. Consequently, the margin of interpretation which the administration gives these civil servants in pursuing certain cases serves more often to toughen up the regulations described in the laws than to soften them.

The Trade Unionist Confronted with Racism

The examples which have just been described suggest possibilities for setting up trade union initiatives, but it is clear that the silence which hangs over everything to do with racism in companies greatly harms the prospects of any campaigns the trade unionist might wish to engage in. An effective unionist intervention should undertake to reorient work relations around the work itself, so that they are less receptive to ideological influences originating from outside. The unionists' room for manoeuvre seems in several respects to be narrow, but it is there nonetheless. This is proved by the reception given to the research, which constantly fluctuated between two types of reaction: relief or tension.

The relief was apparent when the work of analysing existing problems was finished, despite differences of opinion that existed within the unionist section. In this case, the research seemed to be a unique occasion to deal with questions which were difficult, although they were no longer confronted. Throughout the duration of the inquiry, we also noticed that an initial position of relief could be transformed into tension when the more determined unionists took it into their heads to prolong their investigation and tried to change the situations which were uncovered. Where the tension was very pronounced, analysis of the reservations revealed the ideological turmoil in which unionists no longer able to identify themselves openly with an anti-racist campaign found themselves.

This observation brings up traditional questions about the values which guide unionist action, and on the position of the unionist as opposed to the political activist. An appeal to unionist values, the translation of those values into action by the unionists, and the struggle against a political ideal which is opposed to these values are three elements which do not immediately mesh together. Even the unionists who are keenest to engage in a campaign against racism and xenophobia are hesitant when it is a question of undertaking actions in their own workplace, since the definition of their unionist role does not always authorise them to have as much say as they might wish on work relations as long as they are under political influence.

On the other hand, they are quite clear on the point that any formalisation of the racism implicit in work structures is a matter of concern to them, and is something which they can contest. But without real support from their base - in other words without strength - it is impossible for them to contemplate action. For this reason the risk of a unionist becoming isolated grows. There is no answer to this risk other than to rely on federal or confederation structures to influence the social and political climate, at least to the extent that they take a political stand against ideas contrary to the reference values of the militants. On this engagement depends the success of actions on the ground.

References

Bataille, Ph. (1996a), 'De la xénophobie au racisme', *Travailler le social*, No. 17, Louvain-La-Neuve, p. 89-99.
Bataille, Ph. (1996b), 'Le renouveau démocratique par le refus des extrêmes', *Alternatives non violentes*, No. 98, p. 21-8.
Bataille, Ph. (1996c), 'Racisme et entreprise. Notes de recherche', *CFDT Aujourd'hui*, No. 117, p. 34-48.
Bataille, Ph. (1997), 'Le racisme dans le monde du travail', *Esprit* (mai), p. 108-26.
Chicha-Pontbriand, M.-Th. (1992), *Discrimination systémique, fondement et méthodologie des programmes d'accès à l'égalité en emploi*, Commission des droits de la personne, Québec.
Dubet, F. (1987), *La galère: jeunes en survie*, Fayard, Paris.
Dubet, F. and Lapeyronnie, D. (1992), *Les quartiers d'exil*, Seuil, Paris.
Galissot, J. (1986), *Misère de l'antiracisme*, Arcantère, Paris.
Gallissot, R. (1988), *Immigration et mouvement ouvrier en France, les années 1960 à nos jours*, Rapport MIRE.
Jenkins, R. (1986), *Racism and recruitment*, Cambridge University Press, Cambridge.
Lapeyronnie, D. (1993), *L'individu et les minorités*, Puf, Paris.
Lochak, D. (1995), 'Emploi et protection sociale. Les inégalités du droit', *Hommes et migrations*, No. 1187, p. 25-31.
Le Monde, 24 et 25 March 1996, 'Le Front national tente d'élargir ses réseaux dans le monde du travail'.
Le Monde, 3 April 1996, 'L'influence des idées du Front national connaît sa plus forte progression depuis 1990'.
Le Monde, 13 September 1996, 'La majorité et l'opposition sont partagées sur les actions à engager contre le Front national'.
Le Monde, 27 May 1997, 'Le Front national est en mesure de maintenir ses candidats dans 133 circonscriptions'.
Perrineau, P. and Mayer, N. (1989), *Le Front national à découvert*, FNSP, Paris.

Phizacklea, A. and Miles, R. (1980), *Labour and Racism*, Routledge and Kegan Paul, London.
Rattansi, A. and Westwood, S. (1994), *Racism, Modernity Identity on the Western Front*, Polity Press, Cambridge.
Sainsaulieu, R. (1977), *L'identité au travail*, PFNSP, Paris.
Touraine, A. (1996), 'Le nationalisme contre la nation', *L'année Sociologique*, Vol. 46, No. 1, p. 15-41.
Touraine, A., Wieviorka, M. and Dubet, F. (1984), *Le mouvement ouvrier*, Fayard, Paris.
Tribalat, M. (1995), *Faire France*, La Découverte, Paris.
Tripier, M., de Rudder, V. and Vourc'h, F. (1995), 'Discriminations en tout genre', *Hommes et migrations*, No. 1187, p. 12-22.
van Dijk, T. (1993), 'Denying Racism: Elite Discourse and Racism', in J. Wrench and J. Salomos (eds), *Racism and Migration in Western Europe*, Berg, Oxford.
Wieviorka, M. (1992), *La France Raciste*, Seuil, Paris.
Wieviorka, M. (1993), *La démocratie à l'épreuve. Nationalisme, populisme, ethnicité*, La Découverte, Paris.
Wieviorka, M. (1996a), 'Le syndicalisme à l'épreuve de la différence culturelle', *Analyses et documents économiques*, p. 67-70.
Wieviorka, M. (1996b), 'Racisme, racialisation et ethnicisation', *Hommes et migrations*, No. 1195, p. 27-33.
Wieviorka, M. (1997), *Une société fragmentée*, La Découverte, Paris.
Wrench, J. (1996a), 'Organising the Unorganised: Race, Poor Work and Trade Unions', in P. Ackers, C. Smith and P. Smith (eds), *The New Workplace and Trade Unionism*, Routledge, London.
Wrench, J. (1996b), *Preventing Racism at the Workplace. A report on 16 European countries*, European Foundation for the Improvement of Living and Working Conditions, Dublin.